ROUTLEDGE LIBRARY EDITIONS:
THE INDUSTRIAL REVOLUTION

Volume 6

WHAT IS PAST IS PROLOGUE

WHAT IS PAST IS PROLOGUE

Cost Accounting in the British Industrial Revolution, 1760–1850

RICHARD K. FLEISCHMAN AND
LEE D. PARKER

Routledge
Taylor & Francis Group
LONDON AND NEW YORK

First published in 1997 by Garland Publishing, Inc.

This edition first published in 2017
by Routledge
2 Park Square, Milton Park, Abingdon, Oxon OX14 4RN

and by Routledge
711 Third Avenue, New York, NY 10017

Routledge is an imprint of the Taylor & Francis Group, an informa business

British Library Cataloguing in Publication Data
A catalogue record for this book is available from the British Library

ISBN: 978-1-138-63291-2 (Set)
ISBN: 978-1-315-16309-3 (Set) (ebk)
ISBN: 978-1-138-05553-7 (Volume 6) (hbk)
ISBN: 978-1-315-16585-1 (Volume 6) (ebk)

Publisher's Note
The publisher has gone to great lengths to ensure the quality of this reprint but points out that some imperfections in the original copies may be apparent.

Disclaimer
The publisher has made every effort to trace copyright holders and would welcome correspondence from those they have been unable to trace.

WHAT IS PAST IS PROLOGUE

Cost Accounting in the British Industrial Revolution, 1760–1850

RICHARD K. FLEISCHMAN
LEE D. PARKER

GARLAND PUBLISHING, Inc.
New York & London / 1997

Library of Congress Cataloging-in-Publication Data

Fleischman, Richard K..
What is past is prologue : cost accounting in the British Industrial Revolution, 1760–1850 / Richard K. Fleischman and Lee D. Parker.
p. cm. — (New works in accounting history)
Includes bibliographical references and index.
ISBN 0-8153-3015-4 (alk. paper)
1. Accounting—Great Britain—History—18th century. 2. Accounting—Great Britain—History—19th century. 3. Accounting—Great Britain—Case studies. I. Parker, Lee D. (Lee David) II. Title. III. Series.
HF5616.G7F58 1997
657'.45'0941—dc21 97-25287

Printed on acid-free, 250-year-life paper
Manufactured in the United States of America

TO

SANDRA and GLORIA

Contents

Preface

This volume reports the findings of extensive archival and contextual research into the surviving accounting and business records of some 200 British Industrial Revolution enterprises. These data were collected and analysed during the course of sabbatical leaves taken in 1987, 1991, 1993, and 1996. For our release from teaching and administrative duties, the authors wish to thank John Carroll and Flinders Universities. For the funding of incremental expenses in the United Kingdom, the authors express gratitude to Arthur Andersen & Co. LLP and especially to the firm's Cleveland, Ohio partners without whose generous support this project could never have been undertaken. Research support from the KPMG Peat Marwick LLP Accounting Professorship in International Business, endowed by alumni at the firm's Cleveland office, was likewise instrumental for accomplishing this project.

A number of chapters herein contained can be sourced back to published work of the coauthors and their collaborators. Since the majority of sourced articles have appeared in British journals, UK spellings and grammatical conventions have been adopted in an effort to achieve a standardisation of presentation. In those chapters new data and expanded discussion are now offered. Further chapters present evidence and analysis not hitherto made available in the accounting literature, especially with regard to accounting developments in the textiles and extractive industries.

A word of explanation about this volume's title seems appropriate for the preface. The current authors have been criticised by some in the journal literature for failing to eliminate the present in our evaluation of costing practices we have found in the past. Our rejoinder, which will be articulated in-depth in the pages that follow, is captured by the words, *What is Past is Prologue*, which are inscribed prominently on the National Archives, Washington, DC.

The authors are extremely grateful to a host of professional archivists in libraries and public record offices the length and breadth of the UK for their tireless efforts in our behalf. We also acknowledge the contributions of many economic historians whose early investigations of these records have made our job much easier in terms of locating and utilising the archival deposits. The efforts of the Royal Commission on Historical Manuscripts in providing computerised data bases for various industries were of inestimable value. Finally, to Mrs Ethel Epstein, the Secretary to the Department of Accountancy at John Carroll University; to Mrs Ruth Cickavage, the University Secretary at John Carroll University; to Professor Lawrence P. Kalbers of John Carroll University who formatted our tables; and to our long-suffering but tolerant spouses, Sandra Fleischman and Gloria Parker, our most heartfelt thanks.

Richard K. Fleischman
John Carroll University

Lee D. Parker
University of Adelaide

February, 1997

Tables

Figures

What is Past is Prologue

1

Introduction[1]

The accounting profession and its associated research community share in many respects a relatively recent heritage. Their organised, institutionalised structures are largely products of the twentieth century, with the majority of early professional bodies and university programs postdating the 1880s. The preoccupation of researchers and professionals with contemporary accounting and management issues possibly reflects this recency of institutional foundations, as well as the daily-reporting and problem-solving orientations of the discipline. Associated with this ongoing presentism has been the relative neglect of historical research into the discipline's own genesis, development, environmental interactions, and socio-economic role. Yet, such research has the undeniable capacity to establish our professional heritage, to rediscover lessons from the past, and to inform contemporary and future judgements and decisions.

Such concerns do not lie unattended, however. Indeed, this chapter pays due recognition to the work of a variety of accounting historians who have laboured across the decades of the century to lay the foundations for an historical understanding of the accounting discipline. Particularly in the 1980s and 1990s, the challenge of addressing the research agenda has been taken up by a growing number of new entrants to the accounting history research community. Despite these welcome signs of activity, the field of Industrial Revolution costing history has lain remarkably fallow. It has stood relatively neglected, save for fences unwittingly constructed by economic and business historians, beyond which a modest sprinkling of accounting historians have been content to graze, occasionally surmising what might lie beneath the surface of the hitherto fallow field.

This volume offers an extensive exploration, based on archival sources, of the various dimensions of British Industrial Revolution costing history. It presents an overview of cost accounting and cost management practices, whilst investigating these methods in the three dominant industries of the period—iron, textiles, and mining. In addition, it provides two organisational case studies—the Carron Company and Boulton & Watt. Finally, it explores two issues central to Industrial Revolution costing—the relationship between technological change and cost management, and the paradigmatic approaches that have predominated in recent costing historiography.

A WORLD OF CHANGE

The Industrial Revolution, conventionally dated from the mid-eighteenth to the mid-nineteenth centuries, was an epoch during which England, Scotland, and Wales underwent significant economic and industrial transformation. The period is characterised most simply in terms of a population explosion, changes in the nature and organisation of work, and dramatic improvements in transport and communications. Between 1500 and 1700, population increased by less than 75%; yet, the first half of the nineteenth century saw a 200% increase. During the same span of years, Britain was converted from a predominantly agrarian society to an industrial economy serving both home and overseas markets. Larger-scale manufacturing and mining organisations, facilitated by mechanical technology of increasing sophistication, were observable in industries such as mining, iron, and textiles. Some indication of the rate of change is evinced by statistics such as the increased number of cotton spindles in operation, rising from 1.94 million in 1788 to 20.47 million in 1850. Patents on new technological inventions rose from 12 in the year 1760 to 250 in 1825. In 1700, 3 million tons of coal were mined, compared to 50 million tons in 1850. Prior to 1760, there were only 17 blast furnaces in operation; yet, by 1806, there were 215 (Ashton, 1948; Brown, 1991; Flinn, 1966; von Tunzelmann, 1978).

Key facilitating factors in the industrialisation process were significant innovations in the generation and availability of power, mass-production machinery, and transport systems for moving raw materials to production sites and finished products to markets. The advent of steam power freed the industrial sector from restrictions that would otherwise have occurred. The number of steam engines increased nearly sevenfold in Manchester between 1800 and 1825, whilst down the road in Bolton the number quadrupled between 1825 and 1837. Horsepower capacity increased even more dramatically. Between 1800 and 1825, the overall growth in steam power averaged between 6.75% and 7.25% per annum (von Tunzelmann, 1978). Innovations, such as Kay's flying shuttle, enabled weavers to double their output within a decade. Manchester textile firms, combining spinning and weaving, grew to significant size and employed 260 people on average by 1840. Workers' tasks, which became more specialised with a greater division of labour, gave rise to productivity increases, though occurring at different rates across industries. Change was not always dramatic, but often occurred gradually though significantly over years and decades (Brown, 1991).

New modes of transportation facilitated mining and manufacturing developments by virtue of their impact both on the speed of delivery and the diversity of locations serviced (mining sites, shipping ports, manufacturers, and markets). Eighteenth century roads were exceedingly primitive and travel by coach was both slow and uncomfortable. Roads were in such poor repair that they were largely unsuitable for freight cartage. Some sections of roads were improved by private turnpike trusts, but the high tolls charged made for expensive freight costs. Thus, rivers and canals were preferred initially for the transport of coal, iron, timber, cotton, and finished goods. Accordingly, many factories were situated adjacent to these arteries. By 1725, England boasted 1,000 miles of canals. Both coaching and canals were dramatically reduced as modes of industrial transport with the advent of railways in the 1830s. This innovation contributed both to the speed of raw materials and finished goods transport, as well as to reduced freight costs. Manufacturing locations were also freed to spread into the South of England, no longer restricted by proximity to sources of raw materials and water transport (Brown, 1991; Parker & Reid, 1972).

The majority of entrepreneurs who established industrial enterprises could be described as capitalists (e.g., landowners, financiers, merchants) not previously involved in mining or manufacturing. Often they were groups of family members, friends, and business associates who formed partnerships to facilitate the contribution of sufficient personal capital and borrowed funds for the significant investments in plant and equipment required. Rarely were they the inventors of new technologies and processes themselves, though they pursued innovation in order to cut costs and increase productivity. Management of enterprises often involved some partners working full-time on site, whilst others played the role of absentee directors or silent partners (Ashton, 1966; Brown, 1991; Parker & Reid, 1972).

The involvement of partnerships of individual entrepreneurs in setting up industrial and mining enterprises reflected the crude and elementary state of capital markets at the time. Most funds came from owners themselves, family, and friends, supplemented by short-term borrowings from merchants and the occasional financier. Firms attempted to plough back profits as an internally generated source of funds. As prospects for profit improved, merchants played a more prominent intermediary role, such as the tea dealers of London and Bristol who financed much of the early iron industry of South Wales. Suppliers of raw materials were often required to extend long-term credit. Cash flow therefore posed an ever-present problem for industrial entrepreneurs, with constant pressure induced by manufacturing and transport lead times, heavy investment in plant and equipment, a large labour force, and predominantly short-term financing contracts. Banks were still in their infancy (only 70 were in existence by 1800, with many failing in the years 1772, 1793, 1814–1816, and 1825), and the Stock Exchange was not initially established until 1773. Consequently, many individual investors, partners, and enterprises experienced financial collapse during the early Industrial Revolution (Ashton, 1948; Chapman, 1972; Parker & Reid, 1972).

Such was the world of mining and manufacturing in Britain in the eighteenth and nineteenth centuries. This brief pen sketch of some of the key dimensions suggests a scenario of change, opportunity, pressure, competition, and financial success and failure. It is into this dynamic world, at times both inviting and hostile, that our costing history enquiries enter.

UNADDRESSED AND UNCONVINCED

The British Industrial Revolution was a period of unparallelled innovation in a range of economic activities as diverse as the development of distribution and marketing structures, the adaptation of new technology to factory environments, the recruitment and control of labour, and the accumulation and deployment of capital. Given the economic sophistication reflected by these multitudinous advances, it is almost unthinkable that the entrepreneurs of the age would be oblivious to the advantages cost accounting could bring to bear upon their enterprises in terms of accurate product costing, process evaluation and control, planning activities, and managerial decision making. Notwithstanding, venerated surveys of accounting history, now nearly half a century old, date the advent of meaningful cost accounting to the mid-1880s and attribute its birth to the US industrial environment (Crossman, 1953; Edwards, 1937; Garner, 1954; Littleton, 1933; Perren, 1944; Solomons, 1952; Yamey, 1949). The scientific management movement, featuring the theories of Frederick Taylor and applications envisioned by the engineering profession, has previously been cited as the genesis of both modern managerialism and managerial accounting. In accounting terms this 'renaissance' was highlighted by the development of standard costing systems and variance analysis. Whilst the histories mentioned above accorded some credit for the birth of modern managerialism at this time to British theorists (e.g., Garcke and Fells, Norton), no recognition was given to any accounting developments dating from the British Industrial Revolution. Brown's *The History of Accounting and Accountants* (1905), one of the earliest contributions to the field of accounting history, took no notice of industrial accounting methods in over 300 pages of narrative. Stacey (1954, p. 60) was decidedly negative in his flowery description of British reactions to early cost accounting advances in other countries as 'so much burning of incense at the alter of window dressing instead of a tool for the attainment of continually growing production'. Several historians of accounting have argued that the British should have been pioneers in the evolution of managerial accounting practices in view of their level of economic activity, but that this leadership role never materialised (Johnson & Kaplan, 1987; Solomons, 1952). Lister (1983), an outspoken critic of the value of accounting history as a research area, focussed particularly on the British Industrial Revolution in his indictment. Despite the period's legitimate reputation as a golden age of economics, he argued that the primitive state of accounting militated against its meaningful employment for the planning and control of large-scale operations.

The costing historians of a generation or two ago may be excused their lack of appreciation for British Industrial Revolution contributions because they were not privy to the ground-breaking research of economic historians who inaugurated a micro-level examination of the period's surviving business records with an eye to their accounting methods (Campbell, 1961; Flinn, 1962; McKendrick, 1970; Pollard, 1965; Raistrick, 1970; Rimmer, 1960; Trinder, 1973, 1974). However, had they consulted Unwin's (1924) work on Oldknow and the Arkwrights or Roll's (1968) treatise on Boulton & Watt, they might have suspected that significant advances in costing history were escaping their scrutiny. Perhaps any industrial accounting sophistication reflected in the activities of these firms was simply dismissed as exceptional rather than representative.

Notwithstanding the accounting implications of these research efforts of the 1960s and early 1970s, the majority of accounting historians have remained unconvinced that the British Industrial Revolution was a significant formative epoch (Chatfield, 1977; Hopper & Armstrong, 1991; Loft, 1986; Miller & O'Leary, 1987; R.H. Parker, 1969, 1986). It is in light of that skepticism that the effort to rehabilitate the history of this period's cost accounting has begun with increasing earnestness (Edwards, 1989; Edwards & Boyns, 1992; Edwards & Newell, 1991; Fleischman et al., 1991; Fleischman & Parker, 1990, 1991, 1992; Fleischman & Tyson, 1993; Walsh & Stewart, 1993). It is to this effort that this present volume is dedicated.

It should also be noted in the way of introduction that any attempt to establish the period of the British Industrial Revolution as the genesis of modern managerialism should be construed as part of a more general effort on the part of historians to revise the costing chronology to times and events predating the Age of Taylor and the scientific management movement. However, identifications of purposeful cost accounting have largely focussed on the US industrial sector. Chandler (1977) found origins in the heyday of American railroad management. Johnson (1972) narrated elements of sophisticated accounting practices at the Lyman textile mills in the 1850s. Porter (1980) found significant developments in the same industrial sector as early as the 1810s. More recently, a considerable amount of attention has been paid to developments at the Springfield Armory, a munitions manufacturing installation of the US government (Hoskin & Macve, 1988, 1994; Tyson, 1990, 1993). The studies contained in this volume offer a counterbalance to the geographic and temporal foci hitherto dominating the costing history literature.

REVIEWING THE CONVENTIONAL WISDOM

The lack of an industrial accounting literature dating from the eighteenth century makes it understandable that historians who have not widely examined surviving business records might have assumed there was little of substance occurring. The numerous textbooks in print dealt almost exclusively with merchant accounting techniques. Multi-edition texts by Dilworth (1810), Fisher (1799), Hutton (1788), Inglis (1800), Kelly (1802), Mair (1749), Morrison (1834), and Webster (1781) did not even mention industrial applications. Some awareness was apparent in three leading manuals of the age—Thompson's *The Accountant's Oracle* (1777), Hamilton's *An Introduction to Merchandise* (1777), and Cronhelm's *Double Entry by Single* (1978). The most hopeful piece of cost accounting literature during the British Industrial Revolution was Charles Babbage's rather late effort, *On the Economy of Machinery and Manufacturers* (1963). Babbage advised industrialists to maintain accurate cost and time information on each manufacturing process and to institute quality control procedures. Although a few contenders appeared in the half-century after Babbage, most accounting historians have cited Garcke and Fells' *Factory Accounts, Their Principle and Practice* (1887) as the genesis of modern cost accounting literature (Garner, 1954; Johnson, 1972; Littleton, 1933).

Pessimistic historians have felt this literary shortfall reflected a dearth of cost accounting activity. In seeking to explain its absence, a theory frequently advanced was the inattention paid by entrepreneurs to production costs because profit margins were so enormous (Edwards, 1937; Hudson, 1977; R.H. Parker, 1969, 1986; Pollard, 1965). The reality, however, especially in the dominant textile and iron industries, was a keenness of competition, necessitating the advantages that effective costing could provide. It has also been suggested that the orientation of entrepreneurs toward technological innovation distracted them from the more commercial side of their firms (R.H. Parker, 1969; Urwick & Brech, 1964). However, it is our opinion that the captains of industry could ill-afford to be unconcerned about anything potentially providing a competitive edge. It is also inaccurate to suggest that Industrial Revolution firms were insufficiently complex to justify sophisticated cost accounting techniques (R.H. Parker, 1969). The larger enterprises of the period were very substantial in terms of the amount of capital invested, personnel, and integrated processes.

More optimistic were those observers who suspected the presence of cost accounting despite the absence of a literature, but who chose not to do archival research into surviving records. It has been frequently argued that considerations of competitive advantage mandated that strict secrecy be maintained about costing techniques (Chatfield, 1977; Edwards, 1937; Garner, 1954; Urwick & Brech, 1964; Wells, 1977, 1978). Since any public disclosure of pricing could lead to competitive disadvantage, cost accounting methodology could only have passed by word of mouth (Chatfield, 1977; Garner, 1954). In reality, as subsequent evidence will demonstrate, many entrepreneurs were quite forthcoming about their costs, as well as their costing methods.

THE PROFESSIONAL AND ORGANISATIONAL ENVIRONMENT

Besides this shortfall in industrial accounting theory and method, other institutions associated with a maturing profession also lagged. Stacey (1954) pointed out the slow evolution of accounting education in the UK. There were precious few accounting practitioners, and those in practice rarely had manufacturers as clients (R.H. Parker, 1986). Moreover, the presentation of financial data was marginally influenced by accounting professionals; rather, financial reporting more frequently was the determination of management (Brief, 1965). There were no accepted accounting conventions during the entire Industrial Revolution period (Yamey, 1960). Consequently, if managerial accounting was practised at all, it would not have reflected the talents of professional accountants, managerial or financial, but of perceptive businessmen who did costing by the seat of their pants and frequently got it right.

Ultimately, those historians most difficult to refute are those who have argued that cost accounting was attempted, but that the industrial environment was too primitive to allow anything but the most simplistic and unsophisticated methods. One cited omission was the failure to allocate fixed costs, either because the amounts involved were minimal or because there was a fundamental lack of understanding of the relationship between indirect expenses and product costing (Chatfield, 1977; Edwards, 1937; Johnson, 1972; R.H. Parker, 1986; Pollard, 1965). Wells (1978, 1987), though he hypothesised the existence of certain more advanced accounting uses adapted from older merchant, manorial, and domestic system methods, did not concede that sophisticated costing prevailed until such time as the post-Industrial Revolution increase in fixed assets necessitated a more careful allocation of common costs. One historian described overhead allocation attempts before the 1880s as 'unsystematic allowances, wild guesses, or complete omissions' (Hudson, 1977). Other points raised to support a later timetable for cost management development included the delay in divorcing the personal affairs of entrepreneurs from their enterprises (Pollard, 1965; Yamey, 1949), and the absence of an incentive to develop accurate costing techniques until it became imperative to value inventory for financial reporting purposes (Chatfield, 1977; R.H. Parker, 1986). Johnson (1972) and Chatfield (1977) concluded that the integration of cost and commercial accounts was not accomplished until such time as businesses became sufficiently complex to require material cost transfers between departments. We would argue that although costing typically remained a separate function, many concerns had multiple integrated processes and a few even attempted transfer pricing systems to link them.

Judgements of cost accounting in the Industrial Revolution have suffered partly because of the primitive state of the financial accounting of the period. Hudson (1986) detailed the shortcomings of financial reporting before the late nineteenth century. The problem is demonstrated most vividly by Campbell's (1961) description of Carron Company's financial reporting system which reflected serious shortcomings, when, in fact, its cost accounting was exemplary amongst contemporary firms. Pollard (1965, p. 233) was harsh but essentially correct when he identified the failings of financial accounting—suspect profit calculations, 'confusion between capital and revenue', non-recognition of depreciation, and the treatment of interest on owners' investment as a cost. However, these charges need not be extended to costing methods which typically address far different agendas (Edwards, 1989). In writing about the early American experience, Johnson and Kaplan (1987, p. 9) observed that 'the management accounting measures were designed to motivate and evaluate the efficiency of internal processes, not to measure the overall "profit" of the enterprise'. The concept of depreciation, for example, was widely known, and the need to recognise wear and tear was explicitly discussed in publications available to British and US textile mill owners and managers (Montgomery, 1840). Nevertheless, depreciation was not recorded methodically because of the absence of financial reporting requirements. Depreciation numbers were also unlikely to influence asset replacement decisions, given the rapid pace of technological innovation during the later stages of the Industrial Revolution (McGaw, 1985).

THE POLLARD DIAGNOSIS

Pollard in his classic, *The Genesis of Modern Management* (1965, p. 248), concluded on the basis of a comprehensive study of existing business records that 'the practice of using accounts as direct aids to management was not one of the achievements of the British Industrial Revolution'. Pollard conceded that accounting was capable of solving certain problems (e.g., stock control, prevention of embezzlement, departmental comparisons), but that ultimately accounting did not come to guide management decisions. His conclusion was based mainly on arguments previously discussed—large profit margins and the lack of fixed asset accounting. Because of his extensive knowledge of the sources, Pollard is widely revered amongst historians, and his negative comments on managerial accounting during the British Industrial Revolution must be addressed.

Pollard was on firmer ground with regard to two other components of his indictment of Industrial Revolution cost accounting. Whilst conceding that the number of surviving cost estimates was impressive, he judged them to be inexact and useless. This verdict appears to have been conditioned by his perception of a 'cavalier attitude' about costing, a perceived disinterest in accurate costing occasioned by the substantial profit margins he presumed to exist almost universally during the period (Pollard, 1965, p. 265). However, his point that the matching of *ex ante* cost analyses and estimates with *post factum* implementations of action was essential to establish a case for 'purposeful' cost accounting is well-taken. The problem lies in the fragmentary nature of surviving archival material which makes these linkages most difficult to document.

Revisionists are more optimistic than Pollard that they do exist. It might also be argued that during the Industrial Revolution there was less need than there is today to use accounting both as a tool (*ex ante*) and a rationale (*post factum*) for decision making.

A second shortcoming, persuasively cited by Pollard and others, was the failure to integrate the financial and cost accounts (Chatfield, 1977; Garcke & Fells, 1887; Johnsòn, 1972; Pollard, 1965). The jury is still out on the ability of revisionists to answer this charge, though Mepham (1988) wrote of Hamilton's attention to this issue in his first edition (1777), and Jones (1985) and Edwards (1989) found evidence of integration at Mona Mine and the Cyfarthfa ironworks. Furthermore, any extensive effort to demonstrate the impact of costing data on commercial accounts would be doomed to failure because of the acknowledged low standard of financial reporting.

HISTORICAL REVISIONISM: BEGINNINGS

Researchers have only begun to collect the data which may eventually refute the reservations of Pollard, Chatfield, and others regarding the emergence of modern cost accounting procedures in the British Industrial Revolution. Roll (1968) provided evidence of superior cost management at Boulton & Watt's Soho Foundry. He detailed a variety of sophisticated costing methods, featuring the articulation of time-and-motion standards, scientific price fixing, departmental profit analysis, elaborate costing calculations (including the application of overhead), and process efficiency testing.

In one of the earliest examples of historical revisionism, McKendrick (1970) found that Wedgwood, the pottery king, though dealing in a luxury product and a less highly competitive market, employed intricate cost data for determining pricing policy and analysing the economics of large-scale production. Wedgwood was concerned, particularly in periods of economic depression, that the output of certain productive lines be sufficient to justify the fixed costs they bore.

Research into early nineteenth century US textile mills provided fruitful results and the expectation that some methods in evidence there would have been transplanted across the Atlantic from earlier UK enterprises (Johnson, 1972; Porter, 1980; Tyson, 1992). A study of records at the Newmills cloth manufactory at Haddington in Scotland has uncovered the use of costing procedures for process evaluation, product line decisions, raw materials control, and 'rational planning' as early as the late seventeenth century (Marshall, 1980). Stone (1973) uncovered cost accounting methods at the Chorlton Mills in Manchester circa 1810 that were 'not believed to have been in use until the early twentieth century'. These techniques included the allocation of overhead to cost centres on the basis of predetermined rates and rudimentary examples of transfer pricing.

Our current understanding of cost management during the Industrial Revolution is the result of a cooperative effort between economic and accounting historians. The bulk of research into the business history of the period is contained in a substantial number of studies of individual firms and entrepreneurs, typically by economic historians who have invested considerable time, often whole careers, in the effort. These works chronicle the activities of individual companies over extended periods and synthesise disparate topics to form organised and complete economic pictures. Such efforts are of uneven value to the historian of accounting who seeks to discover the emergence of modern accounting practices and the impact of these procedures on economic progress. For example, R.H. Parker (1987) observed the difficulty of achieving renown in both disciplines and argued that some economic historians, as a means of expanding the story of the enterprise under investigation, included accounting analyses in their presentations without a real understanding of basic issues. Johnson (1986) suggested that economic historians, untrained in accounting, have difficulty dealing with the increasing sophistication and complexity of accounting over time. Hudson (1977), in good spirit, expressed hope that a trained accountant would subsequently re-evaluate the business records she had consulted to confirm her finding that there was no meaningful cost accounting in the woollen textile industry.

INFLUENCING HISTORICAL INTERPRETATION

For years, historians of accounting have been remiss in failing to respond to the call for a closer investigation of surviving business records from the period of the Industrial Revolution. Forty years ago, Solomons (1952) urged a careful examination of industrial accounts to see what practical men of business were doing so as to answer the charge of 'feebleness' conveyed by the bulk of accounting history literature. Only very recently have historians of accounting begun to cast a wider net by studying primary source material for Industrial Revolution enterprises.

Notwithstanding, the traditional accounting histories remain influential, and at least one eminent British historian of accounting remained unconvinced by revisionist activities during the two decades between his monographs (R.H. Parker, 1969, 1986). We are thus moved to ask how historians have arrived at such diametrically opposite conclusions. The restricted availability of archival resources has limited research into accounting, and the lack of easy access to accounting documents may also have diminished insights into the existence and complexity of cost accounting systems. Traditional accounting historians appear to have reached their conclusions on assumptions drawn from the instructional manuals of the period. As more financial records come under scrutiny, interpretations are being reconsidered.

Differences in basic research approach can have an important impact on findings. Significant variations in interpretation can arise if the context of the organisation, the industry, and the time period are not explicitly considered as part of the analysis. The methodology of the discipline in which a researcher was trained can also colour the conclusions. Another pertinent factor is the level of sophistication ascribed to the cost systems themselves. In discussing the differential findings of Pollard and early revisionists, Edwards (1989, p. 316) noted the possibility that the economic historian 'has rather grander ideas of the potential of management information systems in use in earlier times and today than does the accountant'.

Also problematic is the lack of congruence regarding the definitions of common accounting terms. For example, some historians employ the terminology 'standard costs' to describe the use of norm-based target costs, whilst others limit the expression to situations in which actual-to-standard cost variances are computed and analysed. Another problem in evaluating the quality of managerial accounting during the Industrial Revolution lies in the requisite components of 'good costing'. A universal acceptance of accounting conventions or techniques would indicate a modicum of sophistication, but it hardly seems an imperative. Given the absence in early accountancy of a core literature, an established curriculum, and recognised professional status, the wheel had to be reinvented in multiple venues. Those charged with the cost accounting function might reasonably have been expected to transmit methods of their own devising rather than to have written textbooks (Garner, 1954). In some instances, the surviving accounting archives suggest that useful ideas and systems developed by individual firms and their bookkeepers died with them, since there were no means of transmitting these practices to the business world in general.

A lack of standardisation would be particularly evident if new methods were developed by the entrepreneurs themselves and adapted to their unique situations. Edwards (1989) pointed out that the variety and ad hoc nature of pre-1830 costing reflected innovative attempts of firms to structure accounting information to their needs. Hopwood and Johnson (1986), as defenders of accounting history responding to Lister's (1983) debunking article, argued that elaborate accounting systems are not a necessary precondition to generate information useful for economic decision making. The questions that need to be asked when evaluating the importance of costing techniques to any older society are fundamental. Was accounting used, at least in part, to make business decisions? Did the accounting, however unsophisticated, lead to correct decisions? How frequently and for what reasons did distorted accounting lead businessmen astray and result in a failure to maximise their firms' goals (Edwards, 1989; Yamey, 1981)?

The uses of cost accounting are varied, ranging from pricing, on the one hand, to planning, control, and decision making on the other. However, there seems to be a prejudice, perhaps a product of our own time, that unless techniques are employed for the planning and decision-making functions, they are unsophisticated and antiquated (Hudson, 1977). Provocative writings, such as Johnson and Kaplan's *Relevance Lost* (1987), have moved accounting history to centre stage, and have raised serious questions about the capability of modern methods to provide useful data, not to mention their ability to serve as yardsticks of cost accounting efficiency in earlier societies. Since a contemporary problem of US management is its inability to determine which product lines are profitable, it may be presumptuous to denigrate the costing efforts of Industrial Revolution entrepreneurs.

Without question, the context of accounting has now changed dramatically with the advent of an accounting profession, the demand for uniformity from regulatory agencies, and the development of computer technology for information dispersion. Accordingly, we see the emergence of protests against traditional criticisms of earlier methods and applications (Edwards, 1989; Hopwood & Johnson, 1986; Johnson, 1981). In reflecting on the chronology of accounting historiography, Hopwood and Johnson (1986, p. 45) wrote:

> Many accounting historians writing before the late 1960s adopted that view [to judge the past in terms of the present] when they evaluated pre-twentieth century accounting artifacts in terms of twentieth century financial accounting categories. Their concern was to trace "origins" on the assumption that the past "evolves" into the present in a logical, ordered fashion.

Perhaps accounting history can be excused its delinquency because it is a relatively nascent research area with a still small cohort of devotees. Even though accounting enjoys the advantage of a focus narrower than economics, the majority of researchers in the area have focussed their analyses and debates upon the application of various conceptual frameworks (Neoclassical, Foucauldian, Marxist) to accounting history, rather than on archival research. Moreover, those researchers initially attracted to accounting history were led to expect little of value in Industrial Revolution business archives.

REDRESSING THE BALANCE

In the chapters that follow, the current authors will attempt to redress the balance by reporting and analysing the results of our broadly based examination of surviving business records from the British Industrial Revolution. In Chapter 2, we offer a survey of the best evidence we have found to establish the case that this era was an important formative period for the development of sophisticated managerial accounting methods. In Chapters 3–5, we investigate developments in the dominant industries of the Industrial Revolution—textiles, iron, and mining. Chapters 6 and 7 are case studies of the accounting systems in place at two firms in the vanguard of Industrial

Revolution costing—the Carron Company and Boulton & Watt. Chapter 8 is an essay on the relationship between accounting and the technological innovations that constituted so important a feature of the age. In Chapter 9, we review the paradigmatic debate that has been so vital a component of the historiography of the Industrial Revolution, and, in so doing, elucidate the methodological perspectives that have informed the research leading to this volume. Finally, in Chapter 10, we summarise our conclusions on the topic, as well as advance suggestions for future research directions.

The chapters in this volume draw on a number of studies conducted by the authors over a period in excess of a decade. Some of the work has been presented in published form, referenced in a footnote to the title of relevant chapters. Oftentimes these chapters represent expanded versions, containing more detail than in the original journal article. Other chapters present research hitherto unpublished. Together they are intended to provide a first macro-level view of Industrial Revolution costing based on archives located and examined to date, as well as insights into practices in particular industries and enterprises. It is hoped that this initial venture will provide future researchers with a foundation embracing both environmental and methodological dimensions of the subject.

NOTES

1. The information contained in this chapter is extracted in part from R.K. Fleischman and T.N. Tyson (1993), 'Cost Accounting during the Industrial Revolution: The Present State of Historical Knowledge', *Economic History Review*, Vol. XLVI, No. 3: 503–517.

2

The Big Picture[1]

This chapter summarises our findings of managerial accounting techniques in 25 major British Industrial Revolution enterprises. For each of the firms represented here, an archive of business records does exist. In some instances (e.g., Crowley, Dugdale, Herculaneum, Nasmyth, Pearsce), the number of surviving documents is minuscule. Holdings are abundant for other firms, such as Ashworth, Boulton & Watt, Carron, Darby, Dowlais, Finlay, Marshall, McConnel & Kennedy, Mona, Strutt, and Wedgwood. Our archival research was immeasurably aided by references supplied in older investigations of these materials undertaken by both accounting and economic historians. Pollard (1965), Hudson (1977, 1986), and Jones (1985) examined Industrial Revolution business records over a broad spectrum. Our research also involved consulting the writings of those historians who concentrated their study on individual enterprises—Boulton & Watt (Roll, 1968; Tann, 1981), Carron (Campbell, 1961), Crawshay (Addis, 1957), Crowley (Flinn, 1962), Darby (Raistrick, 1970; Trinder, 1973, 1974), Dowlais (Edwards & Baber, 1979), Gott (Heaton, 1931–1932), Marshall (Rimmer, 1960), McConnel & Kennedy (Lee, 1972), Nasmyth (Cantrell, 1984), Oldknow (Unwin, 1924), Strutt (Fitton & Wadsworth, 1958), and Wedgwood (McKendrick, 1970). Whilst the efforts by economic historians are of uneven value because of differential attention to accounting detail and variable accounting expertise informing their analyses, their coverage of accounting topics in most instances is a function of the sophistication reflected in the archive with which they had to work.

The two most significant factors involved in the process by which the 25 firms were selected for this sample were (1) references to archival sources provided in earlier works, particularly Pollard (1965), and (2) the proximity of the various repositories to Manchester, our base of operations for the 'discovery phase' of the project (Napier, 1989). Although the surviving records of these firms are not necessarily the most fruitful in the UK, there is a definite bias in that direction given their prominence in the economic history literature.

A majority of extant Industrial Revolution business records are oriented toward financial accounting. Day books, journals, and ledgers were of limited value to us because of the poor quality of the reporting and their infrequent attention to costing issues. Much more fruitful were letters between owners, the notebooks and diaries of prominent personnel, minute books, production reports, and miscellaneous cost estimates. The records of absentee-owned firms typically featured a flow of correspondence between managers and owners that was frequently rich in costing data. Yet, questions will remain about the sophistication of the accounting methods described here because the low survival rate for Industrial Revolution business records has made it extremely difficult to match costing projections with managerial decision making.

It should be noted, however, that 'more' is not always better than 'less' when making a case that surviving records reflect purposeful cost accounting at a particular firm. Voluminous survivals exist for James Finlay & Co., McConnel & Kennedy, and Newton, Chambers & Co.; yet, these firms instill little confidence that the data were actually employed in any meaningful fashion. The bounty of the Boulton & Watt, Carron, Darby, and Wedgwood archives, by contrast, communicates a far different story. In yet other instances, the paucity of surviving records frustrates the researcher because the high quality of the little that remains generates the wish that there were much more; e.g., Greg, Oldknow, Philips, Strutt. We can offer no explanation as to why the archival remains of certain firms are more extensive other than the vagaries of record preservation over the centuries. In terms of the quality differential, we attribute the superior methods to the acumen of those individuals, often the founding entrepreneurs themselves, who devised the various systems. In the absence of a cost accounting literature, an accounting profession, and an educational curriculum, it could have been no other way.

Throughout the course of this volume, we will be making qualitative assessments of costing practices discovered to have existed during the British Industrial Revolution. In evaluating these methods we do establish frequent linkages to contemporary practice and modern idiom. Previous work by the current authors has been criticised on this basis. Miller and Napier (1993, p. 639) charged that 'within the traditional evolutionary model, the now is always present, if only *in utero*, in the then'. This critique suggests that historians are able to separate themselves completely from the present in the process of narrating past events. Indeed, the lofty aim of historians to envelop themselves in the past, and thereby to exclude presentist knowledge and ideology, harkens back to Rankean historicism. Whilst we applaud the efforts of those historians who have attempted this disassociation, we doubt its absolute feasibility. In point of fact, whilst recognising the interpretive risks and limitations involved, we rather unabashedly employ the present as a measuring rod of the past because our purpose here is to discover the foundations of 'purposeful' or 'sophisticated' cost accounting. Present methodology, though not assumed to be best practice, does afford a reference point to aid us in defining the above-mentioned adjectives. Additionally, we would raise the following arguments in defence to the objections raised by Miller and Napier:

- Historians who believe that they are providing an objective account are deluded, for they are 'ignoring the distorting lens through which they observed past history' (Hill, 1986, p. 14). The very process of selecting the data to report is itself subjective.
- Whilst measuring the past is not an exercise historians must perform as an essential component of their craft and whilst using the present as the measuring calculus might not be the most appropriate yardstick, it seems to us that qualitative evaluation on the basis of contemporary norms affords the reader a greater understanding of the past and a greater appreciation for its relevance to the present.

Some of these issues are discussed in much greater depth in Chapter 9. Others are reserved for subsequent debate and dialogue in alternative venues. For now, we turn our attention to the best evidence in support of our contention that the British Industrial Revolution was a pioneering epoch in the development of cost accounting.

Table 1 is a listing of the 25 business enterprises comprising the sample, with accompanying information about the firm's industry, the location(s) of its business records, and the nature of the documents comprising the archive. Although archival references are not provided for the summary analysis attempted in this chapter, the reader is encouraged to consult subsequent industry and firm-specific chapters for further details and documentary disclosures.

Table 1: Manuscript Sources

Firm	*Industry*	*Location of Records*	*Types of Records*
Ashworth	cotton	Staffordshire R.O., Rylands (Manchester), Lancashire R.O.	diaries, mill comparisons, expenditure/production reports
Boulton & Watt	steam engines	Birmingham Central	engine books, estimates, notebooks, letters, miscellaneous
Cardwell, Birley	cotton	Rylands (Manchester)	expenditure/production reports
Carron	iron	West Register House, National Library (Edinburgh)	cost analyses, production reports, minute books, letters, cost estimates
Crawshay	iron	National Library (Aberystwyth)	letters, memorandum books
Crowley	iron	British Museum, Newcastle Central	law book, law book administration
Darby	iron	Ironbridge Museum, Shrewsbury Public, Shropshire R.O.	inventory, minute book, valuations, furnace accounts, journals, cost analysis, memoranda
Dowlais	iron	Glamorganshire R.O.	yields, minute books, notebooks, letters, costings
Dugdale	cotton	Rylands (Manchester)	job costings, expenses, machinery book
Finlay	cotton	Glasgow University	day books, minutes, ledgers, letters
Gott	wool	Leeds University	notebooks, engine expenses, expense calculations
Greg	cotton	Manchester Central	stoppages, mill ledgers, stock books, cash books

Table 1: (cont'd.): Manuscript Sources

Firm	*Industry*	*Location of Records*	*Types of Records*
Herculaneum	pottery	Liverpool Central	minute book
Horrocks	cotton	Lancashire R.O.	trade letters, ledgers, journals, powerloom notes
Marshall	flax	Leeds University	notebooks, departmental accounts
McConnel & Kennedy	cotton	Rylands (Manchester)	output accounts, labour accounts, ledgers, day books
Mona Mine	copper	Bangor University	notebooks, smelting expenses, refining charges
Nasmyths, Gaskell	machinery	Eccles Public	day books, sales, letters
Newton, Chambers	iron	Sheffield Central	colliery accounts, letters, production
Oldknow	cotton	Manchester Central	output reports, costings, mill comparisons
Pearsce	cotton	Nottinghamshire R.O.	cost calculations, mill and operations detail
Philips	tape	Staffordshire R.O.	production budgets, process costing
Strutt	cotton	Manchester Central, Derby Central	expense books, machine ledgers, mill-specific results, letters
Stubs	tools	Manchester Central	production, employment, inventory
Wedgwood	pottery	Keele University	letters, ledgers, inventory, pricings

COST MANAGEMENT PRACTICE IN REVIEW

Surviving business records attest to an extensive use of cost management techniques by Industrial Revolution entrepreneurs. Based upon our investigation of the archives, we have identified eight functional areas in which costing data were deployed—expense control; responsibility management; product costing; overhead allocation; cost comparisons; costs for special decisions; budgets, forecasts, and standards; inventory control. In Table 2 we have linked the 25 firms with the cost management functional activities they reflected to some degree. There was substantial activity in all the identified areas with a preponderance of the businesses practising expense control, product costing, and standard costing.[2] Four firms (Carron, Darby, Oldknow, and Strutt) exhibited activity in all eight functional areas investigated.

These techniques took many forms. Consistent with their development by industrial entrepreneurs, they appeared rudimentary at times. On the other hand, in a considerable number of instances a surprising (to a contemporary viewer) level of sophistication was achieved in both development and application. What must be emphasised is our finding that these cost management methods were not mere historical financial accounting figures for post-event stewardship reporting to absentee owners. The pursuits of cost and quality control, as well as profitability maintenance or improvement, were ongoing management concerns.

Table 3 summarises our qualitative assessment of firms which reflected superior attention to or sophistication in the various categories. When evaluated in terms of the breadth of cost management practices, the quality level achieved, the detail apparent in existing accounting records, and the number of references to cost issues over time, five firms emerged most notably for the quality of their cost management. Pre-eminent were Ashworth and Strutt, followed by Boulton & Watt, Marshall, and Philips.

Boulton & Watt made a special impact on Industrial Revolution accounting, apart from the excellence of its costing methods, because it forced other large firms to be more cost aware. During the 1770s and 1780s, Boulton & Watt based the annual rentals for its steam engines on cost savings relative to the older machines being replaced, adjusted for local coal prices. Though this complex premium was subsequently

Table 2: Utilisation of Cost Management Techniques

	Management Techniques							
Firms	Expense Control	Responsibility Management	Product Costing	Overhead Allocation	Cost Comparisons	Costs for Special Decisions	Budgets, Forecasts, Standards	Inventory Control
Ashworth	X	X	X		X	X	X	
Boulton & Watt	X	X	X		X	X	X	X
Cardwell, Birley		X		X			X	X
Carron	X	X	X	X	X	X	X	X
Crawshay	X		X	X	X		X	X
Crowley	X					X	X	X
Darby	X	X	X	X	X	X	X	X
Dowlais	X		X	X	X	X	X	X
Dugdale	X						X	
Finlay			X				X	
Gott	X	X	X		X	X		X
Greg	X	X	X		X	X		X
Herculaneum	X	X				X		X
Horrocks			X	X		X		X
Marshall	X	X	X	X	X	X	X	
McConnel & Kennedy	X	X				X	X	X
Mona Mine	X		X	X	X	X	X	
Nasmyths, Gaskell	X							X
Newton, Chambers					X		X	
Oldknow	X	X	X	X	X	X	X	X
Pearsce	X		X		X			
Philips	X	X	X		X	X	X	X
Strutt	X	X	X	X	X	X	X	X
Stubs								
Wedgwood	X	X	X		X	X	X	X

Table 3: Qualitative Assessment of Superior Cost Management

	Management Techniques							
Firms	Expense Control	Responsibility Management	Product Costing	Overhead Allocation	Cost Comparisons	Costs for Special Decisions	Budgets, Forecasts, Standards	Inventory Control
Ashworth	X	X	X		X	X	X	
Boulton & Watt	X	X	X		X		X	
Cardwell, Birley				X				
Carron		X			X	X	X	
Crawshay				X				
Crowley	X						X	X
Darby		X				X		X
Dowlais	X		X	X		X		
Dugdale								
Finlay								
Gott	X				X			
Greg	X							
Herculaneum								
Horrocks				X				
Marshall	X	X	X	X	X			
McConnel & Kennedy								
Mona Mine	X				X		X	
Nasmyths, Gaskell								
Newton, Chambers								
Oldknow	X							
Pearsce								
Philips	X	X	X		X		X	
Strutt	X	X		X	X		X	X
Stubs								
Wedgwood			X					

commuted to a lump-sum payment, many leases continued on a cost-based formula. Figure 1 was extracted from a 1770s engine book. Each page contained data for a single engine. Needless to say, these intricate calculations required careful record keeping at the engine sites.

The purchase of any steam engine was frequently a decision based on a cost analysis. Carron and Herculaneum made multiple evaluations of engines for a variety of purposes. In the cases of two firms not included in this study, Davison & Hawkesley and Samuel Walker & Co., correspondence with Boulton & Watt on the subject of steam engine costs is the only surviving business documents we have seen.

Whilst it is easy to highlight outstanding examples of cost management practice, it is the extent which should be underscored. Fifteen firms exhibited activity in five or more of the functions identified. The breadth and variety of cost management techniques employed by British entrepreneurs in the Industrial Revolution bear witness to levels of attention and sophistication not hitherto recognised by accounting historians. We turn now to a discussion of noteworthy activities within each of the eight functional areas of cost management previously identified.

EXPENSE CONTROL

Attention to the tracking of expenses might be expected as a necessary first step in the development of any cost accounting system. The fact that 80% of the enterprises studied made efforts to control costs is indicative of competitive realities during the Industrial Revolution. Some firms did better than others. The Gott enterprise was especially conscientious in scrutinising expenses. The notebooks of Benjamin Gott were replete with cost comparisons reflective of this concern; e.g., the cost/benefit of machine rather than manual methods for converting raw wool into yarn, the savings anticipated from cheaper spinning and finishing methods, and the cost differentials between Spanish and English wools.

John Marshall & Co. made an effort to control expenses by maintaining daily performance cards for each spinning frame, input/output records for every variety of raw material, and semi-annual

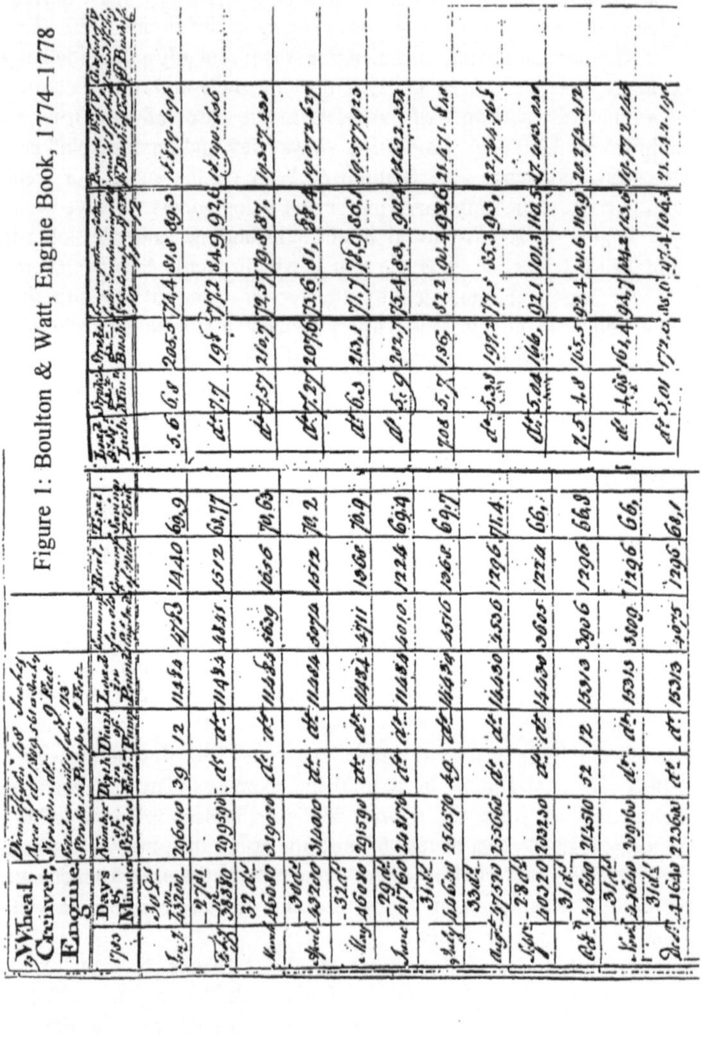

Figure 1: Boulton & Watt, Engine Book, 1774–1778

compendiums of all costs associated with the four major productive processes. The Marshalls were proactive in attempting to influence costs as evidenced by their continuous experimentation with more efficient spinning and hackling machinery and their willingness to restructure workloads to conform to test results relating yarn output to the number of spindles individual workers tended.

The famous law book of the Crowleys, initially compiled in 1692 but continually amended, contained many references to expense control. The surveyor supervised abatements for deficient work and raw materials unaccounted for (Law 45); the nailkeeper reconciled raw materials distributed to finished product (Law 14); and the coalkeeper was cautioned not to purchase coal at times when carriage rates were high (Law 12) (Flinn, 1957). Moreover, the Crowleys monitored output with reports sent weekly to corporate headquarters in Greenwich.

The Gregs maintained intricate wage and expenses books for their Quarry Bank and Caton Mills in which they calculated important control statistics. Correspondence between Robert and Samuel Greg regarding losses in 1829 stressed the heightened production cost of using older machinery, the utilisation of better quality cotton than necessary, and the possibility of halving the number of card rooms to save on overseeing.

Henry Ashworth observed in his 1851 diary that his firm was making no profit on higher quality twist and perceived the problem to be the raw material mixture. It was determined that using more Sea Island cotton instead of the more expensive Egyptian variety would save a penny per pound of yarn, thereby making the product line profitable. The general concern of his firm about costs is reflected in Figure 2, a quarterly expenditure summary, dated 1842.

Numerous other companies tracked costs carefully. The owners of Herculaneum scrutinised weekly wage reports and breakage data. William Crawshay wrote to Cyfarthfa in 1814 that he wanted to see weekly furnace accounts. In 1763, Carron Company's General Court ordered a breakdown of all costs for each product individually, including applied overhead. The Strutts sought to control expenses with separate record books for waste management and wage abatements.

Figure 2: Henry Ashworth, Quarterly Expenditures, 1842

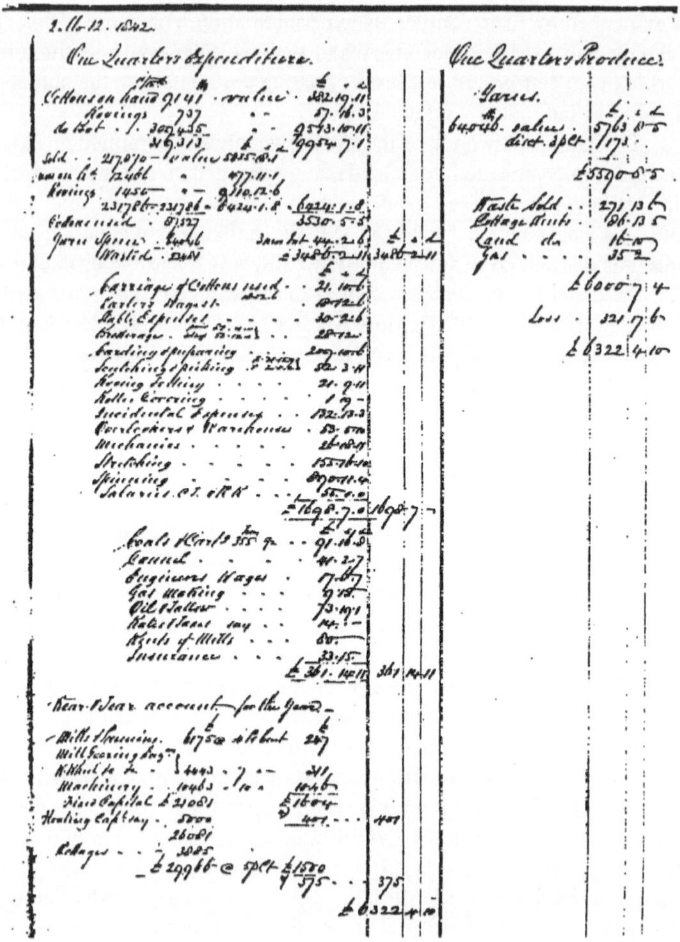
One Quarters Expenditure.

One Quarters Produce.

Carriage of Cottons used

Carters Wages

Rates Expenses

Brokerage

Carding & preparing

Roving Twisting

Roller Covering

Incidental Expenses

Overlookers & Warehouse

Mechanics

Stretching

Spinning

Coals & Cart[s]

Cannel

Engineers Wages

Gas Making

Oil & Tallow

Rates & Taxes say

Agents of Mills

Insurance

Wear & Tear account for the year

Machinery

Fixed Capital

Cottages

Yarns

Waste Sold

Cottage Rents

Land do

Gas

£6000.7.4

Loss . 321.7.6

£6322.4.10

RESPONSIBILITY MANAGEMENT

Though many of the firms studied did not attempt to control expenses for individual cost or profit centres, a slight majority (56%) did. The Gotts established their scribbling, dyeing, mechanics, and milling operations as independent profit centres. The Darbys in the 1820s undertook a management reorganisation which elevated the best men to managerial rank with responsibility for performance reporting. Separate profit and loss statements were not only compiled for individual components of the firm, but for departments within each segment.

The Strutts produced costings by function, by product, and by plant. For instance, commencing in 1831 at Milford, expenses per pound of yarn were recorded quarterly by operation. Averages were maintained to one-tenth of a pence for nine different cost centres. Boulton & Watt compiled weekly expense reports that would allow for the comparison of individual shops of the same function, such as lathes and drilling. There is no evidence, however, that these data were ever used for this purpose. In 1822, Herculaneum Potteries decentralised, allocating operational responsibility amongst five managers. Detailed expense data were demanded from each. Unfortunately, the archive does not contain any of the reports requested.

From its earliest history in the 1760s, Carron Company's ownership insisted that managers be responsible for the performance and profitability of their own departments. In 1765, the blacksmith and plating forge accounts were separated so that the anchor and anvil trades could be evaluated more accurately. Eventually, anchor production, as well as the nail trade, were discontinued on the basis of profit analyses (Campbell, 1961).

PRODUCT COSTING

Precedent to times when formalised financial reporting became required, the primary purpose of cost management was accurate product costing for pricing and profit determination. There are numerous cost calculations in surviving business records, though there is infrequently any narrative about the process by which cost estimates for particular line items were derived or the causal relationship between costs and subsequent selling prices. Consequently, we look for elements of sophistication in the number and frequency of product costings, as well as those individual costs the formulators thought to include. Superior efforts reflected attention to indirect costs and selling expenses, as distinct from the more obvious prime costs.

Perhaps the most spectacular example of product costing was Boulton & Watt's engine books from the early nineteenth century. These enormous volumes contained seven-page printed forms for each steam engine manufactured. Each of the hundreds of components comprising the finished product was individually costed.

Josiah Wedgwood communicated to his partner cost calculations for 31 different vase lots in 1772. These costings were impressive when measured by the range of overhead items and period expenses figured into his reckoning—supplies, indirect labour, breakage, imperfect pieces, selling expenses, and freight (McKendrick, 1970). Unfortunately, Wedgwood's arithmetic was not of similar standard as he frequently misadded his columns of numbers. Perhaps he should not have been so insistent that the accountant he was trying to hire in those days also be able to throw pots (Euphemia, 1973).

Perhaps the most impressive records in this area were not actual costings themselves but accumulations of data for subsequent calculations. John Marshall & Co. kept detailed semi-annual accounts for the spinning, weaving, and bleaching processes, as well as for cheek, flax, and thread production. Over 40 data categories were maintained, including the actual expenses incurred in numerous overhead categories. Abundant information was available for the development of labour efficiency and raw material usage standards though there is no direct evidence that this mass of computations was ever used for this purpose.

Dowlais utilised a three-page printed form entitled 'Cost of Materials and Iron Made' covering five-week periods in the 1840s. Costs per ton were calculated for raw material inputs, as well as for finished and semi-finished output. A formula apparently existed for the application of overhead, called 'general charges', to specific departments. Concern with accurate costing was not a new phenomenon at Dowlais. An 1802 notebook of the firm's manager, J.J. Guest, had a fairly sophisticated tabulation of the expenses for making ten tons of steel. Similar one-off costings were found for William Pearsce (1794—ten pounds of manufactured cotton), Darby (1810—boiler plate cost), Crawshay (1822—one ton of foundry pig iron), Oldknow (1797—'contingency expenses' of spinning), and Gott (1830—costs of processing £1,000 of Hamburgh wool). Such cost estimates were complex, containing line items for incidental supplies, indirect labour, selling expenses, depreciation, taxes, machinery and building repair, rubbish removal, reworking scrap, and interest on capital.

The Greg manuscripts contain an 1831 calculation showing costs associated with producing 18,000 pounds of twist weekly. Included were an allocation to recover the initial outlay for the factory and machinery, raw materials, waste, wages, and an itemised 'contingencies' list. The bottom line, after four pages of computations, was a product cost of 2.27d per pound.

OVERHEAD ALLOCATION

Firms in the vanguard of product costing manifested a superior awareness of which overhead items to include in their pricing analyses and period comparisons. Here we review the efforts of companies which took greater pains in overhead allocation and included overhead when evaluating product lines or productive departments.

Horrocks, Crewdson & Co. deserves special mention as the architect of the most complex procedure for handling depreciation. Each year the current values of the firm's identifiable assets were recalculated, and a predetermined proportion of depreciation was allocated to the productive departments. Furthermore, any diminution in current asset values was charged to departmental accounts.

Three of our large Industrial Revolution firms allocated overhead amongst departments based on formula. The distribution of Dowlais' 'general charges' was mentioned above. Carron Company, as early as 1763, made a similar allocation to its seven cost centres. Carron was also careful to specify which items of expense to include in 'general charges' and which to charge directly to the productive departments. Marshall's Shrewsbury accounts contain the following application of overhead expenses for 1811:

Table 4: Overhead Allocation at John Marshall & Co.

Item	*Total*	*Flax*	*Spinning*	*Twisting*	*Dyeing*	*Finishing*	*Making Up*	*Sales*
Rent	2700	400	1100	550	200	200	50	200
Repairs and Taxes	255	20	140	50	20	20		5
Repair of Machinery and Steam Engine	2200	300	1200	500	100	100	30	20
Coals	2400	100	1400	710	100	100	20	20
Tallow, Engine Men's Wages, etc.	400	20	220	120	40	40		
Mill and Hacklers Sundries	1012	70	500	300	40	40	20	62
Sundries, Clerks, etc.	1200	200	100	70	50	50	30	700
Total	10167	1110	4660	2300	550	550	150	1007
Interest			400	200	20	20	10	3000
Expenses per week	292	47	97	48	11	11	3	96

In 1819, the allocation figures were adjusted as rent expense was reduced £500 and the machinery repair and coals accounts by £200 each. These savings were not proportionately passed on to all the cost centres. Thus, departmental percentage contributions were altered to reflect current utilisation.

The most meticulously kept expense book we have seen is found in the Strutt archive. Belper plant expenses included weekly costings of such items as superintending, dinner breaks, and 'learning' (the only recorded instance we have seen of the latter cost element). Moreover, expenses were reckoned to a thousandth of a pence, with overhead allocated over various processing departments.

Additional firms applied overhead to products in a less systematic fashion. In 1798, Darby management, in an analysis of the relative profitability of various products and departments, observed that many manufactured goods did not have prices proportional to the variety of 'additional charges incidental to manufacturing'. As a result some products appeared less profitable than the pig and bar iron trades, whilst the Coalbrookdale Foundry did not compare favourably to other installations. William Crawshay advised his resident manager in 1814 not to close down a blast furnace because it would decrease production, increase common charges per unit of output, and raise prices. Mona Mine in 1827 was applying overhead costs to products at a standard rate, with the difference between actual and standard cost going into a sundry account.

COST COMPARISONS

Industrial Revolution entrepreneurs never tired of making cost comparisons. Departments were ranked against one another in terms of profitability. In firms with multiple plants, statistics were maintained to evaluate relative performance. Like machines, blast furnaces, steam engines, and card rooms were contrasted as to costs and profitability.

Major iron producers took pains to maintain cost and yield data on their mineral sources. William Lowes, Carron Company's accountant, filed numerous reports during the 1770s about the firm's coal, limestone, and ironstone holdings and leases. Minerals were charged to user departments at transfer prices reflective of the expenses incurred in raising ore in the various fields. Records were kept to support buy-or-lease decisions on mineral fields owned by neighbours. The Darbys knew in the 1820s the costs of mining the several kinds of coal and ironstone the firm utilised. Dowlais did a complete analysis of the efficiency, and hence the cost, of various types of coal available. Included in these calculations were the amount of iron received per grain of charcoal and coal, the volume of residual ash, and the specific gravity of the coal and coke used. The notebook of Thomas Beer, the accountant at Mona Mine, contained data on good copper yields from different ores, taking into account differential costs of raising and smelting.

Textile firms were particularly concerned about raw material mixtures and waste management. Benjamin Gott's notebook contained calculations of the cloth output from various wool mixtures. Henry Ashworth, similarly concerned about profitable cotton blends, was attentive to the cost of waste in his comparative analyses as he determined 3.15 ounces the appropriate standard for each pound of yarn produced. The intricate spinning, flax, and cheek data categories employed by the Marshalls permitted annual waste comparisons. The Strutts had a separate book reserved for computations of waste. The Herculaneum and Wedgwood concerns maintained close track of pottery breakage.

The subject of steam engine efficiency precipitated a number of cost comparisons. Gott compared the expenses of working two engines, one old and one new, taking five-year averages during the period 1833–1857. Supply items (coal, tallow, oil, packing, shovels), tender wages, repair expense, and machine downtime were all taken into account. A Dowlais notebook from 1827–1828 provided intricate detail on the horsepower generated and the coal consumed by each engine. Weekly blast furnace accounts at Darby tracked the downtime of each engine. Records were likewise kept, dating from the 1820s, of coal quantities consumed by individual steam engines.

A number of large firms engaged in macro-level cost comparisons, either of their various function rooms or plants. The Strutt mill at Milford had four carding and four spinning rooms. Quarterly cost comparisons revealed significant variations in expenses. These results were not only used to evaluate the cost control of the respective managers, but became the basis for interperiod and interplant comparisons. Expense data were generated weekly for the multiple lathing and drilling shops at Boulton & Watt. In the 1790s, a supervisor at Carron was transmitting monthly reports of costs per ton of good iron for each blast furnace. These comparisons were accompanied by notes explaining why production might be down, either generally or at a particular furnace.

Figure 3 is extracted from a 14-page report entitled, 'Account of the coals consumed by the Steam Engines at Messrs. Marshalls Flax Mills Leeds Yorkshire, and also the quantity of Yarn spun in the year 1823'. The document, which contained a number of important cost and profit calculations far transcending the narrow scope suggested by the title, was in essence a comparison of three different mills. There is a surviving 15-page report, dated 1846, which contrasted profit/loss, the wear and tear allowance, and profit per spindle (gross and net) for the 12 years past at Ashworth's New Eagley and Egerton mills. A Darby quarterly memorandum of 1820 concluded with the observation that an additional five hundredweights of coal were required for each ton of pigs produced at the Dawley Castle furnace compared to Horsehay.

COSTS FOR SPECIAL DECISIONS

Two giant iron concerns, Darby and Carron, were clear leaders in generating cost analyses to aid special decision making. In the one surviving Darby minute book, dated 1789–1796, the firm's owners ordered no fewer than five cost analyses and acted on most: (1) a combined lease-and-delivery decision for ironstone to Coalbrookdale and Madeley; (2) a repair-or-sell decision on premises called Nailors' Row; (3) a general investigation of several branches of the concern to eliminate leases that impaired profits; (4) a decision not to build a railway from New Work Colliery to Horsehay, but rather to subcontract the service for a charge of 2d per ton per mile; and (5) a cost/profit analysis of Chepstow premises for anticipated subsequent sale. In 1798 and 1825, the firm carefully considered the viability of its Coalbrookdale and Horsehay leases. In 1813, the firm did an intricate calculation of the expenses and savings associated with the use of a boiler to conduct heat from the puddling furnaces, a development Raistrick called a very significant technological advance. In the 1830s,

Figure 3: John Marshall & Co., Mill Comparison, 1823

From the Table of averages, the coals and produce was as follows, I from Jan 1823 to April II April to July; III July to Octr. Octr. to Jan 1824.

Quarter	Hours Work	Pounds of Coals	Coals per Hour		Cost of Coals £ s d	Bundles Yarn	Pounds Yarn	lb per Bundle	Leys per lb
I	922.5	783118	849	–	57-8-4 50-3-9	7582	231385	30.5	6.56
II	973	730061	758	–	56-6-8 46-1-8	8501	235774	27.7	7.36
III	888	735941	828	–	64-17-5 37-15-9	7883	210051	26.8	7.46
IV	932	854610	917	–	[illegible]	8315	219756	26.4	7.58
Year	3716.5	3103710	836	–	433-2-8	32301	894982	27.7	7.22

Hence it appears that this Engine consumed 1385.6 Tons of Coals in the year, which cost 233-2-2 And spun 32301 bundles of Tow yarn, of 27.7 lb. per Bundle; Weight 400 Tons.

This is at the rate of 26.66 tons of coals per Week cost 8.6.8 and the produce 621 bundles per week; weight 17200 lb = 7.68 Tons.

The average price of coals 6-4 per ton; the consumption 836 lb per hour of working, or allowing 1 hours consumption per day the firm revoked subcontracts it had made in the areas of railways, canals, and brick making (Raistrick, 1970; Trinder, 1973).

The Carron archive contains two remarkable documents concerning the firm's coal-mining operations. In 1768, a report was prepared on the extraction and profitability of Kinnaird coal, which included time-and-motion studies on the mining process and laid the foundation for the establishment of standards and transfer prices. In 1770, a more general survey of coal reserves was made and differential costs calculated for the raising of each. This report also included a cost analysis for sinking the Kinnaird engine pit three fathoms and a business forecast comparing profitability between existing production levels and a proposed reduction to 50% of current volume. Carron's management also demanded cost data for a wide range of items including subcontracting, machinery procurement, and repair-or-replace decisions.

At Dowlais in 1859, an in-depth analysis was prepared as to the advantages of purchasing the Penydarran mineral field. In this 12-page report, the estimated raising costs and yields from Penydarran were compared with similar data from current operations. The savings in costs and coal yields per ton were translated into annual cost reductions in the manufacture of both pig iron and forge coal. It was concluded also that the new field would allow the firm to defer current expenses associated with sinking pits.

One aspect of the Industrial Revolution was the growing vertical integration of the larger firms. These decisions to expand operations were frequently the end result of cost/profit estimations. Though the Crowleys concentrated on the manufacture of finished iron products almost exclusively, they did expand into pig iron forging and outright ownership of their own shipping fleet (Flinn, 1962). Samuel Oldknow made informed decisions as the firm added new processes, such as bleaching, printing, and dyeing (Unwin, 1924). The Philips' made cost estimates for all additions to their tape-making operation. Wedgwood considered stove manufacturing but concluded that the expansion would not be cost effective for the amount of space required (Euphemia, 1973).

Similar cost information facilitated existing product line decisions. Boulton & Watt utilised numerous subcontractors to manufacture engine components and frequently reversed these decisions as situations changed (Tann, 1981). Carron withdrew from the nail trade and anchor production. Wedgwood either abandoned or de-emphasised crests, figurines, and painting (Euphemia, 1973).

Transportation costs were a matter of consequence to some firms. Herculaneum imported all coals via the Sankey Canal after alternative routes had been investigated. Wedgwood did a cost/benefit analysis in 1765 of constructing a canal into Staffordshire (ibid.). Mona Mine did a cost comparison of selling at Swansea as opposed to Liverpool in 1827.

One last example of costs for special decisions demonstrates much ado about nothing. There are virtually no surviving business records or economic histories about the Wilkinson iron concern.. One remnant is an 1807 comparative costing for raising coal and ore from a pit using ropes and chains respectively. The calculation is so detailed that even the salvage value of the old ropes is taken into account (Randall, 1879).

FORECASTS, BUDGETS, AND STANDARDS

Evidence of Industrial Revolution firms employing production and costing standards is plentiful, though forecasts and budgets are relatively rare. The records of J.&N. Philips contain a remarkable set of production standards for the year 1771, showing monthly input quantities projected over a 20-month period to achieve a desired level of output. The computation was all the more exceptional because the looms used were of different types with differential productive capabilities.

Henry Ashworth established standards for 40, 50, and 60 count twist in his 1849 diary. In each case Ashworth calculated a 'prime cost' per pound based on actual fortnightly expenditures divided by the spinner's labour standard, which for 60 twist was 250 pounds weekly or 15 hanks per spindle. A raw material standard, based on an equal mix of Egyptian and Bahia cotton and a one-sixth allowance for waste, was added. The result was a 13½d per pound cost, compared to a 14d selling price. This 'haepenny' profit per pound is indicative of the narrowness of profit margins in cotton textiles. The Ashworths also attempted to forecast the firm's financial performance for the seven years following 1846, as illustrated in Figure 4. Though similar prognostications were infrequently found, the Carron owners requested

Figure 4: Henry Ashworth, Profit Forecast, 1846

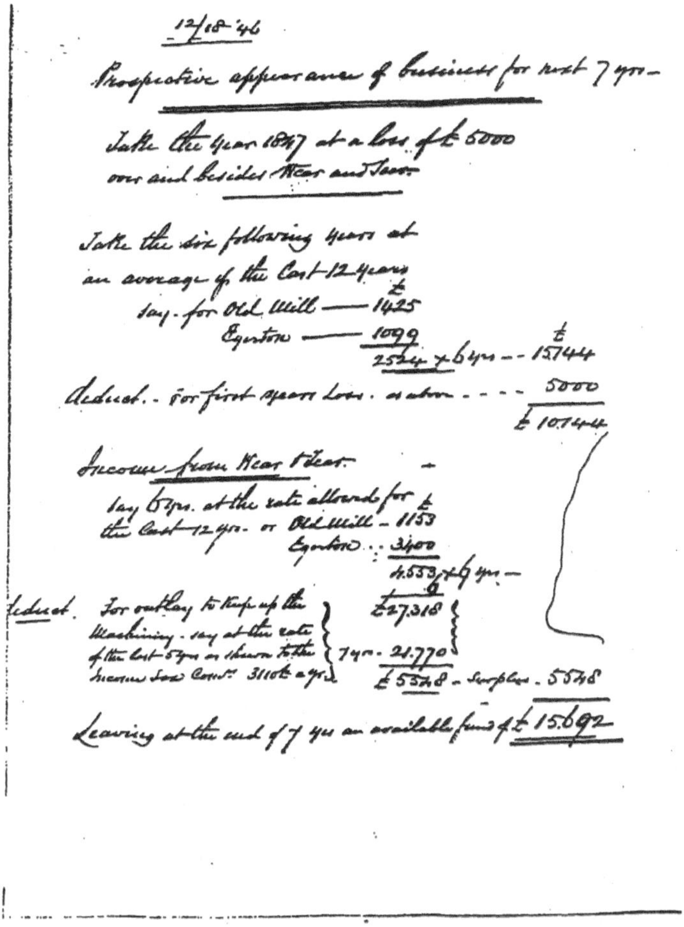

12/18 '46

Prospective appearance of business for next 7 yrs –

Take the year 1847 at a loss of £5000
over and besides Wear and Tear

Take the six following years at
an average of the last 12 years
say – for Old Mill —— £ 1425
Egerton —— 1099
2524 × 6 yrs – – £ 15144
deduct. – for first years loss . as above 5000
£ 10144

Income from Wear & Tear –
say 6 yrs. at the rate allowed for the last 12 yrs. – or Old Mill – £ 1153
Egerton . . 3400
4553 × 6 yrs –
£27318

deduct. For outlay to keep up the Machinery – say at the rate of the last 5 yrs as shown to the Income Tax Comrs 3110£ a yr – 7 yrs – 21770
£ 5548 – Surplus – 5548

Leaving at the end of 7 yrs an available fund of £ 15692

a 13-year projection of income for the Quarole Colliery in 1767. It is unknown if they ever received it.

At Crowley an inventory, taken every ten weeks, became the basis of production plans drawn up by its accountant, who was cautioned 'not to demand uneconomical runs of particular quality and sizes' (Law 36). The surveyor and nailkeeper had ultimate authority to determine the finished goods to produce, whilst corporate approval was required for the quantity and quality of iron inputs (Law 66). This system of inventory control and budgeted production runs was operational because the firm had 12 standardised rod gauges for all its iron (Law 9) (Flinn, 1957).

Boulton & Watt maintained a book of moulders' estimates for orders covering the years 1815–1839. Raw materials were logged at standard cost per hundredweight with some quality variations. Estimates for labour processes (e.g., drilling and grinding) were charged at standard. The risk of irreversible damage during the boring process was charged at one-twelfth of the costs above, tools at 25% of job cost, with a bottom-line markup of 40%. The firm also employed labour standards as evidenced by a calculation of the moulders' time required for each step of constructing a 20-horsepower engine, measured in quarter-day units (Tann, 1981).

Standards were a particularly important component in the determination of labour costs at Darby and Mona Mine. In the 1830s, Darby furnacemen agreed to a bounty system. A norm was set at 60 tons per week, with bounties paid for excess production and abatements levied below (Trinder, 1974). Mona Mine contracted 'tribute bargains' with its miners every two months. A standard price per ton of ore was calculated for each mine and each shaft.

Standard costing was almost universally applied by large Industrial Revolution manufacturing firms, particularly for product pricing and inventory valuation. The record was not always impressive, however. McConnel & Kennedy employed standard costs for valuing components of their self-constructed spinning machinery. Despite the size and success of the firm, however, there was no allowance made for overhead items.

INVENTORY CONTROL

Industrial Revolution entrepreneurs used accounting techniques to maintain inventory control. Inventory costs were carried at standard almost universally and frequently flowed through work-in-process prior to product completion. Managers were concerned about appropriate inventory levels though theories differed between enterprises. The Crawshays, for instance, were willing to commit capital to maintain high inventories of raw materials as hedges against future price increases. This policy was modified in the 1820s, however, as price fluctuations became less severe and too long-term (Addis, 1957). Most firms appreciated the downside of this approach, though there was fear frequently expressed of stockout dislocations.

The Strutts had the most sophisticated inventory control we have seen. They recorded varieties of cotton in their raw materials inventory at average and standard cost. They knew the location of all materials in various stages of production. Yarn in the finished goods inventory was measured according to quality, rated on a one-to-five decimal scale.

Entrepreneurs had a clear understanding of the risks inherent in carrying excessive or inadequate inventories. Dowlais correspondence in 1815 referred to the need for a well-assorted stock to promote cash sales, but at the same time a Mr Barnes was chastised for maintaining excessive stocks that incurred heavy interest charges (Elias, 1960). This concern about inventory carrying costs was echoed in Wedgwood correspondence in 1771 when a call was made for inventory reductions at London and Liverpool. The next year Wedgwood accused his management of inattention to the growth in the volume of stock which was becoming obsolete, breaking, and otherwise diminishing in value daily (Euphemia, 1973). On the other hand, the risk of stockouts was recognised by some firms. In 1792, the Gregs did an analysis of importation volume, cotton consumption, and stockout ramifications. The Herculaneum owners, fearful of the dislocations caused by coal stockouts at the pottery, resolved to maintain 50 to 100 tons on hand at all times.

A number of firms were outstanding in specific aspects of inventory control. Some Industrial Revolution firms had the good accounting sense to write obsolete items out of inventory, even though not required to do so by public reporting standards. Both Carron and

Darby regularly pruned their stocks of obsolete goods. Nasmyths, Gaskell & Co. conducted quality checks on raw materials received (Cantrell, 1984). Cardwell, Birley & Hornby took great pains to track and include twist and weft-in-process. At Darby's Ketley Foundry the transition of output from work-in-process to finished goods was recorded on a daily basis.

CONCLUSION

Whilst firms varied in the extent and sophistication of their cost management practices, the foregoing analysis provides evidence of a full spectrum of activities during the British Industrial Revolution. Expense control governed labour and machine costs, waste, general expenses, efficiency, and productivity. Responsibility cost management was aided by the establishment of profit and cost centres at the department, plant, function, and product levels and, occasionally, by comparisons of managerial performance. Overhead costs were subject to detailed listing and tracking and, in some instances, were allocated to cost centres.

Cost comparisons were made between different material inputs, production methods, mills, managers, time periods, transport methods, and supply routes. Cost data and analyses formed the basis for a wide variety of management and owner decisions (e.g., cost-based pricing of output; fixed asset, product line, and subcontracting decisions; and determination of potential cost savings from proposed new production methods).

The calculation of standard costs appears to have been widespread. Standards were set for work time, general expenses, material, and labour inputs. Inventory was typically carried at standard cost. With respect to inventory itself, there is evidence of considerable attention having been paid by entrepreneurs to both its level and quality. Risks of obsolescence were recognised, as were the perils of overstocking and stockouts.

It is also noteworthy that elements of job costing and process costing can be found during the British Industrial Revolution. Dugdale & Bros. kept a job costing book for the years 1848–1852. A page in the book was committed to each job and included the cost of bleaching at standard prices, an itemisation of raw material cost, and the calculation of total cost per piece. J.&N. Philips attempted process costing in their bleaching operation as each of the nine steps in the process was individually costed.

Whilst some entrepreneurs' efforts at cost management were primitive and incomplete, others demonstrated both innovation and attention to detail. Certainly cost management was accorded a high priority by many. The recording of operating statistics and costs was often carried out in intricate detail and included both financial and non-financial data, expressed both in quantitative and narrative forms. Such reports and correspondence also tended to indicate the direct involvement of many entrepreneurs in the ongoing management of their firms. Their discussions of cost incurrence suggested an underlying preoccupation with the economy and efficiency of their operations. Many appeared to have had a sophisticated understanding of the impact of product cost and quality on their profits. Many appreciated the relationship between product quality, cost, and selling price.

The comprehensiveness and variety of cost management practices during the British Industrial Revolution attest to their high priority with industrial entrepreneurs. We present them as hitherto unrecognised forerunners of today's management accounting tradition. The innovative genius of British entrepreneurs was not confined to their well-documented technological advances, but extended to their approach to cost management in a dynamic and competitive environment.

NOTES

1. The material in this chapter is drawn heavily from R.K. Fleischman and L.D. Parker (1991), 'British Entrepreneurs and Pre-Industrial Revolution Evidence of Cost Management', *Accounting Review*, Vol. 66, No. 2: 361–375.

2. It should be noted that there is considerable disagreement about what is meant by 'standard costing'. The current authors, for purposes of our qualitative assessment of a firm's activity and/or excellence in this area, view standards as costing norms based upon past actual results which come to be utilised for product costing, inventory valuation, and pricing. Within the context of this definition, a number of British Industrial Revolution business enterprises succeeded in establishing a functioning 'standard costing' system. If standards are construed to connote targets attainable with reasonably efficient performance, firms fitting that test would be considerably rarer. Boulton & Watt and Carron Company did conduct time-and-motion studies of a sort to gauge labour efficiency, whilst a number of textile firms were attuned to the quantity of raw materials consumed. Other researchers interpret standard costing to mean a system in which actual costs are compared to predetermined ones in order to generate cost variances. Those who date the inception of standard costing from the late nineteenth century, for example, hold that actual-to-standard variance analysis is an integral part of standard costing systems.

3

The Industrial Revolution Iron Industry[1]

Iron was second only to cotton textiles as the dominant industry of the British Industrial Revolution. Measured in terms of the magnitude of initial investment, the ratio of fixed to circulating capital, and the degree of vertical integration, it is arguable that the major iron enterprises far outstripped their cotton counterparts. Thomas Attwood, the scion of the prominent Birmingham family of iron makers, observed in 1812 that a typical initial outlay of £50,000 was necessary for an iron works, an amount of fixed capital which made it extremely difficult for entrepreneurs to enter or withdraw from the industry (Ashton, 1963).

It is particularly in the iron industry that one might expect to find evidence of purposeful cost accounting. The economic units were substantial, necessarily so because of the heavy investment in fixed assets. A presumption exists that the founding entrepreneurs were talented individuals as evidenced by their ability to raise the initial sums needed for iron enterprises. We reiterate the point that in the absence of an organised accounting profession, an accounting literature, or an accounting curriculum, the inspiration for cost accounting methods came in many instances from the entrepreneurs themselves.

The need for attention to cost accounting techniques may have been greater in the iron industry than in other Industrial Revolution pursuits. Any laxness motivated by high profit margins was less likely to have existed in this sector. Even Pollard (1965) conceded the presence of low margins in textiles and iron.

It was also the case that with the passage of time during the Industrial Revolution, the leading iron concerns became increasingly integrated with respect to raw materials control and product distribution. It has been hypothesised that accounting could not be sophisticated until such time as businesses became sufficiently complex to require material cost transfers between departments (Chatfield, 1977; Johnson, 1972; R.H. Parker, 1969). If this argument is true, then the textiles and iron industries alone should reflect sufficient entity complexity to offer the prospect of more advanced costing methods.

The current authors have investigated the surviving business records of four dominant iron producers from the Industrial Revolution period. Cyfarthfa and Dowlais, located in South Wales, were the largest concerns in the UK. Cyfarthfa was the largest producer in 1806 by a wide margin, whilst Dowlais, with its labour force in excess of 5,000, was identified as the 'largest manufactory in the world' by 1830 (Birch, 1967, p. 290; Scrivenor, 1967). Carron Company, one of the largest Scottish iron concerns, was popularly known as 'the arsenal of Europe' following its development of the Carronade cannon (Campbell, 1961). The Darby iron enterprise was a dominant force in the eighteenth century in terms of technological innovation and production. It is more difficult to measure the firm's impact in the nineteenth century as various Shropshire properties (Coalbrookdale, Dawley, Madeley Wood, Horsehay, Ketley) moved in and out of the possession of the Darby and Reynolds families.

The four iron enterprises featured in this chapter were examined without any prior assumptions being made about the degree of their individual involvement in cost management. Their selection was based solely upon the volume of surviving archival records. Indeed, the chapter reports supplementally on cases such as Newton, Chambers where a lack of cost management practices, despite a voluminous archive, directly contrasts to patterns observed in the other large firms.

This chapter has been structured to proceed from individual case studies to an analysis of the relationship between iron industry cost management and its environmental influences. First, this pattern is intended to provide some insight into the practices observed in particular individual firms of general industry significance during the period. Second, an attempt has been made to employ traditional historical methodology in identifying and arguing probable environmental influences upon the cost management techniques observed. This approach recognises certain historical analytical limitations; namely, that general rather than specific practices of individual firms are being considered and that deterministic or 'proven' environmental links to method are neither possible nor justifiable in the historical approach to causal attribution. Given that historical knowledge can never be complete or ultimately certain, such analysis of influence must necessarily be argued and justified in terms of *probable* influences (Previts et al., 1990a, 1990b).

THE MAJOR FIRMS

Carron Company[2]: In 1759, two Birmingham industrialists and a former Cockenzie merchant formed Carron, destined to become the largest Scottish iron enterprise. The minutes of semi-annual General Court meetings and the correspondence between the resident manager and the absentee partners contain numerous reports featuring cost accounting utilisation. In Chapter 6, we will examine Carron's cost accounting in minute detail as a case study. For now, we will review certain key features to underscore Carron's significance to the overall picture of cost accounting in the Industrial Revolution iron industry.

Arising from the severe financial difficulties that were to plague Carron in its early years, managers instituted control mechanisms to limit expenses, such as classifying receipts for cash expenditures and charging labourers for defective work (GD 58/2/2/1, p. 165; GD 58/14/2). Carron's management generated detailed product costings with numerous indirect expense categories (GD 58/2/1/1, pp. 73–78).

The viability of Carron's individual branches was evaluated on an ongoing basis. For example, nails, anchors, and anvils were three product lines discontinued due to unsatisfactory levels of profitability (Campbell, 1961; GD 58/2/1/1, p. 171; GD 58/2/3/1, p. 7). The abandonments of air furnaces, the plating forge, and charcoal forging were also contemplated (GD 58/2/3/1, p. 15; GD 58/2/1/1, p. 165; GD 58/4/1/1, p. 54). Detailed job descriptions were articulated for all senior managers and their responsibilities clearly delineated (GD 58/6/4/2).

Carron was one of the very few Industrial Revolution firms which based overhead allocations on predetermined formula.[3] In 1763, 'general charges' amounting to £2,000 were allocated to various cost centres (GD 58/2/1/1, p. 63). In 1769, the General Court restricted the number of expenses to be included in that account, mandating that a variety of costs be charged directly to departments (GD 58/2/3/1, p. 16). In 1771, excessive overhead charges, which had produced losses to the air furnaces and the plating forge, were reallocated to the blast furnaces (GD 58/2/1/1, p. 398).

As was mentioned in Chapter 2, the Carron archive contains two extremely detailed technological reports related to coal production, dated 1768 and 1770, which transcended any cost analyses we have seen in the eighteenth century (ACC 5381, Box 28, Folders 1 and 2). In the 1770s, Carron's accountant was providing monthly reports on the differential costs of extracting ore from the firm's various mineral holdings (GD 58/6/4/1). These reports furnished data leading to the abandonment of cost-inefficient fields, the support of numerous lease-or-buy decisions, and, most impressively, the establishment of transfer prices to the blast furnaces. Somewhat later, the blast furnace supervisor was transmitting monthly cost-per-ton comparisons of the five furnaces under his direction (GD 58/6/4/4).

Additional cost analyses involved the subcontracting of road repair (GD 58/2/3/1, p. 23), proposals to blow out and repair blast furnaces (GD 58/2/3/3, pp. 185–186), a comparison of output costs of two ironstone quarrying managers (GD 58/6/4/1), a cost/benefit analysis for a blacking kiln repair (GD 58/2/3/3, pp. 37–38), several procurement and repair decisions for steam engines (GD 58/2/3/1, p. 15), a proposal for a new boring mill (ibid., p. 26), and an analysis of the power requirements to raise water to the furnaces (ibid.).

Carron management from earliest times employed standard costs for transfer pricing and inventory control. Sporadic efforts at income forecasting and budgeting were even attempted (GD 58/2/1/1, pp. 43, 63). The records collectively reflect sophisticated levels of cost management through the firm's first quarter-century, even though the surviving evidence is reduced to a trickle following a change in firm management in the mid-1780s.

Cyfarthfa[4]: The Crawshay installation at Cyfarthfa was the largest in the kingdom in the late eighteenth and early nineteenth centuries. The managerial structure, with the senior Crawshays typically absentee owners resident in London, duplicated those conditions so appropriate for documenting cost accounting at Carron. Indeed, the correspondence between the London-based Crawshays and the resident managers, often younger Crawshays, was sufficiently voluminous that the standard history (Addis, 1957) of the firm has been written almost entirely from this source.

Recent work by Jones (1985) and Edwards (1989) recounted significant cost management beginnings in the 1790s. In particular, the firm was in the vanguard with respect to overhead cost allocation. The company distinguished overhead expenses directly related to production, which were allocated to 12 cost centres, from those incurred in non-productive functions, which appeared as sundry items in the profit-and-loss account (Edwards, 1989; Jones, 1985). However, Jones (1985) concluded that in the absence of evidence as to how the apportionment was made, the allocations appeared arbitrary and inconsistent from year to year.

Accounting historians, critical of Industrial Revolution cost accounting, have cited the lack of integration between cost and financial records as symptomatic of an unsophisticated methodology. However, the development of standard transfer prices at Cyfarthfa in the 1790s has caused Edwards (1989) to claim that at Cyfarthfa the earliest known integration of cost and financial records was achieved. Notwithstanding, the Crawshay correspondence does not reflect the awareness of cost management possibilities that characterised the Cadell/Garbett exchanges at Carron. Furthermore, the Cyfarthfa archive contains less of those types of materials which best evince mature costing—production reports, management diaries, directors' minute books. There are plentiful financial accounting records, but these sources are rarely helpful. Profit-and-loss statements from the 1810s did provide distinct earnings numbers for four blast furnaces at Cyfarthfa and two at Ynnisfach suitable for comparative purposes (A2, Box XII). By contrast at Hirwaun, also a Crawshay subsidiary, separate figures were not kept for individual furnaces (ibid.).

Jones (1985, p. 136), who studied the Crawshay ledgers meticulously for the 25 years following the 1790s, found no evidence of 'accounting progress'. This view may be unduly pessimistic. There continued to be advances in dealing with overhead issues. William Crawshay wrote to his partner Benjamin Hall in 1814 concerned that the reduction of output associated with closing down a blast furnace would increase 'common charges' per unit of output and, consequently, mandate higher selling prices (A2, Vol. I, #162). Like other large iron producers, managers at Cyfarthfa tracked the yields of different types of coal in the smelting process and the amounts of waste associated with each. William Crawshay wrote to Matthew Wayne in 1814 that he wanted to see blast furnace accounts on a weekly basis (A2, Vol. I, #233). Unfortunately, these reports, if ever prepared, no longer survive.

In a memorandum book dated 1822–1828, there are several isolated cost calculations and yield comparisons which give faith that there was better data tracking than reflected in the financial reports and letters. One computation includes the differential quantities of coal, ironstone, and limestone required to produce a ton of pigs from four different mineral fields. These quantities were then multiplied by a standard cost for that raw material input to give costs per ton. In all instances a mean quantity/cost was also calculated. Additionally, there is an 1828 report of the quantities of coal mined at seven different Cyfarthfa and four Ynnisfach sites, coupled with the yield of good iron and associated waste for each of the 11 varieties (A2, Vol. II, #14–15).

The Cyfarthfa operation did fall upon hard times in the 1830s as the Crawshays committed errors which might have been avoided with more attention to cost factors. For example, the elder William Crawshay was willing to stockpile finished iron products without apparent concern for the cost of capital committed to inventory or the erosion of value from rust. Addis (1957) observed that the pricing structure for Crawshay iron products did not correspond to costing analyses prepared for that purpose.

Darby[5]: The Darby iron enterprise is one of the most famous Industrial Revolution firms because of its longevity and its prominence in the development of new technology. The written record of the company, patchy at best, includes a serious gap in the last quarter of the eighteenth century. The archive does span 150 years, however, and relates to various furnaces and collieries in the neighbourhood of the main Coalbrookdale installation.

An immaculately maintained inventory survives from 1718 and reflects what Trinder (1974, p. 24) called 'traditional Quaker meticulousness'. Similar care was manifested in a variety of other documents. Overhead costs were charged directly to individual productive departments ('Summary of the Value of the Concerns Belonging to Coalbrookdale Co., 1805–52'). Departmental costs were subsequently transferred to inventory. For expenses such as the maintenance of workers' cottages, by contrast, a 'General Charges' account also existed (item 330). There is a detailed analysis of the labour costs incurred in the manufacture of bar iron, dating from 1719 (Raistrick, 1970).

Commencing with these promising beginnings, Darby management employed its accounting system to control labour costs and, in association with technology, to reduce other production costs. An 1810 cost compilation showed how the coal requirements for a ton of coke had been significantly reduced from 3.1 to 2.5 tons. The substitution of slack for higher quality coal post-1830 saved 600 to 700 tons per month at Horsehay (Trinder, 1973). In the 1820s, a bounty system was established which specified a quota of 60 tons as the standard furnace make per week, with bonuses added and abatements subtracted for deviation. Likewise, puddlers were bound by standards to a given yield. In this way as well, the accounting system was used to evaluate worker performance and to allow for the promotion of the more talented to positions of greater managerial responsibility (Raistrick, 1970).

Darby's management maintained many of the same types of comparative statistics we have seen at Carron. Data were kept on the output of individual blast furnaces (1987, Box 20). The quantity of coal consumed by individual steam engines, as well as respective downtimes, was known ('Commentary' by unknown author, circa 1875, p. 5). The costs of raising various kinds of coal and ironstone were regularly calculated (ibid., p. 6).

A memorandum was prepared for management in 1799 on the occasion of a lease renewal on premises at Coalbrookdale. The document announced in general terms that it was necessary to maintain expense records for each distinct work and branch of trade to determine which were advantageous. The forges at the Dale were found to be profitable, but not so the foundry activity. It was hypothesised and then dismissed that the greater profitability of Horsehay's foundry was a function of a superior capital/employee ratio. It was then observed that the transportation costs from the iron ore and coal pits were 10s per ton greater because of location, though the Dale did enjoy an advantage in limestone carriage charges. It was also demonstrated that many manufactured goods did not bear prices proportionate to the variety of additional charges incidental to their manufacture. Consequently, these product lines appeared less profitable than semi-finished branches (e.g., the pig and bar iron trades). The opinion was expressed that if the lease was renewed and if the foundry function was not moved entirely to

Horsehay, it would be necessary to raise the selling prices of the Dale's finished products to cover the general expenses charged (1987, Box 20).

Raistrick (1970) reported a similar 1825 analysis designed to evaluate a proposal to de-emphasise Coalbrookdale activities in favour of a greater centralisation of operations at Horsehay. Joseph Reynolds, who undertook the study, took into account such elusive factors as the opportunity cost of lost Coalbrookdale housing rentals, expenses associated with the repair and rent collection on these premises, and the value of scrap if the buildings were demolished.

Departmental accounting records were extraordinarily detailed and beautifully maintained. As raw materials and semi-finished goods passed through the productive process, weights and transfer prices were recorded (items 336–337). Though there is no evidence illustrating the build-up of these prices, the Darby enterprise was more highly integrated in this regard than any Industrial Revolution firm we have seen. Inventory control was tight at Ketley where daily reports were prepared on raw material inputs, a wide range of foundry outputs, and the volume of scrap associated with that production (1987, Box 20). The firm's archive contains some 1810 boiler plate production costs (245/43). Included were standard costs for depreciation (wear and tear), rubbish removal, and scrap reworking. Likewise, an 1813 calculation of savings from using boilers to conduct waste heat from the puddling furnaces included depreciation, a cost component infrequently found at such an early date in Industrial Revolution accounting (Raistrick, 1970).

The desire of the firm's directors to base decision making on cost analysis is reflected in the one surviving minute book from the late eighteenth century. In a four-month period in 1794, the board utilised cost estimates to support diverse actions, including renewing mineral field leases, analysing the profitability of productive branches, sub-contracting the construction of a railway, establishing a transportation cost standard, and effectuating repair-or-sell decisions on workers' housing (Minute Book 1789–1796, pp. 25–27, 37, 40).

Dowlais[6]: Though the Dowlais Iron Company was founded in the same year as Carron (1759), the pattern of existing business records was totally dissimilar. There were virtually no remains from the first 70 years of operations, followed by reasonably sophisticated costing documents thereafter. In light of England's charge (1959) that the company advanced slowly due to its policy that partners could veto improvements, it is difficult to know definitively if the initial dearth of records resulted from managerial incompetence or the vagaries of record survival.

John (1950) has written an economic history of Dowlais based primarily on a vast quantity of business letters (estimated by Elias [1960] to number 563,000) and some miscellaneous surviving documents. From these materials it is possible to piece together some evidence that early managers had good costing instincts. There is an 1802 costing for ten tons of steel from J.J. Guest's notebook, which contains in addition to prime costs an overhead allocation ('general charges') and a number of selling expenses (D/DG, Section C, Box 1). The firm employed technology to reduce costs as indicated by the reduction of the required coal input from eight to nearly three tons per ton of finished iron between 1791 and 1831 (John, 1950). A letter from William Lewis to J.J. Guest in 1809 urged greater managerial responsibility at Dowlais by requiring managers to provide reasons for production shortfalls (Elias, 1960). Another letter, dated 1815, from Thomas Guest to William Taitt reflected a good working knowledge of inventory control and the capital costs associated with overstocking (ibid.).

Like with other iron firms, Dowlais' management was vitally concerned with the productive potential of different raw material inputs. In 1812, David Mushet, a prominent nineteenth century entrepreneur and engineer, prepared analyses of various types of coal with respect to sundry informational categories, such as ash residue, specific gravity, iron production per grain, and volatile matter (D/DG, Section B, Box 8). One of the most provocative survivals in the Dowlais archive is another Guest notebook, dated 1827–1828. This document intricately details the quantity of coal consumed by each steam engine and the corresponding cost per horsepower for each. More significantly, Guest undertook a comparison of the output from each of the firm's five rolling mills in which he contrasted total production to a budgeted volume (D/DG, Section C, Box 1).

Pains were taken at Dowlais to control transportation costs. A 1795 estimate for the construction of a turnpike included specific engineered costs of 5.25d per cubic yard for banking and 4.25d for cutting and wheeling (D/DC, Section E, Box 8). In 1827, a Mr Harrison generated a three-page report on the estimated construction costs of a new road, accompanied by an analysis of its anticipated cost/benefit to Dowlais (D/DG, Section D, Box 1/2/2). The first page of this report appears as Figure 5. There is an 1836 analysis of the costs of transporting finished iron to Cardiff for shipment with the various components costed to one-tenth of a pence. Included is an allocation for road repairs (D/DG, Section C, Box 4).

Still, it was not until the 1840s, when the firm commenced preparing a report every five weeks entitled 'Cost of Materials and Iron Made', that the costing moved into high gear. These reports, formatted upon three-page printed forms, recorded input costs for ten cost centres. The average costs per ton of mining operations (coal, ironstone, and limestone) and production (finers' metal, puddled bars, bar iron, and pig iron) were calculated precisely for each period, again to one-tenth of a pence. These costings were a combination of standards and actuals. For instance, the average actual cost per ton of coals for a period became the standard cost for all coal inputs to productive departments, such as puddled bars and bar iron. Figure 6, dated November 1845, is a page from one such report. Dowlais, like Carron, was one of the few Industrial Revolution firms which allocated overhead costs on the basis of predetermined formula. The apportionment remained consistent in percentage terms between 1845 and 1851, though the amount allocated had risen significantly by the later date. The limestone and finers' metal cost centres inexplicably bore none of the charges (ibid.).

The study of Dowlais by Edwards and Baber (1979) included few references to the archive predating the 1850s. There are, however, several extremely detailed cost analyses from the 1850s, such as a 12-page report to support the purchase of the Penydarran mineral field (D/DG, Section B, Box 8). Efforts such as these, combined with the cost reporting of the 1840s, justify their view (ibid., pp. 147–148) that, commencing with the 1850s at least, Dowlais' management had sufficient cost data to support 'major strategic decisions' which proved 'startling successes'. Though the physical remains from the first half of the century are considerably more sketchy, there appears to be good reason for optimism about Dowlais' costing sophistication.

Figure 5: Estimated Road Costs, Dowlais, 1827

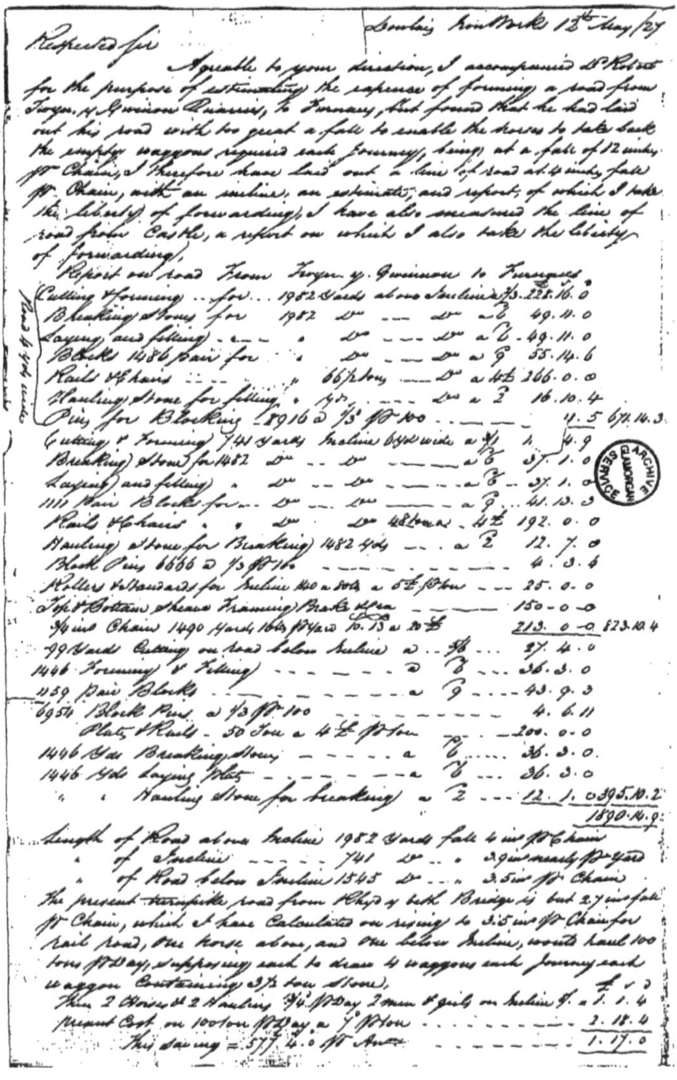

Dowlais Iron Works 12th May /27

Respected Sir

Agreable to your direction, I accompanied Mr Robert for the purpose of estimating the expense of forming a road from Forge-y-Gwinion Quarries, to Furnaces, but found that he had laid out his road with too great a fall to enable the horses to take back the empty waggons required each journey, being at a fall of 12 inches pr Chain, I therefore have laid out a line of road at 4 inches fall pr Chain, with an incline, an estimate, and report of which I take the liberty of forwarding, I have also measured the line of road from Castle, a report on which I also take the liberty of forwarding.

Report on road from Forge-y-Gwinion to Furnaces

	£ s d	
Cutting & forming .. for .. 1982 Yards above Incline a 2/3	228.16.0	
Breaking Stones for 1982 do --- do a 6	49.11.0	
Laying and filling .... do --- do a 6	49.11.0	
Blocks 1486 Pair for do --- do a 9	55.14.6	
Rails & Chairs ---- 66½ tons --- do a 4£	266.0.0	
Hauling Stone for filling yds --- do a 2	16.10.4	
Pins for Blocking 8916 @ 1/3 pr 100 ------	4.5	671.14.3
Cutting & Forming 741 Yards Incline 6 yds wide a 4/1	[illegible] 4.9	
Breaking Stone for 1482 do -- do ----- a 6	37.1.0	
Laying and filling do -- do ----- a 6	37.1.0	
1111 Pair Blocks for -- do -- do ----- a 9	41.13.3	
Rails & Chairs do do 48 tons - 4£	192.0.0	
Hauling Stone for Breaking 1482 yds --- a 2	12.7.0	
Block Pins 6666 @ 1/3 pr 100 ----------	4.3.4	
Rollers & Standards for Incline 1140 a 30lb a 5£ pr ton ---	25.0.0	
Top & Bottom Sheave Framing Brake &c ------	150.0.0	
¾ inch Chain 1490 Yards 16lb pr Yard 10.13 a 20£	213.0.0	873.10.4
99 Yards Cutting on road below Incline @ .. 5/6 ...	27.4.0	
1446 Forming & Filling ------- @ 6 ...	36.3.0	
1159 Pair Blocks --------- a 9 ----	43.9.3	
6954 Block Pins a 1/3 pr 100 ----------	4.6.11	
Plates & Rails - 50 Tons a 4£ pr ton ----	200.0.0	
1446 Yds Breaking Stones ------ a 6	36.3.0	
1446 Yds laying Plates -------- a 6 ...	36.3.0	
" " Hauling Stone for breaking a 2 ---	12.1.0	395.10.2
		1890.14.9

Length of Road above Incline 1982 Yards fall 4 ins pr Chain
" of Incline ------ 741 do .. " 3.9 ins nearly pr Yard
" of Road below Incline 1545 do ... " 3.5 ins pr Chain

The present turnpike road from Rhyd y bedd Bridge is but 2.7 ins fall pr Chain, which I have Calculated on rising to 3.5 ins pr Chain for rail road, One horse above, and One below Incline, would haul 100 tons pr Day, supposing each to draw 4 waggons each journey each waggon Containing 3½ ton Stone,

	£ s d
Then 2 Horses & 2 Haulers 3/4 pr Day 2 men & girls on Incline 4/- a	1.1.4
present Cost on 100 ton pr Day a 7d pr ton ----------	2.18.4
This saving = 577.4.0 pr Annum ----------	1.17.0

Figure 6: Cost of Materials and Iron Made, Dowlais, 1845

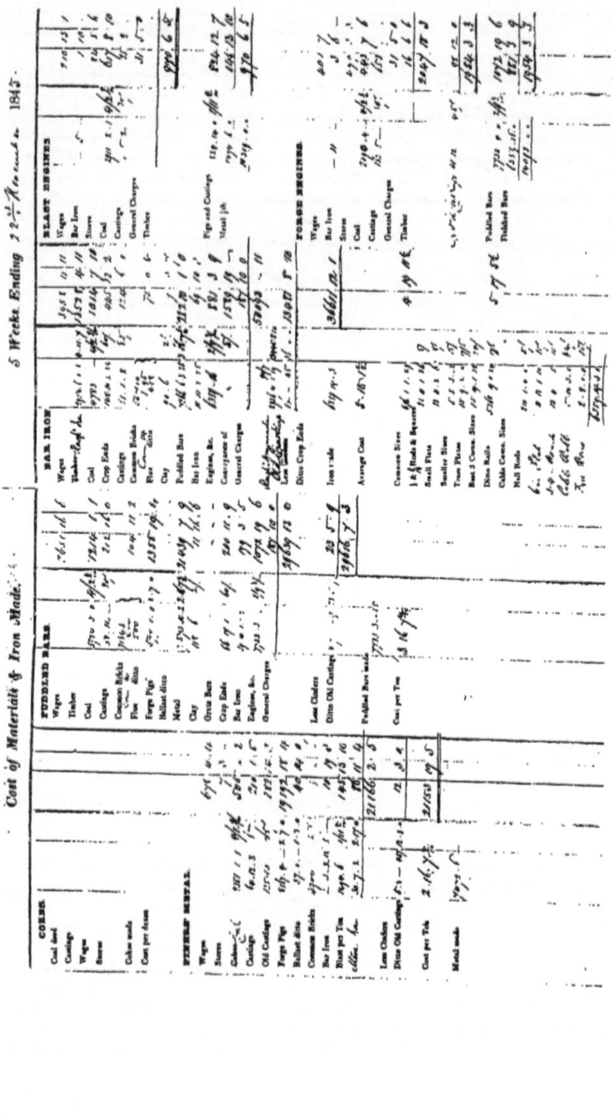

OTHER IRON ENTERPRISES[7]

The current authors have examined existing business records of some 20 iron firms of lesser stature than the four aforementioned. Certain of these companies were smaller comparatively, whilst others were quite substantial. However, a common characteristic was a lesser volume of archival material. For example, the only surviving record for Lancashire-based Backbarrow Iron was an old furnace book whose most sophisticated feature was a recipe to cure the bite of a mad dog (DDMC, 30/1).

Newton, Chambers: This firm, headquartered at Thorncliffe (near Sheffield), was the second largest iron enterprise in Yorkshire. Its substantial archive includes those categories of records that typically provide fertile ground—a foundrymen's work book, pig iron vouchers, carriage accounts, furnace books, colliery accounts, weigh books (TR 63, 64, 76, 292, 295, 445). However, the collection reflects a cost accounting wasteland. The holdings are sufficiently extensive and varied to suggest that adequate costing was just not attempted, rather than to suppose that better evidence had simply failed to survive. Newton, Chambers is offered as the clearest example that the methods herein discussed did not receive universal application.

Crowley: This Tyneside iron enterprise was distinct from other leading producers in its orientation toward finished iron goods to the exclusion of mining and forging activities. There are few extant business records, but an excellent company history (Flinn, 1962) based on widely scattered evidence and one major survival, the firm's law book, an extensive code of rules initially written in the late seventeenth century and continually revised (Flinn, 1957). In its effort to make the labour force calculable, the law book might have been a prototype for what Hoskin and Macve (1988) subsequently described at the Springfield Armory.

Flinn (1962) asserted that the Crowleys were very attentive to costs to achieve profit maximisation, whilst Young (1923–1924) concluded that in their attention to detail and general industrial outlook, they were a century in advance of their contemporaries. From the law book and secondary source material, it would appear that the Crowleys utilised cost accounting methods most evidently to prepare ten-week production plans, to articulate and achieve conformity to waste standards, and to make vertical integration decisions (e.g., pig iron forging, ownership of transport vessels) (Flinn, 1957, 1962). We have already seen in Chapter 2 how the law book mandated that various company officers (surveyor, nailkeeper, coalkeeper) participate actively in inventory control. There was also an accountant whose job it was to take inventory of existing raw materials on a regular basis and to prepare schedules of budgeted needs. The accountant was also instructed to collaborate weekly with the surveyor and the nailkeeper to plan production for the slitting mill, with the additional directive that 'care must be taken not to demand uneconomic runs of particular sizes or qualities' (Law 36) (Flinn, 1957, p. 114).

Butterley: A leading Derbyshire producer, Butterley evinced good cost accounting from the 1830s forward by maintaining comparative statistics on the productive capability of blast furnaces individually and of the firm's two plants (Butterley and Codnor Park) more generally (D503B, 'Forge Book', pp. 19, 23). Commencing in the 1840s, detailed listings of forge prices appeared periodically in which each productive function and input was costed. These costings were mill-specific (ibid.).

Notwithstanding, Butterley's cost accounting was not universally so useful. Estimates of expenses associated with new construction were crude; inventory control of raw materials was poor; waste management was not good compared to other firms; and differential transfer prices were not developed for ores from different mineral fields (D503B/A1, A8).

Vivian: This Welsh conglomerate had copper and tin operations in addition to iron. Like many large contemporaries in the industry, a monthly schedule of cost of materials and iron made was prepared in the 1840s (item E18). This report was more sophisticated than many in that there were internal allocations apart from general charges. For example, blast engine expenses were apportioned 40% to the blast furnaces and 30% each to finers' metal and the charcoal finery. The costs of shipping and conveyance were allocated to profit centres at a standard rate per ton. Moreover, some of the transfer prices reflected standard costs rather than the actual costs for the period. However, the allocation of general charges was quite rudimentary in comparison to other iron enterprises, both with regard to the amounts distributed and to the small number of cost centres (five) that bore a portion.

Clydach: An impressive, albeit small archive defined operations at the Clydach Iron Company, South Wales. The firm made year-to-year comparisons of raw material costs, production costs, and carriage expenses of finished goods to Newport (Maybery 1961–1968). Other firms generated the data necessary for these comparisons, but in Clydach's case there is actual evidence that something was being done with the information. Clydach's management also prepared sales budgets and was concerned about transport. Cost estimates for limestone and coal delivery via a proposed new railway were contrasted to then current charges for canal transport (Maybery 918). It is noteworthy that at Clydach good cost accounting methods were in use circa 1810, rather than a generation later as typified the industry.

Abersychan: The only surviving document from this subsidiary of the sizeable British Iron Company is a '9-Month Cost of Materials and Iron', dated 1844, which appeared on a printed form typical of the South Wales iron industry (D454, 939) (see Figure 7). The average costs calculated for coals, ironstone, pig iron, refiners' metal, puddled bars, and bar iron became transfer prices to other cost centres. For some inexplicable reason, overhead was allocated only to four cost centres. However, this form did have lines for overtime work and 'dead' work, reflecting an awareness of indirect labour not usually in evidence.

Clyde/Cramond: These two Scottish iron companies were components of the Cadell family empire and, as such, inherited the cost accounting sophistication in evidence at Carron. There were blast furnace reports at Clyde in the 1780s, a decade earlier than at Carron, but they were of lesser quality in that the material inputs were maintained in weights only (ACC 5381, Box 39, Folder 2). These reports did track and explain furnace downtime and frequently related the results of experimentation with different raw material inputs. The Cramond archive, though very sparse, features the briefs of an 1837 law suit wherein Robert Porter sued Messrs Cadell Sons & Company (ACC 5381, Box 32, Folder 3). The plaintiff's document was 14 pages of minute detail and figures

Figure 7: Cost of Materials and Iron, Abersychan, 1844

ABERSYCHAN IRON WORK.

Cost of Materials and Iron 9 Months ending 21 September 1844

	Materials Used Tons	Cwts.	Qrs.	lbs.	Rate	Amount £	s.	d.	Quantity Tons	Materials Used per Ton of Iron Tons	Cwts.	Qrs.	lbs.	Rate	Cost per Ton £	s.	d.
REFINERY. DR.																	
To Cash paid for labor Refining, &c.						277	3	1	3950							1	4½
Sundries, for Pig Iron and Castings	4392	7			71/7¼	15725	10	6		1	2	.	26		3	19	8
Foundry, for Castings	29	8	3	8	100/-	147	3	11					15				9
Colliery, for Coal used	1713	1			3/11¼	337	5	..			8	2	18			1	8½
Horse Account, for Horse labor						92	3	2									5½
Stores, for sundries used						6	19	1									½
						16504	14	9		Refined Metal, Per Ton					4	11	-
PUDDLING FORGE. DR.																	
To Cash paid for labor Puddling, &c.						2062	3	7	4605							8	11½
Ditto paid for Engine expenses																	
Refined Metal, for Metal used	4061	17	3	12	84/-	17059	19				17	2	15		3	14	1¼
Pig Iron, for Pig Iron used	740	11	3	24	71/7¼	2651	9	10			3	.	24			11	3¼
Puddled Bars, for Scraps used																	
Colliery, for Coal used at																	
Furnaces … 4374 5											19	.					
Engine … 1372 5	5746	10	.		3/11¼	1131	7	10			6	.				4	11
Foundry, for Castings	72	17	2	9		364	7	8								1	7
Bar Iron, for Iron for Tools	8	14	2	19		52	7	11									2¼
Brickyard, for Bricks and Clay						196	9	2									10½
Timber, for Timber used						27	6	10									1¼
Horse Account, for Horse labour						112	7	1									5¾
Stores, for sundries used						209	10	10									11¼
						23867	9	9							5	3	5¼
By old Castings returned	16	1	1	..	65/	52	4	1								.	2½
						23815	5	8		Puddled Bars, Per Ton					5	3	2¾
ROLLING MILL. DR.																	
To Cash paid for Mill labor						1465	9	9	5725							5	1½
Ditto paid for extra labor on Rails						1373	14	10								4	9¾
Ditto paid for Engine expenses																	
Puddled Bars, for Bars used	[illegible]	6		11	77/3¼	4461	1	5			8		2			15	8½
Colliery, for Coal used at	5[illegible]77	10	1	22	77/11	22464	14				19		23		4	16	0½
Heating Furnaces 3106 19											10	3	11				
Rail Furnaces … 542											1	3	16				
Engine … 1256	4904	19			3/11½	965	13	4			4	1	14			3	4½
Foundry, for castings	72	17	2	9		364	7	9								1	3¼
Bar Iron, for Iron for Tools	8	14	2	19		52	8	1									2¼
Horse Account, for Horse labor						112	7	2									4¾
Timber, for Timber used						25		11									1
Brickyard, for Bricks used						196	19	4									8½
Stores, for sundries used						209	11	2									8¾
Galeage	5343	5	3	26		557	4	5								1	11¾
Rent of Williams's Land						108											4½
Charges						1026										3	7
						38382	12	2							6	14	3½
By old Castings returned	16	1	1		65/-	52	4	1									2½
						38330	8	1		Bar Iron, Per Ton					6	14	1

DR. BAR IRON. CR.

	Tons	Cwts.	Qrs.	lbs.		£	s.	d.		Tons	Cwts.	Qrs.	lbs.	£	s.	d.
To Common Iron	582	1	1	13	[illegible]	3268	13	4	By Common Iron	582	1	1	13	3026	5	11
To ditto extra sizes	66	9			[illegible]	404	1	3	By ditto extra sizes	66	9			402	5	.
To Best Iron	3	.		.	[illegible]	24	4	10	By Best Iron	3				23	15	.
To ditto extra sizes									By ditto extra sizes							
To Rails and Tramplates	5073	8	3	15	[illegible]	34653	8	8	By Rails and Tramplates	5073	8	3	15	29136	8	8
To Boiler Plates									By Boiler Plates							
To Carriage to Newport						1300										
To Profit and Loss									By Profit and Loss							
	5724	19	1	.		39630	8	1								

regarding productive trials, waste calculations, and comparisons of current to past costs. The rebuttal at 21 pages contains more narrative, but still includes incredible detail in its attempt to gainsay Porter's claims for compensation from the firm.

We shall now turn our attention to an exploration of certain environmental influences which occasioned, in part, this observed commitment to cost accounting in major iron industry enterprises. Factors which appear to have precipitated a closer attention to cost management include the regional character of the iron industry, the typical firm structure of the period, the prevailing relationship between technology and productivity, and a preoccupation with resources control.

A REGIONAL INDUSTRY

Though many management decisions for the Carron, Cyfarthfa, Crowley, and Dowlais iron enterprises were made from afar, the industry as a whole was distinctly regional in its organisation. As typified most economic endeavours during the British Industrial Revolution, the iron industry developed in close geographical propinquity to its raw materials—coal, ironstone, and limestone (Briggs, 1959; Marshall, 1973). Carron has been identified as a noteworthy example of an iron industry operation dependent on local supplies of natural resources (Slaven, 1975), though the same could be said of most of the companies examined during this time period. This concern with raw material availability was reflected by the attention all the leading iron firms paid to the differential costs of ore extraction and yield potentials. We have seen lease-or-buy decisions on mineral fields at Carron, Darby, and Dowlais. The detailed cost analyses of transportation alternatives were likewise related to raw material procurement and control. This reliance often meant that the viability of an industrial region could be tested, particularly when a major resource failed. A regional iron industry could decline dramatically when beneficial leases expired, local ore resources became exhausted, or new technologies and sources of ore supplies led to a heightened demand for new sites (Pawson, 1979). Of course, the canal age (1760–1830) and the advent of the railroads (post-1830) decreased the cost of moving heavy commodities and made remote regions more accessible (Ashton, 1966).

Still, by 1806, 90% of iron production was concentrated in Shropshire, Yorkshire, Staffordshire, South Wales, and Scotland (Brown, 1991). Edwards and Baber (1979), in their study of Dowlais, noted that the location of the iron works was initially determined by the availability of essential raw materials in the Merthyr district.[8]

Another aspect of iron industry regionalism was the limited industrial capital and commercial credit markets (Hudson, 1989). During the eighteenth and early nineteenth centuries, capital rarely flowed outside the geographical region in which it was generated (Pawson, 1979). The costing instincts of iron industry owners and managers may well have been sharpened by this restricted availability of capital. Where access to local finance was limited or subject to fluctuation, the motivation for close attention to cost control and production costs may well have been stimulated. There is no shortage of illustrations in the foregoing case studies of expenditure controls. Abatements for deficient work, waste/scrap calculation and control, and the careful classification and allocation of indirect costs were just some of the examples in evidence.

Certain distinct accounting usages likewise reflected iron industry regionalism both chronologically and methodologically. For example, the Scottish iron firms (e.g., Carron, Clyde) in the late eighteenth century concentrated on the comparative capabilities of their productive factors, such as steam engines and blast furnaces. Likewise, in the 1840s, there appeared an almost standardised production report form throughout the Welsh branch (e.g., Abersychan, Cyfarthfa, Dowlais, Vivian) of the industry which represented a coming of age in departmental cost allocation and standard costing.

FIRM STRUCTURE

Developments in the iron industry's firm structure again related to the costing concerns of owners. The enterprises were traditionally family firms, most frequently partnerships, drawing labour from the surrounding countryside (supplemented by some experienced workers from outside the region) and capital from regional sources (supplemented by self-generated profits). These firms expanded their markets, diversified their product lines, and vertically integrated their operations as they matured. Iron industry firms are distinguished from most manufacturers of the period because of the larger scale of the enterprises. As the coming of the railroads accentuated the demand for iron, even larger factories emerged to supply the required output (Brown, 1991; Marshall, 1973). In attempting to generate and control the resources required for such developments, close attention to the labour costs, raw materials, funding sources, and productive processes was clearly a priority for owners and managers.

Major iron industry firms were not only large but typically vertically integrated, controlling almost all their productive factors from raw materials to transportation mechanisms. A number of analyses have survived illustrating integration decisions, most notably in mineral field procurement (Carron and Dowlais) and transport subcontracting (Clydach, Crowley, and Darby). Expanded activities did not imply that iron firms were restricted to one geographical site. Some of the larger iron masters were able to establish sophisticated interlocking partnerships that coordinated the output of geographically scattered iron works servicing a variety of markets (Harris, 1988). Typically these linkages were regional. The Crawshays expanded to include the Hirwaun and Union furnaces in the 1790s, as did the Carron-based Cadell family to incorporate Clyde and Cramond. The Wilkinsons, for whom no accounting records survive, had multiple sites (Bersham, Bradley, Broseley, Brymbo) in Shropshire and the Black Country. We have seen at Darby continuous managerial attention to the empire's structure, resulting in the abandonment of certain operations and increased product specialisation amongst those remaining. The formation of the British Iron Company in 1824 saw an amalgamation of nine concerns (Abersychan was one) which transcended a regional base. However, the enterprise was not successful long-term (Birch, 1967), though the fraud that riddled the organisation is a more likely explanation of its failure than the dispersion of its operations.

Iron production was most frequently a specialised operation conducted by relatively small units of production (Lee, 1986), with long-run escalations of demand accommodated by an increase in the number of productive units rather than an expanded scale of operations at the original site (Pawson, 1979). This pattern of development mandated increased capital outlays, utilisation of retained profits, and improved operational efficiency. Sophisticated accounting systems for the coordination of activities were necessary as illustrated by the comparative data generated for sundry productive units forming the Butterley, Cyfarthfa, and Darby concerns.

MANAGING TECHNOLOGY AND PRODUCTIVITY

From 1700 to 1760, there was a relatively slow rate of growth in pig iron production as only 17 furnaces were functioning by the later date. After 1760, production accelerated in response to increased demand for munitions. Accommodation of this demand was made possible, in part, by improved technology in heating pig iron, utilising local British coal supplies. By the early 1820s, iron concerns were expanding the volume of their manufacturing in response to the requirements for gas and water pipes, railways, bridges, ships, and machinery. Until 1830, production primarily serviced the domestic market, but subsequently the scope was expanded to cater to export markets in Europe, the US, Australia, and India. Export products included heavy rails, pins, nails, chains, cutlery, and hardware (Ashton, 1966; Brown, 1991; Marshall, 1973). This growth in the iron industry and its constituent firms reflected the confluence of market demand, technological change, and related advances in productivity.

We have seen, particularly in firms such as Carron and Cyfarthfa, how correspondence between absentee owners and resident managers revealed concerns with improving the efficiency and effectiveness of operations through the control of productivity, the reduction of waste, the minimisation of input costs such as raw materials and related transportation, and the application of new technology. Iron was one of the relatively 'newer' industries of the period wherein the observed growth in productivity was not confined to the specific industry alone but to expansion also occurring in more traditional sectors (Mokyr, 1987). Thus, some productivity growth was achieved without automatic recourse to technological change. In this respect it is interesting to note that most expansion in the nineteenth century iron and steel industry was due to minor rather than major improvements in technology (Allen, 1983). Change following this scenario is typically gradual rather than dramatic. In this context analyses of raw material costs, labour costs in relation to final output, and costs of alternative sources of supply were responses to concerns about the productivity of existing processes.

Efforts to employ accounting data for the implementation of cost-cutting procedures were universal in the iron industry firms investigated. Motivation for cost management was both a function of a perceived need for securing greater efficiencies from existing methods, as well as for investigating the possible advantages accruing from the adoption of new technology.

In the latter respect technological innovation was clearly related to owners' assessments of the impact on overall process costs. When new technology was introduced in the iron industry, it was often related to demonstrable cost savings. Results of technology experiments have survived in the Carron and Darby archives (see also Slaven, 1975).

The efforts of the iron masters were not confined solely to a focus on restricting costs and improving outputs for existing processes and products. By the nineteenth century several had developed new casting techniques and had popularised new cast iron products for both household and industrial use. The large, integrated iron firms produced and marketed a wide range of specialised shapes unknown in the previous century (Hyde, 1977; Trinder, 1973). Although product line decision making was most advanced at Carron and Darby according to surviving evidence, the care taken by most firms to allocate overheads reflected an effort to generate the data necessary to gauge the long-run profitability of individual products.

CONTROLLING RESOURCES

Three particular factors of production occupied much of the iron masters' attention—sources of raw materials, labour, and capital. All motivated a recourse to various cost calculations to determine the feasibility of expanded operations.

Surviving records, particularly correspondence and management reports, contain frequent references to the comparative costs of various sources of raw materials and attendant raising and transporting expenses. We have seen how the regional character of the industry developed as a function of cost differentials occasioned by the availability of natural resources, particularly in Scotland and South Wales (see also Hudson, 1989; Slaven, 1975). Whilst early advantages may have been conferred on such firms, there is still a considerable volume of evidence that their owners continued to pay close attention to the costs associated with various sites of supply. In the 1840s, for example, as the cost of native iron ore was beginning to rise in South Wales, companies looked to more distant sources (Baber & Atkinson, 1987).

Labour was also an input of fundamental importance to Industrial Revolution iron masters. Dowlais, for example, had 10,000 employees in 1849. Mokyr (1987) has observed that workers who gravitated to the factories often came from countryside households already engaged in non-agricultural occupations. Though iron firms had to make large capital expenditures, they nonetheless relied on significant labour inputs. These labour requirements were often for highly skilled workers, recruited from outside the local region (Lee, 1986). This importation certainly happened in the case of Scottish firms where specialised English labour was relocated to teach skills to the local labour force. Since iron production was labour-intensive, managers found it a relatively easy option to cut labour inputs when attempting to contain operating costs. The case studies afford ample evidence of the attention paid to controlling labour costs. One of the two massive technological reports at Carron circa 1770 contains a series of time-and-motion studies designed to establish standards for particular mining functions. Darby's intricate system of shaft-specific bounties and the detailed Crowley abatement structure are also offered as classic examples of this focus.

Iron industry firms were concerned not only with sources of supply and costs of labour, but with the availability of appropriate expertise as well. For example, Carron Company succeeded technically because it hired experienced workers from Coalbrookdale, from the Wealden gunfoundries, and even from as far away as Sweden (Pawson, 1979). Hence, the approach to labour management was not simply one of cost minimisation. It was balanced with a concern for expertise and quality of output that led to a continuous attention to cost control relative to productivity and quality.

Capital for business maintenance, operations expansion, and new plant and machinery investment was of fundamental importance to the iron masters. Sources of capital inputs were limited by the regionalism of capital markets and the prevalence of family partnerships as the founding basis for most firms. The joint-stock company had barely arrived on the scene. Thus, an important source of capital injection lay in the reinvestment of earned profits and by further investments of capital from partners in the business (Slaven, 1975).

Given the important role of retained profits in financing further infrastructure investments in these firms, close attention to cost management in maintaining adequate levels of profitability was of vital significance. The multitude of cost controls chronicled here reflected the necessity to have ploughed-back capital available for investment in vertical integration opportunities, regional expansion, and/or technological innovations of both major and minor types (Crouzet, 1985). In summary, the iron industry entrepreneurs were vitally affected by their resources of raw materials, labour, and capital. They demonstrated attention to the planning and control of these resources, both in operational terms and in their appreciation of input costs. Cost accounting, in its various forms, was for them an important means of responding to and surviving in their environment.

CONCLUSION

This study of Industrial Revolution iron industry firms has revealed clear evidence of purposeful costing activities undertaken by owners and managers. In the cases studied the sophistication of cost accounting reflected in archival records appears to have been commensurate with the sophistication of marketing strategies, operating processes, and technological innovations. Their attention to costing reflected and was influenced by the industrial environment within which they operated. Key factors included the competitiveness of their industry; the restrictions upon their access to capital inputs; the variation in periodic profitability and access to resources in different regions; the relationship between productivity and material supplies, labour availability, and technological innovation; and the progress of new technology in productive processes.

Based on the currently available evidence, there appears to be ample justification for regarding the British Industrial Revolution iron industry as being a major contributor to the development of cost accounting and cost management practices in the industrial environment. Certainly, important foundations were laid for subsequent methodological advances that were to occur in the era of scientific management.

NOTES

1. This chapter draws heavily from material which appeared in R.K. Fleischman and L.D. Parker (1992), 'The Cost-Accounting Environment in the British Industrial Revolution Iron Industry', *Accounting, Business and Financial History*, Vol. 2, No. 2: 141–160.

2. The Carron archive is located at West Register House, Edinburgh. The important Cadell/Garbett correspondence is located in the National Library of Scotland, Edinburgh. Secondary source material can be found in Campbell (1958, 1961).

3. This assertion is based on the current authors' survey of the surviving records of over 200 Industrial Revolution business enterprises.

4. The Cyfarthfa archive is located at the National Library of Wales, Aberystwyth. The bulk of the Crawshay correspondence has been published. Secondary source material can be found in Addis (1957), Edwards (1989), and Jones (1985).

5. The Darby archive is located at the Shrewsbury Public Library, the Shropshire Public Record Office (Shrewsbury), and the Ironbridge Gorge Museum Library (Telford). Secondary source material can be found in Raistrick (1970) and Trinder (1973, 1974).

6. The Dowlais archive is located at the Glamorganshire Public Record Office (Cardiff). Secondary source material can be found in Edwards and Baber (1979), Elias (1960), and England (1959).

7. The only secondary sources consulted in the section on other iron enterprises were Flinn (1957, 1962) and Young (1923–1924) on Crowley. The Newton, Chambers archive is located at the Sheffield City Archives; Butterley at the Derbyshire Public Record Office (Matlock); Vivian and Clydach at the National Library of Wales (Aberystwyth); Abersychan at the Gwent Public Record Office (Cwmbran); and Clyde/Cramond at the National Library of Scotland (Edinburgh).

8. Reliance on indigenous material inputs gradually declined and, in order to minimise transportation costs, the decision was taken in 1887 to relocate the steel-making capacity of the firm to a site adjacent to Cardiff docks (Owen, 1972).

4

The Textile Trades

The single most significant component of the British Industrial Revolution was the mechanisation of the cotton industry and the increased productivity that ensued. Having long taken a back seat to woollens, cotton underwent an expansion in the last two decades of the eighteenth century that was to leave it the undisputed leader amongst Britain's textile trades. Finished cotton goods became the most important export in the nation's foreign commerce. The factory system in cotton was in evidence from 1780, a date selected by some historians to signal the beginning of the Industrial Revolution. Larger-scale operations were necessary to capitalise and house the new spinning machines, a major technological innovation of the age. The impact of Boulton & Watt's steam engine in the fullness of time freed textiles from a dependence upon water power and allowed its transition to urban venues where cheaper and more centralised supplies of labour were available.

ARCHIVES REVIEWED

Given the new demands for capital accumulation, distribution systems, and technological innovation in the emerging cotton industry, it might have been anticipated that the fresh entrepreneurship would have spawned more sophisticated managerial accounting. Such was not the case, however, in comparison to the iron and extractive industries where large-scale operations were in evidence decades earlier. Table 5 summarises the comparative positioning of 13 textile enterprises in four cost management areas amongst the 25 firms as we qualitatively evaluated them in Fleischman and Parker (1991, p. 364).

Table 5: British Industrial Revolution Firms Reflecting Activity and Excellence in Cost Management Areas

(13 textile firms in parentheses)
12 non-textile firms without parentheses

	Cost Control		Overhead		Decision Making		Standard Costing	
Activity observed	10	(8)	7	(9)	8	(6)	11	(9)
% with activity observed	83	(62)	58	(69)	67	(46)	92	(69)
% evaluated excellent	42	(38)	25	(15)	33	(23)	25	(23)

It was only in accounting for overhead that the textile firms reflected a higher incidence of activity. In terms of excellence, the non-textile firms had a slight qualitative edge in all categories.

The accounting sophistication reflected in the surviving archives of textile firms we have examined run the gamut from excellent to deplorable. Amongst the best are the methods employed by Ashworth, Marshall, and Strutt. The few scattered remnants that survive for Philips reflect outstanding methodology in diverse areas. Archival holdings for Dugdale and Horrocks are likewise promising, but are too meagre in quantity to allow definitive judgement. The records for Finlay and McConnel & Kennedy, both extremely sizeable enterprises, are voluminous in quantity, but are reflective of a managerial accounting wasteland. Table 6 indicates the location(s) and types of firm records examined, as well as the branch of the trade plied by the individual enterprises. It will be noted that our sample size has been increased beyond the 13 firms evaluated in the 1991 study.

Table 6: Manuscript Sources (Major Collections)

Firm	*Branch*	*Location of Records*	*Types of Records*
Richard Arkwright & Co.	cotton	Chesterfield P.L.	wage books
H.& E. Ashworth	cotton	Lancashire R.O., Staffordshire R.O., Rylands L. (Manchester)	cost estimates, diaries, production reports, mill comparisons, expense reports
Cardwell, Birley & Hornby	cotton	Rylands L. (Manchester)	stocks, production reports
James Finlay & Co.	cotton	Glasgow U.L.	production reports, minutes, wage books, mill comparisons
Benjamin Gott & Sons	woollens	Brotherton L. (Leeds)	notebooks, production reports, expense comparisons
R. Greg & Co.	cotton	Manchester C.L.	stocks, letters, wage books, mill books, expense books
Horrocks, Crewdson & Co.	cotton	Lancashire R.O.	calculations books, journals, powerloom notes
Lanark Twist Co. (Owen)	cotton	Glasgow U.L.	production reports, wage books
Marshall & Co.	flax	Brotherton L. (Leeds)	process reports, expense books, notebooks, mill comparisons
McConnel & Kennedy	cotton	Rylands L. (Manchester)	production reports, stocks, wage books, ledgers
Samuel Oldknow & Co.	cotton	Rylands L. (Manchester)	production reports, costings books, mill comparisons, process reports
J.& N. Philips & Co.	tape	Staffordshire R.O.	cost estimates, process reports, production standards
W.G. & J. Strutt	cotton	Manchester C.L.	expense books, mill comparisons, stocks, production reports

Table 6: Manuscript Sources (Minor Collections)

Firm	*Branch*	*Location of Records*	*Types of Records*
T. & M. Bairstow	worsteds	W. Yorkshire A. (Leeds)	expense books
John Barraclough	silk	W. Yorkshire A. (Calderdale)	notebooks
James Bury & Co.	calico	Manchester C.L.	diaries
J.T. Clay & Sons	worsteds	Manchester C.L.	stocks, production reports
Robert Clough (Keighley)	worsteds	Brotherton L. (Leeds)	wage books, notebooks
Nathaniel Dugdale & Bros.	cotton	Rylands L. (Manchester)	job costings, expense books
John Foster & Sons	worsteds	Brotherton L. (Leeds)	memoranda books
William Gray & Son	cotton	Bolton Archives	stocks, machinery books
James Kenyon & Son	woollens	Lancashire R.O.	production reports
Henry Kirkland	cotton	Strathclyde Archives	diaries
John Murgatroyd & Sons	worsteds	W. Yorkshire A. (Calderdale)	production reports, minutes
Owen Owens & Son	cotton	Rylands L. (Manchester)	sales books, memoranda books
William Pearsce	cotton	Nottingham R.O.	mill evaluation
Henry Pease & Co.	worsteds	Durham R.O.	experiments, trials
Pettigrew & Dickie	cotton	Strathclyde Archives	costings books
Rylands & Sons	cotton	Rylands L. (Manchester)	property valuations
Stansfeld family	woollens	W. Yorkshire A. (Calderdale)	wage books

HISTORICAL PERSPECTIVES

Gleanings from the archival collections have been supplemented by the findings of historians who have studied individual firms or specific segments of the textile trades. Accounting historians have not delved wholeheartedly into Industrial Revolution business records, perhaps deterred by the prevalent belief that sophisticated cost accounting methodology awaited later development. However, Stone (1973) reported on the Chorlton Mills of Birley & Co., a forerunner of Cardwell, Birley & Hornby. The accounting records upon which this significant early study was based are housed at the University of Florida, Gainesville. More recently, Walsh and Stewart (1993) have compared the accounting methods of the Newmills cloth manufactory at Haddington (based on Marshall, 1980) in the late seventeenth century with those of Owen's factory at New Lanark a century later. Accounting historians have more actively examined the business records of US textile enterprises (e.g., Johnson, 1972; Porter, 1980; Tyson, 1992).

A great debt is owed to economic historians who have reported on accounting methodology in broader studies of British textile firms. Pollard's (1965) monumental search for the 'genesis of modern managerialism' included a close investigation of accounting at the Gott and Marshall enterprises. Chapman's (1967) study of the early factory masters provided vital insights into the Arkwright empire. Hudson's (1977, 1986) work on the West Riding wool industry reflected a keen appreciation for accounting history despite her call for a trained accountant to verify her findings. Valuable work of a firm-specific nature has been done by Unwin (1924) on Oldknow, Heaton (1931–1932) on Gott, Fitton and Wadsworth (1958) on Strutt, Rimmer (1960) on Marshall, Lee (1972) on McConnel & Kennedy, and Rose (1977) on Greg.

The quality of the accounting history in these studies tends to vary as a function of the historian's interest and expertise in accounting and/or the sophistication of the studied firm's record keeping. Interpretations can conflict as evidenced by two analyses of the earliest UK textile firm whose records have been closely scrutinised, the Haddington works. Marshall (1980) observed that the firm used costing data for process evaluation, product line decisions, control of raw materials, and 'rational planning' as early as the late seventeenth century. Walsh and Stewart (1993, p. 795), by contrast, evaluated this accounting as little more than a series of rules to ensure discipline, to discourage individuals from 'transgressions by a series of contracts and punishments'. As practitioners of the 'new accounting history', like Walsh and Stewart, make their initial forays into the arena of British Industrial Revolution cost accounting, paradigmatic influences will result in conflicting interpretations of the data.

ANALYSING A COMPETITIVE ENVIRONMENT

Two other preliminary points may serve to furnish background for the environment in which the accounting methods of textile enterprises developed. First, profit margins were extremely narrow in the textile trades, necessitating a careful attention to expense control. Henry Ashworth in his 1849 diary calculated the cost of making 60-twist cotton yarn. He estimated his 'prime cost' to be 13½d for a quantity that sold for 14d. However, it should be noted that Ashworth included both interest on capital and 'wear and tear' (depreciation) at 1½d in this computation (D3016/2/1). Communication between Robert and Samuel Greg in 1829 indicated that losses at Quarry Bank could be attributed in part to an input factor as seemingly insignificant as its raw cotton mixture, the firm having 'thrown away something' (C5/8/12).

Second, despite the competitive nature of the industry, neither the accounting methods nor the accounting numbers were considered trade secrets. The Ashworth archive contains an 1845 survey of Bolton-area mills, summarising 26 actual returns and 14 estimates for firms not responding. Data categories included the number and size of machines (mule spindles, throstle spindles, looms), the amount of raw cotton annually used, the weight of yarn produced, and the volume of coal consumed (DDAs 2/3). Moreover, Ashworth gathered statistics at six rival mills he personally visited (DDAs 2/1), and noted in his 1849 diary that James Burton cleared 3d per pound profit for 40-twist, taking into account wages paid and ordinary working expenses (coals, oil, tallow, straps, etc.), but excluding interest on capital and wear and tear (D3016/2/1). Similarly, Philips in the 1820s knew the price structures of three competitive tape firms sufficiently well to conclude that it undersold two, but were beaten competitively by the third (D644/1/5).

Pease was aware of the costs and prices of competitors in Manchester, London, Paisley, and Bradford in the late 1840s (D/HP/21). Though there were no textbooks detailing accounting methods for industrial concerns, it would appear that information about competitors was readily available. Yet, the variety of methodologies in evidence throughout the industry would suggest that techniques were home-grown, designed to convey the information that individual entrepreneurs thought vital to their respective operations.

Distilling the archival survivals of some 30 Industrial Revolution textile firms is a daunting organisational task. In order to facilitate this discussion, we propose a four-part classification scheme: expense control, product costing, responsibility accounting, and non-routine decision making. Under the category of *expense control*, we will consider the various techniques employed to report and control expenditures. In the textile industries particularly, the control of raw materials and finished goods inventories were of the utmost importance. Closely linked to the expense control function was *product costing*. Subtopics here include the allocation of overhead, the cost recovery on fixed assets, and the preparation of production reports. *Responsibility accounting* was used frequently during the period to generate data which might have been used to evaluate the efficiency of machines and production rooms of the same function, as well as multiple plant installations. The opportunity to gauge the performance of the operatives and managers involved was present. Within this classification of responsibility accounting, we will also consider early standard costing. Finally, a number of textile firms did detailed cost analyses to aid in *non-routine decision making*. Many of these evaluations were specifically linked to the technological innovations which revolutionised the textile trades in the late eighteenth and early nineteenth centuries.

EXPENSE CONTROL

It might be expected that accounting methods designed for the new factory system in textile spinning would feature expense control as a primary objective. For decades after technology mandated a factory environment for spinning, the weaving function was still organised under the domestic system. Here accounting was used to control the 'putting-out' process. The method described by Unwin (1924) in place at Oldknow was typical. A weaver's account was debited for the twist and weft received and credited for the quantity of cloth and waste returned. Each returned warp was numbered so that poor workmanship could be traced.

The earliest documents we have seen evincing expense control in a textile factory environment tracked materials (ashes, starch, oil nitriol, powder blue) used in the bleaching operation at the Philips' factory at Tean in 1791 (D644/7/1). Unit costs for each material input were calculated per pack of bleached tapes. When quantities varied from an expected level, explanations were provided. By the 1820s, Philips was displaying current and the previous year's expenditures for comparative purposes.

Sir Richard Arkwright was a pioneer of spinning technology and factory organisation in the early Industrial Revolution. Unfortunately, virtually no accounting records from his various enterprises exist. One of the rare survivals is a wage book (D644) circa 1811, which is relatively undistinguished but for its careful segregation of overtime hours worked. There are separate categories for 'extra hours worked' and for 'extra hours allowed'. Finally, reflective of the family economy in cotton textiles, a column is included for total income when there were multiple operatives from the same family.

The most impressive expense compendia are the Marshall process reports, prepared annually or semi-annually for the spinning, bleaching, weaving, cheek, and flax departments, commencing in 1806 (MS 200/Book 6). These documents include a substantial number of data categories, including raw material consumption, amount of production, daily or weekly output per worker, percentage of waste, allocation of general expenses, and many others. Rimmer (1960, p. 122) said of these reports that they 'were tantamount to developing a radar system for the business'. Rimmer claimed that a daily performance card was maintained for each spinning frame at Marshall. Though we have not seen any of these records, they do seem in keeping with the panoptic gaze typical of the firm. Marshall required accounting information on various processes to determine which operations were the most profitable and to gauge how technological innovations, such as new hackling machinery, were doing. Ultimately, these data permitted year-to-year comparisons, 'to keep the laggards up to scratch', as Rimmer put it.

The Greg archive contains a 'Stoppages Ledger' (C5/1/16), dated 1815–1847, in which a careful separation is made between regular and overtime wages, as well as 'lost time'. A wages and expense book (C5/1/7/1) has spinning statistics for time worked, output per spinner, labour cost per pound of yarn, and expenses for apprentices for 1834–1838. Following 1838, similar information is provided for the weaving branch, including labour cost per loom.

The Strutt enterprise had a sophisticated system of expense control, but one which was deployed at peak efficiency only sporadically. An accounting of costs per pound of different yarn qualities did provide monthly results and yearly averages, commencing in 1809, but gave no specific breakdowns of overall expense. Starting in 1831, however, expenses were reported quarterly with a build-up in terms of nine specific operations, costed to one-tenth of a pence (01/Box 1). Even more detailed expense reporting appeared in other Strutt records. Expense numbers specific to product line, process function, and individual mill were kept for some twist varieties from 1815 on (01/Box 2). A statement of weekly expense components, 1811–1821, includes costings to three decimal places for items such as 'learning' and dinner downtime (01/Box 4).

Some Ashworth papers, dated somewhat later in the 1840s, reveal a number of temporal comparisons of expense items. There is one analysis of certain cost elements contrasting levels of associated expenditure in 1812, 1830, and 1845 respectively (DDAs 2/1). There is a 12-week study of the earnings of four spinners in 1835 and 1841, accompanied by corresponding changes in productivity. A rather elaborate 38-week investigation was undertaken in 1845–1846 to calculate the total fixed charges per week for the firm's 148 looms (ibid.). It must be conceded, however, that there is no evidence that these analyses were carried out on a regular basis or that managerial action was ever taken on them.

Since raw material inputs were major product costs and since profit margins were typically modest, most textile manufacturers paid significant attention to raw material mixtures and waste control. Various archival collections feature product costings, many of which include a standard cost for waste. A 1789 Greg calculation indicates a £26/11/3 weekly expense for waste on the production of twist costing £321/17/6

(C5/1/8). McConnel & Co., Ltd. (1906) estimated for 1795 a waste component of 4½d in the 2/6 cost of raw cotton needed to produce 100-count twist valued at 7/2½. A precise Ashworth calculation in 1850 divided the yield from a pound of spun cotton into 12.85 ounces of yarn and 3.15 ounces of waste (D3016/2/1).

In similar fashion, the more sophisticated production reports of the period contain columns for waste data. The Marshall process evaluations (MS 200/Book 6) all include waste information, occasionally multiple pieces of data as in the case of the spinning department. The Lanark fortnightly production reports have waste columns for the spinning and reeling operations, as well as waste per pound of rovings and yarn in the weaving branch (UGD 42/31/3). The Strutts went a step further by actually maintaining a separate waste book (01/Box 6).

Many textile entrepreneurs took efforts to reduce their raw material costs. An early nineteenth century Gott diary contained a calculation of the volume of wool loss in the scouring process, differentiating Spanish and English wools (MS 193/117a, p. 59). The same diary also included the differing yields of various wools in the production of assorted goods. We have already seen how the Gregs explained 1829 net operating losses in terms of a more expensive than necessary cotton mixture, though the archive does not indicate remedial action (C5/8/12). Henry Pease & Co. undertook a number of wool mixture trials in the 1836–1846 period (D/HP/11; D/HP/21). John Barraclough, a silk entrepreneur, maintained notebooks detailing the results of 'experements' he conducted and 'esteemates' of various costs (SPL 203). In 1851, Henry Ashworth noted in his diary that a savings in raw materials was necessary if his firm was to continue the production of heavier yarns (70, 80, and 90-counts). He reported the savings of 1d per pound of yarn by using Sea Islands instead of Egyptian cotton (D3016/2/1). It should be noted, however, that some firms refused to sacrifice quality to effect raw material cost savings. McConnel & Kennedy and Strutt chose to compete on the basis of quality rather than price (Fitton & Wadsworth, 1958; Lee, 1972).

Various textile firms took innovative actions by way of handling their raw materials. Greg was depreciating ('tare') raw cotton in inventory during the 1790s at differential annual rates (e.g., 2½% for Surinam, 4% for West Indian) (C5/1/1). Moreover, in a narrative regarding its raw material consumptions, the firm evinced concern about the deleterious effect of stockouts (C5/8/2). New Lanark had accounts which distinguished waste from 'loss', defined as raw materials unaccounted for (UGD 42/31/3). Rimmer (1960) contended that Marshall & Co. actually found it cost beneficial to run its machines more slowly in order to minimise the amount of waste. The Strutts, commencing in 1839, generated weekly reports which included both the average actual price and the standard price for raw cotton stocks consumed (01/Box 5).

Notwithstanding the rather sophisticated accounting for raw materials evident in some firms, the pattern was inconsistent. Cardwell, Birley & Hornby, for instance, carefully tracked twist and weft-in-process as well as in stocks, but did not apparently account for waste (MS 1201/1). The Gotts, who experimented extensively with wool mixtures, failed to include waste expense in a rather intricate product costing they undertook in 1830 (MS 193, item 210/1). Robert Clough paid careful attention to the quantities of soap and wool distributed to the combers, but was less attentive to the quantity and quality of goods returned by domestic system employees.

The attention accorded raw materials by certain textile enterprises was mirrored by some interesting inventory transactions and methods in evidence during the period. Rimmer (1960) wrote of Marshall's extensive inventory manipulations in the early nineteenth century. John Marshall bought huge stocks of flax and other raw materials on speculation. This inventory was regularly revalued not so much, says Rimmer, to reflect price fluctuations, but to influence profit-and-loss numbers. His was not an isolated case (see also Fitton & Wadsworth, 1958; Lee, 1972). Some smaller firms, such as William Gray & Son, J.T. Clay & Sons, and John Foster & Sons, reflected amongst very meagre record collections considerable sophistication in accounting for work-in-process (2GR/6; CLA 10; S.B. Foster's Memorandum Book). Following a disastrous fire in 1799, Gott's records were sufficiently precise that the firm could state the amount of the casualty loss on work-in-process inventory to the shilling (MS 193/117a, p. 89). Horrocks, Crewdson & Co., following a substantial raw materials purchase in 1803, wrote down its inventory the next year to reflect subsequent price declines (DDHs 1/1).

Several firms applied novel accounting methods to their finished goods inventory as well. The Owen Owens & Son archive includes a salesbook, dated 1831–1846, which reflects consignment accounting (H30). McConnel & Kennedy maintained finished goods inventory accounts net of discounts and commissions. Its 1805 stock taking, for example, contained deductions ranging from 7½ to 15%, apparently depending on destination and broker (Inventory Book, 1797–1811). Most remarkable was the rating system employed by Strutt to value its inventory qualitatively. In a record known as a 'Complaint and Remarks Book' (01/Box 4), the firm attempted techniques that were modified over time. In 1798, the firm used descriptive adjectives ('bad, bad middling, middling, pretty good, good') to rate various products. In 1799, the firm turned to a 1–5 numerical scale for qualitative evaluation. In 1801, the process was refined a step further as decimals were introduced to the five-point rating scheme.

In summary, we find plentiful evidence of detailed attention paid by textile manufacturers to their accounting for expense control. However, the focus of expense control efforts, the level of accounting detail, and the complexity of calculations appeared to have varied considerably amongst firms in this industry. As might be expected given tight profit margins in relation to raw material costs, particular attention was most often paid to the recording and tracking of the costs, usage, mixture, and waste of raw materials. Even in this respect, however, the degree of attention paid by the various manufacturers fluctuated considerably. Our investigations also reveal evidence of expense control records in relation to wages, time worked, input/output relationships, process costs, and cost comparisons between current and past years. In several firms expense control also involved relatively detailed accounting for work-in-process and finished goods inventories.

PRODUCT COSTING

The highly competitive nature of the textile trades mandated careful attention to product costing as well as expense control. However, the preparation of production reports and the allocation of overhead to products as necessary prerequisites to purposeful product costing represent a quantum leap in terms of the degree of sophistication reflected by the accounting. The surviving records of textile firms reveal far fewer production reports and product costings than were in evidence for iron enterprises of the same period. Only Marshall could rival the major iron founders in coping with the intricacies of overhead allocation. The track record in textiles for depreciation ('wear and tear') accounting was truly hopeless.

Firms in the vanguard of product costing were those which maintained accounting records that could aid them in measuring the costs of the individual processes through which finished goods passed. We underscore again certain methods used by several firms in the previous section. Marshall maintained intricate expense records for various productive departments from 1806 on (MS 200/Book 6). Philips tracked indirect materials costs for the nine steps that formed the bleaching process in the 1830s (D644/1/16). Likewise, Strutt in the 1830s costed to one-tenth of a pence the various productive processes through which assorted numbers of twist passed on a quarterly basis (01/Box 1). Several smaller firms as well maintained costing records for the individual productive processes that contributed to finished goods. John Bury, the calico printer, kept in his 1811 diary the specific costs of bleaching, cutting, printing, colouring, duty, dipping, dyeing, grounding, extras, and commission/risk/interest associated with shawl production (L4/2/4/1). At the same point in time, Pettigrew & Dickie costed processes individually to determine selling price. Included here was a category called 'agency' (TD 242/4).

We have seen that iron industry enterprises regularly did cost analyses for various types of output. In the textile industry these costings appeared far less frequently, perhaps because the finished goods were more homogeneous in regard to costs. The most notable was an effort undertaken by Benjamin Gott in 1830 (MS 193/210/1), when he calculated the costs associated with converting £1,000 of raw wool on board at Hamburgh (sic) into saleable cloth. The list of added-on expenses included duty, freight, taxes, interest on fixed and moveable capital, depreciation, indirect materials, an allotment for repairs of machinery and buildings, and direct and indirect labour. These expenditures totalled £1,681. Consequently, each £8 of raw material resulted in finished cloth valued at £21/9/0. Although the most elaborate costing exercise we have seen in the textile archives, Gott inexplicably omitted an allowance for waste despite the general awareness of this cost factor throughout the industry and his own specific attention to its importance in other documents.

It will be recalled also that many iron companies were utilising full-scale production reports in the 1830s and 1840s. By this time a fairly standardised printed form was in evidence amongst producers in

South Wales (see, as an example, Figure 7). Whilst some textile firms, such as those mentioned above, compiled information about various processes, these data were rarely integrated into a production report for the operation as a whole. The Oldknow archive does contain a monthly mill statement for its Mellor plant in 1797 (Item 826), which appears as Figure 8. The report commenced with the number of spindles set up in each of four spinning rooms. Then, a mill-wide number was provided for average spindles in operation, the amount of cotton consumed, the volume of waste, the hanks and pounds spun, and the wages paid. Raw cotton was costed at a standard 2/1½ per pound and waste at 1/4, reflective of its salvage value on disposition. Contingent expenses of 1s per pound were added and specified separately as hands in the mill (direct labour) 5½d; management, clerk, smiths, joiners, etc. (indirect labour) 1½d; wear and tear 1½d; interest on money 2d; rent, insurance, carriage of stores, postage, etc. 1½d. A 10% deduction was allowed, comprised of discounts to purchasers (5%), commission for selling (2½%), and risque of debts and carriage to Manchester (2½%). Finally, an 'apparent gain' was calculated on operations. It should be noted that Oldknow's accounting system supported these reports because daily production summaries for individual workers were generated. The actual quantity of output for each spinner was multiplied by a standard value (Item 829).

Another prototype of a textile industry production report, that has been reproduced elsewhere, is the fortnightly statement of the New Lanark enterprise (UGD 42/31/3; Walsh & Stewart, 1993, p. 794). These reports, dating from the first decade of the nineteenth century, were mill-specific for one of Lanark's three plants. The data categories included the number and location of various spinning rooms, number of spindles, type of cotton, quantity of rovings, utilisation of power (water wheel), actual production (weight, fineness, hanks, hanks per spindle, waste in spinning and reeling, yarn and waste per pound of roving, waste per pound of yarn), and wages (theoretic, spinning masters, total picking, total carding, total spinning, total reeling and sorting, total preparation). Despite the analytic possibilities provided by these statistics, there is little evidence that the firm did anything with them. In point of fact, the volume of omitted data over the series (1803–1805) is unsettling. One column that was never filled was 'theoretic', a subcategory of wages. Perhaps Lanark's accountant, like the current authors, had no clue what the designation meant.

Figure 8: Mellor Production Report, Oldknow, 1797

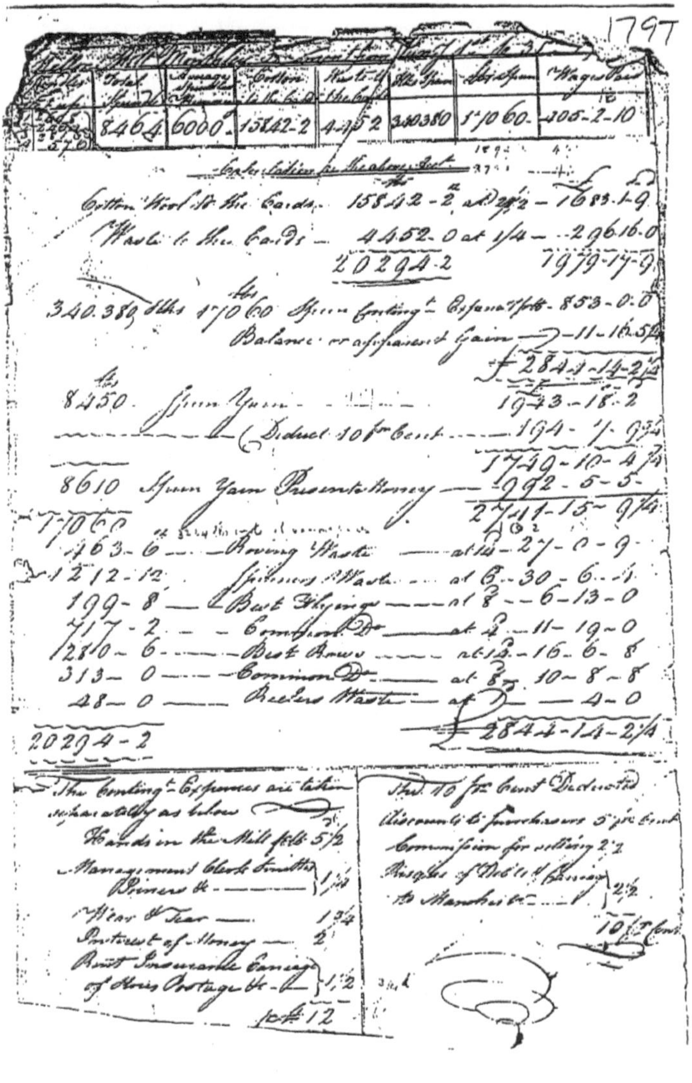

A smaller producer, James Kenyon & Son, had a printed production book for the period 1820–1846 (DDX 823/6/1). There were 22 different data categories. With the passage of time, more and more of these were left blank. However, a corresponding blanket book (DDX 823/2/4), with 18 categories, was assiduously maintained. McConnel & Kennedy maintained a weekly production report in a document called 'Yarn Output Book', dated 1808–1818.

A good measuring rod of the level of sophistication reflected by product costings and production reports is the handling of overhead, both with regard to which expense items rightly constitute overhead and the process by which overhead is allocated to products and/or cost centres. Marshall was clearly the leader in overhead allotment amongst the textile enterprises surveyed. An 1811 allocation formula (MS 200/ Book 7, pp. 261–262) distributed eight overhead cost components to seven cost centres (see Table 4). In 1819, a revision occurred wherein certain overhead costs were reduced, reflecting changing price levels in the post-Napoleonic period. Not only were the annual costs changed, but so also were the percentage apportionments to the various departments. These tabulations were a continuation and refinement of the Marshall process reports, dating from 1806, wherein general expenses were allocated according to predetermined formula. When John Marshall II became the prime mover in his father's firm in the early 1820s, attention came to be focussed increasingly on overhead costs to achieve competitive advantage. Although general expenses were then being charged at one-sixth production costs, the younger Marshall felt that reality dictated a number closer to one-fourth. Under his administration overhead expenses fell one-third between 1827 and 1830 (Rimmer, 1960).

The only other firm that evinced overhead allocation on the basis of *ex ante* estimates was Birley & Co., as reported by Stone (1973). At the Chorlton Mills, overhead was apportioned to 14 cost centres according to formula, again dating from 1811. A substantial volume of underapplied overhead was written off to a buildings account in 1813, and the estimated annual amount amended upward to avoid future shortfalls. At the other end of the spectrum is the example of Dugdale where no cognisance of overhead costs was taken well into the 1840s despite detailed accounting in other diverse areas. Even more startling was the inconsistency of certain Strutt records in the handling of overhead. An expense book that compared costs at Belper and Milford (01/Box 3) contained no overhead items despite the fact that in an earlier document for Belper only (01/Box 4), various overhead components were costed with astounding precision (one-thousandth of a pence).

A number of firms were taking account of overhead components in a variety of ways. Previously mentioned examples include Oldknow, whose production reports incorporated a build-up of contingent expenses (Item 826); the weekly expense reporting of Strutt, which precisely costed indirect labour on a process-specific basis (01/Box 4); and the indirect materials costing for nine bleaching processes at Philips in 1830 (D644/1/16). Additionally, Horrocks, Crewdson & Co., commencing in 1817, did an annual calculation of specific overhead cost items for the spinning function that included wear and tear, coals, taxes, insurance, interest on fixed assets, and interest on prime costs. These calculations were done to a base of one-twentieth of a pence (DDHs 75). Commencing in 1831 with the advent of the powerloom, weaving overhead and power costs were similarly calculated. The Greg archive contains a detailed four-page estimate for the construction and operation of a spinning factory to produce 18,000 pounds of twist weekly (1831) (C5/1/1/3). A calculation of weekly 'contingency expenses' includes 15 overhead items.

An entire chapter could be written on the vagaries of textile industry depreciation as a component of overhead costing. Most firms were conscious of this cost factor, though 'wear and tear' was often amalgamated with interest on capital. Depreciation accounting was by no means universal, however. The Strutt enterprise, though extraordinarily sophisticated in its expense control, was taking no depreciation in its 1821–1823 machinery ledger (01/Box 51). Finlay was not depreciating its assets as late as the 1860s.

Depreciation accounting was a learned experience in the record-keeping chronology for the majority of textile firms. McConnel & Kennedy day books made no mention at all of depreciation in the period from 1795–1802. Following a gap in the records, the 1811–1814 day book indicated a depreciation rate of 2½% on all assets except lighting (7½%). Differential depreciation rates on various asset categories appeared for the first time in a document called 'Real Ledger, 1817–1827'. Cardwell, Birley & Hornby was not taking depreciation in the 1790s, but again following a gap from 1798–1813, was depreciating its Chorlton Mill at a flat rate of £2,500 per annum (MS 1199/R106303/Book 3). Greg actually used the word 'depreciation' (rather than 'wear and tear') in 1816, but was depreciating only its inventory until 1819 (C5/1/2/5).

Most firms used straight-line depreciation of historical cost for their cost recovery. There were exceptions, however. McConnel & Kennedy, in taking its standard 2½% on most assets, based its depreciation expense on net book value (Day Book, 1811–1814, p. 328). The Gregs also used net book values rather than historical cost when taking 5% on machinery and 2½% on buildings semi-annually (C5/1/2/5). In an 1831 machinery book (C5/1/1/3), replacement cost rather than historical cost was used. William Gray & Son employed current appraisal value for the depreciation of certain property holdings (2GR/6). Dugdale revalued machinery in 1842 for cost recovery purposes (MS 1200/R106303/Book E). McConnel & Kennedy also adjusted machinery valuations up and down between 1804 and 1806 to reflect current cost, but commencing in 1807, the firm ceased making these annual adjustments (Inventory Book, 1797–1811).

Two firms were particularly concerned with depreciation accounting. Horrocks, as we have seen, was carefully calculating wear and tear from 1817 on. In 1839, the firm began an elaborate depreciation calculation for its spinning department. Fairly typical depreciation rates of 12% on steam engines, 10% on buildings, 4% on land, and 7% on pipes were taken. Additionally, there were chargebacks to spinning of a portion of the depreciation expense incurred by weaving and the steam engines in common use. All this numeracy resulted in an overhead allocation of 1.801d per pound of spun goods in 1857, for example (DDHs 65). Ashworth did a 12-year comparative study of performance at its New Eagley and Egerton installations for 1835–1846 (MS 1201/R106303). Performance was gauged by adding profit to wear and tear. Bottom-line profit at New Eagley was given at 11/9 per spindle, but at 21/4 with wear and tear added. The corresponding figures for Egerton were 5/1 and 20/8 respectively. One is skeptical of the accuracy of these calculations, however, not only because of the wide discrepancies in depreciation rates (10/5 per spindle at New Eagley, 15/7 at Egerton), but also because in some years (1839–1842), no wear and tear was taken at all.

In summary, product costing and production reporting were far less frequently undertaken in textile firms as compared to what we have found in the iron industry. Enterprises that did pay attention to these aspects costed departments and processes; some calculated conversion costs from raw materials to finished goods. They were in a distinct minority amongst textile firms, however. Our investigations revealed little evidence of the production record books or the standardised production reports that came to typify the iron industry by the late Industrial Revolution. Some components of overhead cost were recorded and tracked in a variety of ways, with particular attention to depreciation accounting. However, few firms appear to have employed cost allocation techniques for overhead.

RESPONSIBILITY ACCOUNTING

Some historians who seek the genesis of modern managerialism look to the utilisation of cost accounting as a means to enhance disciplinary control over workers and managers. This point of departure would require an effective panopticism which Hoskin and Macve (1988, 1994) found at the Springfield Armory in the 1830s and 1840s, but which was not evinced in their opinion at Boulton & Watt in the first decade of the nineteenth century (see Chapter 7). Fundamentally, two questions must be answered positively for these historians to accept a specific environment as the origin of modern managerialism. First, did the accounting system generate the types of data necessary to order people about? Second, did the firm employ these data for such a purpose? We would suggest from our review of British Industrial Revolution textile records that in some instances there was adequate information available to support a system of responsibility accounting. However, there is virtually no evidence that the data were ever specifically deployed to create a disciplinary regime or a 'panoptic gaze'.

There exist in the archives a substantial number of statistical compilations that would allow for a comparison of individual operatives, machines, managers, function rooms, and/or mills to lay the foundation for responsibility accounting. In some instances the focus seemed to be on the performance of operatives. At Strutt there was an accounting record known as 'Quarterly Gift Forfeits' in which fines were levied against workers for 'doing work badly' (01/Box 34). McConnel &

Kennedy tracked the daily quantity of cotton picked, delineating fine from coarse output and recording shortfalls in the productivity of individual workers (Cotton Pickers Account Book, 1795). Meanwhile, at Oldknow a pejoratively labelled 'Disgrace Account' was a log of operatives' mistakes (Unwin, 1924). Henry Ashworth had sufficient statistics at his disposal to compare the productivity of four spinners in 12-week periods in 1835 and 1841 (DDAs 2/1). Two smaller firms, Stansfeld and John Murgatroyd & Sons, were particularly conscientious in tracking worker productivity. The latter firm had a printed weavers' ledger in the 1840s with a page given over to the pay and output of each operative (STA 225/8; FH 421; FH 429/1; JM 174).

Other times the record keeping centred on the productive efficiency of individual machines. Rimmer (1960) reported that at Marshall & Co. every frame had a daily performance card so that its efficiency could be measured. Likewise, the periodic reports of overseers to the factory manager on the work performed in their individual function rooms could have served important comparative purposes, though there is no evidence that they were ever used that way (MS 200/Book 6). William Gray & Son, as early as 1803, maintained detailed information on its machinery, including the expected weekly production of various hanks (2GR/7). Ashworth kept a record of loom downtime to permit production changeovers. An average of 4.67 set-ups was required for each six-month period (DDAs 2/1). The knowledge Gott had at its disposal regarding the output expectations from various raw material inputs and machines induced A.B. Hunter to comment optimistically (MS 193/117a, pp. 66–67, 71):

> ...indeed it may be said that in Mills in this Country today there is little or no attempt to procure the statistical data which Benjamin Gott obtained and noted in this book a hundred years ago.

Several major textile firms maintained statistics that would have permitted the comparison of the efficiency of multiple function rooms. A weekly expenditure book at the Strutt's Milford Mill (1821–1828) tracked expenses for four carding rooms and four spinning rooms, and reflected significant variations amongst them (01/Box 3). Quarterly compilations further provided aggregated information that might have been used to gauge managerial performance. Stone (1973) intimated that the establishment of the five carding rooms and eight spinning rooms at the Chorlton Mills as individual cost centres would likewise have furnished data for comparative, evaluative purposes.

Five of the largest firms with multiple installations maintained a record-keeping system which afforded comparisons of operations at the mill level. In a document dated 1771–1787 (D644/1/1), Philips developed production budgets for its two factories at Tean and Radcliffe/Whitefield. Included were data on the number of looms expected to be in operation at each, the types of output anticipated on a mill-specific basis, and production standards for operatives at each installation. For example, the anticipated output of No. 39 tapes in 'weavers dozens in a month for one loom of a sort' was 21 at Tean but only 18 at Radcliffe/Whitefield. Ten different tape varieties 'supposed to be made per month' were considered. Expectations at Tean were universally higher, though there is no proportional relationship between budgeted output in the ten categories.

The monthly production reports at Lanark Twist for the first decade of the nineteenth century were specific to three mills and to individual spinning rooms within each (UGD 42/31/2). Expense books in the Strutt archive compared operations at Milford and Belper. There are three volumes of statistics, dated 1821–1845, with essentially no reporting modifications over the two and one-half decades (01/Box 3).

Marshall had prepared a 14-page document entitled 'Account of the coals consumed by the Steam Engines at Messrs. Marshalls Flax Mills Leeds Yorkshire and also the quantity of yarn spun in the year 1823' (MS 200/39). This analysis, a page of which is offered as Figure 9, provided individual statistics of power utilisation and output for mills A, B, and C, plus a 'Comparison of the Mills A and B with the Mill C'.

The Ashworths were vitally interested in contrasting operations at their two plants. We have discussed the 12-year profit and depreciation analysis for New Eagley and Egerton (MS 1201/R106303). In addition, a comparative raw materials usage study was undertaken in 1845. It was found that at New Eagley, each pound of raw cotton resulted in 12.125 ounces of yarn. At Egerton the yield was only 11.4 ounces. This analysis was also compared to data from a dozen competing firms. The range of yield varied from 10.8 to 15 ounces of yarn per pound of cotton, averaging 12.72. However, four of the others apparently did not approach the calculation with the precision of Ashworth as their returns were rounded to the nearest ounce (DDAs 2/3).

Figure 9: Flax Mills Comparison, Marshall, 1823

11

to drive 3441 spindles = 57.35 spindles to a Horse Power. without allowance for millwork

Comparison of the Mills A and B with the Mill C.

As Mill A is entirely employed in spinning tow and Mill B by spinning the line from the same flax they must be added together in order to compare with Mill C which is for line and tow.

Mills	Engine	mill work	Spindles	Bundles	Pounds	pounds	leas
Mill A	50 HP	10 HP	1735 tow	33301	894982	27.7	7.22
Mill B	96 HP	22 HP	3853 line	85750	1116029	13.03	15.35
A and B	146	32	5588	118051	2011011	17.04	11.74
Mill C	76.	16	3441	58128	729337	12.55	15.94
Total	222	48	9029	176179	2740348	15.56	13.85

The expence of fuel for the year 1822 was 1822-18-2 for 5940.65 tons, price 6-1½ per ton for 230 HP = 15-17-2¼ per Horse power per annum

Mill A	433-2-2
Mill B	710-12-1
A & B	1143-14-3
Mill C	679-3-11
Total	1822-18-2

The deployment of a standard costing system is a method for assessing operative and managerial responsibility, though considered to be a largely twentieth century practice. The question has been raised elsewhere as to what constitutes sophisticated standard costing. Is an established norm or expectation based upon past results sufficient? Must standards be based upon observations, stopwatch in hand, as typified by the scientific management movement of the Age of Taylor? Must a purposeful standard cost system be accompanied by variance analysis suggestive of remedial action?

There are numerous examples from the Industrial Revolution textile trades of firms employing cost standards of the more rudimentary type. In most cases it is not possible to gauge whether these efforts were the result of careful evaluations of past results or mere guesses. As early as 1768, Cardwell, Birley & Hornby valued inventory at standard cost (MS 1199/R106303/Books 1 and 2). Marshall used standard costs for both raw materials and finished goods inventories in 1793 (MS 200/Book 1, pp. 11–15). Finlay was carrying finished goods inventory (both yarn and castings) at standard circa 1810 (UGD 91/422). An 1848–1852 account book of Dugdale (MS 1200/R106303/Book G) evinced the usage of standards for job-costing purposes. Other firms were using standards for the application of labour costs to products. Oldknow in the 1790s was maintaining a daily record of worker productivity by multiplying actual output by a standard cost (Item 829). Marshall's process reports (MS 200/Box 6) calculated output per operative in a time series which would have allowed, at least, for the articulation of labour efficiency standards. The elder John Marshall attempted to increase the output and efficiency of his spinners by focussing production on coarser yarns. With the ascension of the younger John Marshall, the firm sought to enhance worker productivity through time-and-motion studies and the efficient arrangement of machine layouts (Rimmer, 1960). These efforts parallelled the innovations James Watt Jr introduced at Boulton & Watt two decades earlier (see Chapter 7). Pease & Co. in the 1830s and 1840s was applying non-direct labour at a standard cost per hundredweight of output (e.g., 'lookers over' at 2s) (D/HP/11). Gray & Son typified a number of firms which valued machinery at standard rather than historical cost (e.g., spinning machines at so much per spindle) (2GR/6; see also R. Greg & Co., C5/1/1/3).

Three textile enterprises took standard costing to a higher level of sophistication. Two Strutt volumes, dated 1827–1828 and 1839–1841, provided on a weekly basis the average and standard prices for raw cotton consumed (01/Box 5). As usual, however, there is no evidence to indicate that anything was ever done with variances between the numbers. We have seen previously how intent Henry Ashworth was with the calculation of standards for various components of his business. He was most attentive to waste norms (D3016/2/1). Moreover, he tracked output per spindle in terms of raw cotton utilisation and coal consumption (DDAs 2/3). In 1845–1846, he undertook a 38-week study in which he established a 2/3 per loom per week 'fixed charge' to which he added 1/9 for rent and power to derive a total overhead cost (DDAs 2/1).

By far the most exceptional standard costing was undertaken at Philips at a date early in the Industrial Revolution. The document that served as the basis for production standards (D644/1/1, 1771–1787) is in very poor condition, having suffered considerable water damage over the ages. Herein contained are a number of output projections. For 1771, there is a forecast of the hanks of warp and weft to be used in a 20-month period given a certain level of production. There is a calculation of the volume of tapes 'supposed to be made' per month and the quantity of warps and wefts required. The expected output of looms of different types and differing capabilities are stated in 'falls per week'. Finally, the expectations per loom at two locations (Tean and Radcliffe/Whitefield) are provided. Here the possibilities for variance analysis were very real since the expected output columns were set next to columns in which actual output was provided.

In summary, we find evidence that the textile firms developed information for responsibility accounting purposes, covering all inputs of materials, labour, and overheads. Statistical compilations that could have facilitated performance comparisons between operators, machines, managers, and mills were present in abundance. Some firms tracked worker and machine productivity, loom downtime, and set-ups per period. They compared the efficiency of multiple function rooms and of different mills with respect to such factors as raw materials usage, power consumption, and output. The archives yield numerous examples of the employment of rudimentary cost standards for raw materials, labour, and finished goods. Some more sophisticated records demonstrate evidence that variations from standard were calculated, but we are unable to conclude the extent to which such data may have been utilised by management.

NON-ROUTINE DECISION MAKING

If there were two areas that typified the focus of Industrial Revolution cost accounting, these would be the generation of statistics to aid management in controlling expenses and in making non-routine decisions. A major problem in trying to evaluate highly episodic calculations that appear in the archives is establishing relationships between *ex ante* analyses and *post factum* action based on the accounting numbers produced. In the absence of these linkages, we may be faced with a situation not unlike early Victorian days when Parliamentary investigators collected hundreds of volumes of statistics that were hardly ever translated into action. 'Data for data's sake' does not bespeak a high level of sophistication in managerialism, though the process does at least suggest an appreciation for some accounting purpose.

Many textile manufacturers were vitally concerned with technology costings, especially in light of the numerous innovations that spawned the birth of the factory system, first in spinning and subsequently in weaving. We have seen how statistics were maintained on individual machines of the same function in the section on responsibility accounting. Marshall, the prime mover in this regard, additionally had technology-related cost analyses prepared periodically. We have discussed the firm's coal consumption study dated 1823 (MS 200/39). A detailed analysis in 1821 computed the loss sustained by spinning wet rather than dry. Factoring in depreciation on the additional machinery requirements for wet spinning and incremental drying costs, Marshall estimated that the existing process technology cost 4½d per bundle more on a volume of 145,000 bundles (MS 200/32). Unfortunately, the records are silent as to whether the firm made the change indicated.

Heaton (1931–1932, p. 46) said of Benjamin Gott that he 'studied costs carefully'. Gott knew exactly the disposition of the power generated by his 40-horsepower Boulton & Watt engine to various productive departments (MS 193/117a, p. 7). Also, he was reputed to have spent thousands of pounds experimenting with steam dyeing as an alternative to water (Heaton, 1931–1932). The Gott archive contains an 1833–1857 analysis of comparative costs of working an old and a new steam engine (MS 193/Item 221). Average expenses for each were taken for five-year intervals and included the costs of coals, tallow, oil, packing, shovels, tenders' wages, and repairs. Notwithstanding this attention to power sources, textile entrepreneurs were not generally as concerned as the iron founders with these issues. There is evidence of only two firms having had negotiations with Boulton & Watt on the purchase of a steam engine. Unwin (1924) claimed that Oldknow had secured estimates for various horsepower engines. Chapman (1967) reported a lengthy negotiation between Boulton & Watt and Davison & Hawkesley, a large worsted manufacturer for whom we have been unable to locate any surviving records.

A major technological decision for textile firms in the 1820s and 1830s was whether or not to adopt the new powerloom. This issue was an extremely emotional one in the cotton textiles area, and led to Lancashire's brand of Luddism in 1812 and the subsequent tragedy of the domestic handloom weavers (Bythell, 1969; Fleischman, 1985). The premier cost analysis leading to this important technological innovation was undertaken at Philips in 1820 (D644/1/5). Here a table of comparative costs for the two weaving alternatives was constructed for a variety of different tapes. It was determined that the powerloom would result in a weekly savings of £90, mostly the result of direct labour reductions (the number of weavers could be halved from 450 to 225). In this instance we know that Philips did indeed make the transition, though we have no information as to whether the firm's expectation as to the volume of redundancies was realised.

Other firms were likewise concerned with their technology. The Strutts in 1809–1810 had prepared two cost analyses for different processes (01/Box 1). In 'An Epitome of Bleaching Sewing Short Skeins', differential costs between 'done the old way' and 'done the new way' were considered. 'A Comparison of Bleached Sewing Dram Balls' contained statistics on costs associated with production 'done by water machines' and 'done by hand'. The attempt of Greg to account for its net operating losses in the late 1820s included an awareness of the productivity shortfalls associated with using old machinery (C5/8/12). Horrocks, Crewdson & Co. carefully tracked power utilisation by different departments and powerloom expenses in the early 1830s (DDHs 75). We have mentioned previously Ashworth's study of 143 powerlooms in 1845–1846 designed to establish weekly overhead charges per loom (DDAs 2/1).

Capital construction was an expense item very carefully attended to by many Industrial Revolution textile entrepreneurs. The archive of T.&M. Bairstow, although very meagre in quantity and otherwise undistinguished in quality, contains some unbelievable expense logs for various capital improvements (Items 44, 52, 159). Repairs to the Sutton Mill in 1836–1838 are detailed in 337 line items, whilst a shed enlargement in 1848 involved 112 different costs. Warehouse repair in 1839 cost £298, with 78 items of expense specified. Another improvement, totalling a modest £92, was supported by no fewer than 125 discrete charges. The Gott manuscripts contain similar costings whose detail would cause an observer to ponder the cost/benefit considerations of their build-ups. An 1814 document (MS 193/Item 223) recorded the amount of window glass in feet and inches at the Park Mill in Bean Ing. There is also an 1832 costing, 'Account of Expenses of Making the Well and Boreholes at Park Mill', which details expenditures of the original construction in 1812–1813, as well as additions subsequently made in 1819–1821 and 1830. One can only marvel that these data were conveniently at hand for a compilation undertaken two decades after the initial construction (MS 193/Item 212). The Strutt enterprise also maintained detailed expense records of construction projects (01/Box 47). McConnel & Kennedy did a goodly amount of self-construction. Throughout the 1790s, the firm built its own machinery, but only commenced cost analyses of these efforts decades later (Lee, 1972). In 1798, the company began construction on an entire factory on which it recorded a healthy profit over the next five years (ibid.).

Two impressive cost analyses appear in the archives to support major expansion decisions. Greg's 1831 proposal to construct a four-storey, fireproof spinning factory and stock it with appropriate equipment has been previously discussed (C5/1/1/3). Another 'soup-to-nuts' expansion analysis appears in an account book of Pearsce's Pleasley works (DDBM 197/2; also bears reference DD4p/79/63). The proposal here was to purchase an abandoned cotton mill near Papplewick circa 1795. There is a full description of the factory's specifications, as well as an estimation of the costs and output associated with full production. Included are considerations of raw materials, waste, various costs associated with individual processes, wear and tear, and labour requirements. Output expectations were based on the productivity of 'very good' or 'best' spinners. The capability of the water wheel to generate sufficient power was observed, watch in hand.

Ashworth was typically in the vanguard of firms that used accounting for non-routine decision making. We have seen Henry Ashworth's 1851 diary entry in which a product line abandonment of higher count twists was contemplated in the absence of savings on the raw material mixture (D3016/2/1). In 1846, the firm made a business forecast for the next seven years in a document of some 15 pages in length (MS 1201/R106303). This look into the future was the best example of a very small number of business forecasts undertaken by Industrial Revolution enterprises. Furthermore, the Ashworth archive contains an 1842 document, comprising three huge folio pages, entitled 'Estimated amount of loss sustained at New Eagley Mill by deficiency of Power occasioned by abstraction of Water since the year 1833' (DDAs 2/2). This statement includes actual production levels with *pro forma* prognostications of what might have been achieved without the power deficiency. Figure 10 is a reduction of the summary page of the analysis.

A number of textile firms were using other financial and managerial accounting techniques atypical of the age. Unwin (1924) reported how Oldknow employed accounting estimations for making vertical integration decisions to expand its operations into bleaching, printing, dyeing, warping, sizing, and trimming. Philips likewise secured estimates for all additions to operations (D644/8/1). In the financial accounting realm, Owen Owens & Son was dabbling in foreign currency translation. An 1840–1845 memo book dealing with upland cotton provided purchase prices in dollars and pounds, along with prevailing exchange rates (L41a). Finlay, despite extremely primitive accounting methods for a firm of its size and profitability, used transfer pricing for the movement of goods internally between Catrine, Deanston, and Ballindalloch (UGD 91/422, 423). Stone (1973) reported transfer pricing amongst cost centres at the Chorlton Mill as well.

In summary, the records of various textile firms reveal a substantial number of examples of cost analyses for non-routine decision

Figure 10: Estimated Loss due to Power Deficiency, Ashworth

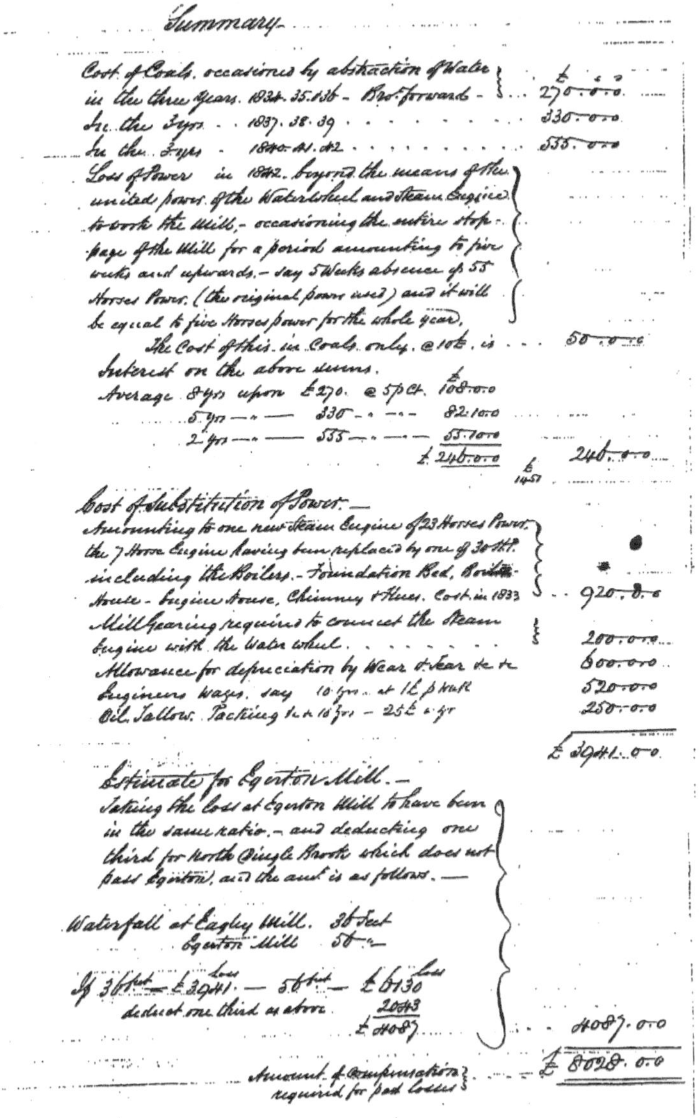

Summary

Cost of Coals, occasioned by abstraction of Water in the three Years. 1834. 35. 1836 – Bro. forward – £ 270.0.0
In the 3 yrs 1837. 38. 39 330.0.0
In the 3 yrs 1840. 41. 42 555.0.0
Loss of Power in 1842, beyond the means of the united power of the Waterwheel and Steam Engine to work the Mill, – occasioning the entire stoppage of the Mill for a period amounting to five weeks and upwards. – say 5 Weeks absence of 55 Horses Power, (the original power used) and it will be equal to five Horses power for the whole year,
The Cost of this in Coals only, @ 10£. is 50.0.0
Interest on the above sums.
Average 8 yrs upon £270. @ 5 p Ct. £ 108.0.0
5 yrs — " — 330 — " — " — 82.10.0
2 yrs — " — 555 — " — " — 55.10.0
£ 246.0.0 246.0.0
£ 1451

Cost of Substitution of Power. —
Amounting to one new Steam Engine of 23 Horses Power, the 7 Horse Engine having been replaced by one of 30 H.P. including the Boilers. – Foundation Bed, Boiler House – Engine House, Chimney & Flues. Cost in 1833 920.0.0
Mill Gearing required to connect the Steam Engine with the Water wheel 200.0.0
Allowance for depreciation by Wear & Tear &c &c 600.0.0
Engineers Wages. say 10 yrs at 1£ p Week 520.0.0
Oil. Tallow. Packing &c &c 10 yrs – 25£ a yr 250.0.0
£ 3941.0.0

Estimate for Egerton Mill. —
Taking the loss at Egerton Mill to have been in the same ratio. – and deducting one third for North Dingle Brook which does not pass Egerton, and the amt is as follows. —

Waterfall at Eagley Mill. 36 Feet
Egerton Mill 56 "

If 36 feet – £3941 loss — 56 feet – £ 6130 loss
deduct one third as above 2043
£ 4087 4087.0.0

£ 8028.0.0

Amount of Compensation required for past losses

making. The evidence most often informs us as to the purposes of the calculations undertaken, but infrequently as to their actual usages and outcomes. Entrepreneurs calculated potential profits on losses or proposed actions, evaluated costs of alternative technologies, and experimented with alternative production techniques. Costs were accumulated for decisions concerning repairs, plant expansion, and product line abandonments. Even examples of opportunity cost and transfer pricing calculations can be discerned in some instances.

TEXTILES: THE CONTEXT OF THE TIMES

The reader is referred to Chapter 1 in which the key characteristics of the British Industrial Revolution are discussed. Numbered amongst the innovations that rendered the age so discontinuous with its past, at least in economic terms, were the marked growth in population, the application of science to industry, the more efficient accumulation and deployment of capital, the revolution in transportation systems, and the wide expansion of marketing and distribution networks. Inventors, entrepreneurs, and industrialists generated a cornucopia of new enterprises, technological advances, process improvements, and applications. Such was the environment within which the textile industry developed (Ashton, 1948; Flinn, 1966).

The cotton industry, born from the older linen and fustian branches of the textile trade, underwent spectacular growth in three distinct stages. From 1700 to 1740, growth averaged 1.4% per annum, largely due to legislation prohibiting the importation of Indian calicoes. The growth rate doubled over the next four decades before reaching a peak of approximately 8.5% per annum, maintained well into the nineteenth century. This expansion featured the introduction of the earliest powered spinning mills in the 1770s. Whilst the technological innovations housed in these factories fuelled the industrial take-off, the productivity increases are as much explained by the growth of domestic demand and the expansion of export markets (Brown, 1991; Flinn, 1966).

By the late eighteenth century, cotton textiles had eclipsed the linen and fustian branches. Silk followed a path of peaks and troughs during much of the Industrial Revolution. The real story, however, was the magnitude of cotton's growth relative to the old staple, woollens. By

1800, each of the two branches constituted about 10% of total British industrial output. Subsequent to that point of equal contribution, cotton became king (Brown, 1991; Deane & Cole, 1969).

Originally the textile industry had been organised around a merchant clothier who employed putters-out to distribute materials to domestic spinners and weavers. Gradually, throughout the first half of the eighteenth century, operatives gathered in workshops and water-powered protofactories. Subsequently, larger enterprises emerged that were characterised by a greater integration of various manufacturing processes (Ashton, 1948). Mechanisation was introduced within this environment (Briggs, 1959; Fleischman, 1985). As cotton emerged supreme by the end of the century, Lancashire became established as its heartland, with more minor levels of activity apparent in Derbyshire, Nottinghamshire, Norwich, Scotland, and North Wales (Brown, 1991; Fleischman, 1985).

The structure of the textile industry varied considerably as a function of location, chronological period, and the specifics of particular branches. The linen and silk industries remained essentially home-based and rural well into the nineteenth century. There were some substantial flax, woollens, and worsted enterprises (e.g., Gott and Marshall), though the pattern in the West Riding was one of smaller firms dependent upon a domestic labour force (Hudson, 1977, 1986). The first generation of cotton factory masters (e.g., Arkwright and Oldknow) oversaw substantial installations that dominated the industry. However, by the beginning of the nineteenth century, the industry was typified by more middle-sized firms. This pattern resulted from financing constraints, as well as geographic separation and specialisation—spinning in South Lancashire and Stockport and weaving north of the Ribble. However, firms such as Murrays and McConnel & Kennedy could boast of labour forces in excess of 3,000 operatives. Cotton manufacturers in Carlisle employed 3,500 handloom weavers scattered across border counties in England, Scotland, and Ulster. The advent of the powerloom in the 1830s and 1840s not only occasioned the tragedy of the handloom weavers, but encouraged several larger-scale operations (e.g., Horrocks) as the spinning and weaving branches could now be amalgamated in a single factory. At the same time, the huge capital requirements for combining the processes resulted in the growth of enterprises with functional specialties (e.g., spinning, weaving, bleaching, dyeing). Thus, unlike in the iron industry, there continued to exist many small and medium-sized manufacturers (Ashton, 1948; Brown, 1991; Chapman, 1972; Fleischman, 1985).

To some extent, the geographic diversity of enterprise locations, the separation of different functions within textile firms, the variation in degree of mechanisation of different processes, and the persistence of a large number of small and mid-sized firms may together have contributed to the varying amount of attention apparently paid to expense control. These factors may also partly explain the lesser frequency of product costing and overhead cost allocation when compared to the iron industry. Textile firms may have simply been more diverse in size, location, and internal functions, so that they were less able or inclined to engage in these cost-recording and management activities.

TECHNOLOGICAL CHANGE

Cotton spinning in its early days depended upon hitched horses to provide the power for roller drawing. With the advent of the spinning jenny and subsequently the mule, humans provided the motive power on machines that handled ever-increasing numbers of spindles. Arkwright, the architect of the factory system in cotton spinning, commenced operations with horses but switched to water wheel power by the 1790s. Thus, most major technological breakthroughs in cotton spinning centred on power sources other than steam, at least during the developmental phase (Musson, 1972; von Tunzelmann, 1978). Steam became more important in the longer run, but it was not until the mid-1830s that the water wheel had been supplanted in Lancashire, Cheshire, Derbyshire, and the West Riding. Steam power not only reduced spinning time and cost, but also permitted machine spinning of finer quality yarns, which had previously been done manually (Brown, 1991). With respect to weaving, Cartwright developed the powerloom in 1787, though the first prototypes did not appear in Manchester mills until circa 1800. Powerlooms became widespread in the 1820s and 1830s, though there were more handloom weavers than powerloom operators in 1840 (Marshall, 1973). That statistic does not really tell the tale, however, as the productive potential of the powerloom far outstripped the handloom.

Brown (1991) described three distinct phases in the evolution of the factory system in the cotton industry. During the first phase, entrepreneurs such as Arkwright built their mills along fast-running streams in Nottinghamshire, Derbyshire, North Wales, and parts of Scotland. Steam power was the central feature of the second phase as the industry became increasingly concentrated in Lancashire, freed from its dependence on running water. After 1815, firms increasingly combined the spinning and weaving functions. The spinning branch was mechanised throughout, whilst weaving was organised as a domestic system craft until the widespread adoption of the powerloom in the 1830s. During the 1840s, however, the geographic separation of spinning and weaving once again occurred as the central development of the third phase. Weaving was the riskier of the two processes, requiring a greater managerial control to match inputs with outputs. Consequently, weaving enterprises tended to be smaller and remained in the North of England where labour was cheaper, coal more readily available, and railway access superior. By 1884, 62% of the looms were in the North, 78% of the spindles in the South. Thus, it would appear that technology, industry structure, and location were all closely linked factors.

Woollens industry spinning followed a similar course to cotton, albeit more slowly. Its shorter staple and the matted nature of the fibres forestalled roller application. The Jersey wheel was employed until it was superseded by Hargreaves' jenny, which was the dominant machine until circa 1825. The mule was never really adaptable to wool spinning because of its greater cost. For woollen and worsted weaving, the flying shuttle was adopted more slowly than in cotton. Technologically then, the woollens industry lagged behind cotton for a number of reasons: (1) a more conservative attitude toward production, (2) an oversupply of labour, (3) greater technical difficulties in applying power machinery to wool fibres, and (4) more slowly expanding markets (Brown, 1991; von Tunzelmann, 1978).

The motivations for technological change in the textile industry, as with iron and steel, were various. They included the desire to substitute scarce resources with ones more readily available, to liberate capital for more efficient use, to reduce labour costs, to transfer circulating into fixed capital, and to conserve raw materials (Ashton, 1966). Multiple motivations not only drove technological innovation, but did so in a domino-like pattern. Change in one manufacturing process often induced or required innovation in associated processes. For example, the invention of Kay's flying shuttle in 1733 necessitated new spinning technology to keep the handloom weavers occupied. The mechanisation of spinning subsequently necessitated a growth in the numbers of domestic weavers and eventually the development of the powerloom (ibid.; Brown, 1991).

The various stages of technological change through which textile manufacturing, particular cotton, progressed clearly required the close attention of entrepreneurs to the development of information sources and the application of their own analyses for purposes of responsibility accounting and non-routine decision making. Archival investigations of the primary sources of some firms have revealed an accumulation of statistical records in which comparisons of productivity, materials usage, output, and power consumption is made across mills, machines, and operatives. The records have also included evaluations of costs and potential profits from alternative technologies, processes, and expansion plans.

COSTS AND PRODUCTIVITY

Technological innovation in cotton manufacturing had the effect of contributing to the lowering of the average price of cotton yarn from 38s per pound in 1786 to 2/11 in 1832—a massive decline by any standard (Flinn, 1966). Interestingly, von Tunzelmann (1978) argued that the cost savings associated with this price decline did not include reduced expenditures for power. Power did not have a significant impact on spinning costs until the 1830s, and even then took the form of economics of scale in large mills, many of which remained water-powered. Steam power did cheapen the spinning of finer yarns, an effect dated from the late 1780s. On the other hand, labour productivity in cotton spinning improved dramatically over time due to mechanisation. Chapman (1972) reported that the hours required for operatives to process 100 pounds of cotton changed as follows:

Indian hand spinners (eighteenth century)	50,000
Crompton's mule (1780)	2,000
100-spindle mule (circa 1790)	1,000
power-assisted mule (circa 1795)	300
Roberts' automatic mules (circa 1825)	135

The dramatic improvements in spinning productivity (and associated cost reductions) triggered a sequence of technological and organisational changes across many branches of the industry. Other processes, such as weaving, knitting, bleaching, and dyeing, struggled to keep pace. Von Tunzelmann (1978) demonstrated how proportionate labour costs of various processes fluctuated widely in the woollens industry. Spinning accounted for 41.2% of total labour cost in 1790, but only 22% in 1830. Meanwhile, the cost of weaving labour rose from 33.2% to 40.1% and finishing from 20.7% to 31.3%.

Wages had risen to high levels in the cotton industry by 1800 and remained so for two decades. By 1830, however, wages had sunk to one-half their former level for the industry generally, with the wages of handloom weavers falling ever more precipitously to one-third. Perhaps one explanation for this decline was an oversupply of labour in cotton where the number of operatives rose from 250,000 to 425,000 in the first three decades of the nineteenth century. Between 1831 and 1847, the labour force declined by 25%, whilst wages rose 15% on average. The woollen and worsted industries followed similar patterns, though the recovery of wage rates lagged behind that of cotton (Deane & Cole, 1969).

The high and rising wage levels of the late eighteenth century may have contributed to entrepreneurs' attention to expense control and to some observed attempts at setting labour cost standards. The evidence of non-routine, decision-making calculations located in firm archives would have again been triggered by technological change decisions, as observed in the previous section, but also by the evaluation of productivity changes and the impact on profitability of various process and organisational changes. The lack of attention to product costing and overhead cost allocation apparent in the records may also reflect the greater attention to identifying and managing materials and labour costs specifically for different functional segments of the overall manufacturing process.

CAPITAL AND FINANCE

Capital investment in the textile industry changed slowly over time. Until the mid-eighteenth century, the expansion of output was linked to increasing the size of the labour force. Subsequently, technological change required greater capital inputs although large-scale factories were still in the minority. Thus, for most early Industrial Revolution firms, capital investment was mainly in the form of working capital. Fixed capital generally accounted for only 5–10% of total capital circa 1750, rising to approximately 50% by the end of the century (Brown, 1991; Flinn, 1966). Flinn (1966) estimated total investment in the cotton industry to have been £8 million between 1783 and 1802.

Textiles drew very little capital from landed sources, securing its capital instead from the investments of entrepreneurs (and their friends, family, and business associates), accumulated profits, and long-term credit extended by raw material suppliers. The lack of a developed banking system aggravated the problems of financing factories, particularly as the requirements for large fixed asset expenditures increased with the introduction of more sophisticated technology. Industrialists such as the Arkwrights actually established their own private banks to help obtain cash for wages and other remittances. However, such enterprises generally failed during periods of economic downturn (Ashton, 1948; Flinn, 1966).

Thus, as with other industries such as iron, the textile industry gradually came to require larger and larger fixed capital investment, albeit at a slower rate than iron. Sources of finance for such major commitments were short-term, high risk, and generally inadequate. The pressures of attempting to finance large-scale organisations with heavier investment in capital intensive operations must surely have taxed the financial and operational management skills of these early industrialists. For them, expense control and responsibility accounting constituted available means to maximise the cost efficiency of operations so as to minimise demands on working capital as the pressures for fixed capital grew.

CONCLUSION

Rather than rehash the vast amount of data presented in this chapter, we would like our conclusion to focus on comparative aspects of cost accounting between the iron and textile industries. The importance of this comparison is underscored by the dominance of these two sectors in the British Industrial Revolution. In point of fact, of the 25 firms that constituted our early broad-based sample, 19 were iron or textile enterprises. This concentration of economic activity affords the opportunity to investigate industry-specific factors in the development of cost accounting. Both industries shared a number of common characteristics. They were largely comprised of family firms or partnerships whose main source of capital was ploughed-back profits (Pawson, 1979). These firms were often headed by entrepreneurs who were innovators both in technology and cost operations management. Both industries required large capital expenditures on plant and equipment and a sizeable work force in comparison with other industries (Lee, 1986). Access to cheap supplies of raw materials and the employment of technology to reduce costs through efficient use of raw materials were central to profitability (Farnie, 1979; Hyde, 1977). Although the textile trades were much slower to embrace steam power because of the substantial investment represented by factory venues near running water, the need to avoid production bottlenecks precipitated high levels of mechanical inventiveness. Overseas trade and the development and exploitation of new markets were also essential (Chapman, 1972; Harris, 1988). Although may firms in both industries had multiple installations, the geographic concentration of individual enterprises necessitated interrelationships with the transport industry (Lee, 1986; Pawson, 1979).

Certain similarities in methodology between textile and iron firms are evident in the foregoing discussion of cost management activity. Businesses in both industries were utilising costing data for non-routine decision making. Crowley (iron) and Oldknow (textiles) made vertical integration decisions, and Darby (iron), Marshall (textiles), and Greg (textiles) evaluated technological innovations and improvements. Cost analyses were prepared to justify lease-or-buy decisions on steam engines, and statistics were maintained to evaluate the performance of multiple engines; e.g., Gott (textiles), Dowlais (iron), Darby (iron), and Carron (iron).

Regular cost comparisons were a feature of the accounting systems in both industries. Marshall (textiles) and Darby (iron) compiled annual comparative statistics on their multiple plants. Strutt (textiles) made managers responsible for operations in the various carding and spinning rooms, whilst the Cyfarthfa (iron) and Carron (iron) owners demanded weekly blast furnace reports for similar evaluations.

Enterprises in both industries reflected cost accounting sophistication in daily operations. The Carron (iron), Darby (iron), and Greg (textiles) archives contain frequent and intricate product costings. Overhead was applied to product on the basis of predetermined formula at Carron (iron), Dowlais (iron), Marshall (textiles), and Birley & Co. (textiles). Production scheduling was done at Philips (textiles) and Crowley (iron). Care was taken in process evaluation at Carron (iron) with product line decisions and blast furnace records, at Marshall (textiles) with daily performance cards for all machines and workers, and at Strutt (textiles) with precise expense accounts. Standard costing and inventory control techniques were commonplace.

Cost accounting differences between textile and iron concerns appear to have been a function of firm complexity. Because there were more major technological innovations in iron, cost analyses tended to be more frequently conducted and lengthier. There were also more lease-or-buy and transportation subcontracting decisions. Notwithstanding, textile firms did experiment with new technology on a cost/benefit basis. Gott (textiles) analysed the cost/benefit of mechanical rather than manual methods for converting raw wool into yarn and anticipated savings from cheaper spinning and finishing methods.

Firm size does not appear to have been correlated with the volume of cost management activity, though more work on smaller firms may show significant differences. In textiles, Ashworth and Philips were smaller than McConnel & Kennedy and Finlay, but manifested superior cost management. In particular, McConnel & Kennedy, the huge Lancashire textile firm, and Newton, Chambers, a premier Sheffield iron concern, both exhibited unsophisticated cost accounting.

An obvious role for cost accounting in both industries was the control of raw material costs. Major iron producers took pains to maintain cost and yield data on their mineral sources. Carron

Company's accountant filed numerous reports during the 1770s about the firm's coal, limestone, and ironstone holdings and leases. Minerals were charged to user departments at transfer prices reflecting the expenses incurred in mining ore. By the 1840s, Darby and Dowlais knew the mining costs and yields of the several varieties of coal and ironstone the firm utilised. Textile firms were particularly attentive to raw material and waste management. We have seen how Gott calculated cloth output from various wool mixtures, whilst Ashworth was particularly conscious of the savings forthcoming from the use of cheaper varieties of raw cotton. Ashworth was also very precise in the determination of waste standards. The data categories maintained by Marshall and Strutt likewise included waste comparisons.

The foregoing comparative analysis has not revealed a significant number of differences between the costing procedures employed by textile and iron industry concerns. There tended to be more variability in textile industry accounting as, for example, in differential attention to expense control. This difference might be explained in terms of the large number of small and medium-sized firms, the greater geographical diversity of the industry, and the varying degrees of mechanisation. Yet, the overall picture is one of firms analysing costs for making routine and special decisions, engaging in cost comparisons, employing product costing techniques (including overhead allocation), and attempting to control raw material costs. This outcome in all likelihood resulted from the common, periodic exposure of firms in both industries to strong competition, market-driven pricing, and narrow profit margins.

5

The Extractive Industries[1]

Years ago in an attempt to narrow the field for our early investigations of Industrial Revolution cost accounting, we stated, 'large companies whose primary orientations were transport and extraction were generally not studied because of our expectation that nascent cost accounting would flourish most notably in a factory environment' (Fleischman & Parker, 1991, p. 363). We had thought that in the more structured environment of a factory, accounting systems would more likely be present to control labour productivity and to chart the transition of products through integrated processes. Even more significantly, it seemed to us that the wider variety of products typical of industrial enterprises would necessitate a greater attention to costing, if only for pricing purposes.

However, we were misguided in this view. Our own subsequent research into mining operations, the results of which are presented in this chapter, has revealed a sophistication in accounting for certain activities that transcends what we have found in textile mills and iron foundries. McLean (1997) has successfully challenged our earlier expectation in his study of the Tanfield Moor Colliery in Tyneside, whilst Oldroyd's (1996) investigation of the Grand Allies in the same region has likewise contributed to that refutation, though this intent was not specifically stated. Now, from the vantage point of hindsight, we can offer several explanations as to why costing in the extractive industries was heretofore lost to us. First, the mining operations of integrated, iron-producing firms have not received as much attention from historians as subsequent activities related to production, perhaps because the costs associated with raw materials extraction were a minimal component of total product cost. Second, we failed to appreciate that large-scale mining predated the advent of the factory system so that a substantially longer time frame existed during which costing systems could be developed and improved. Third, the most extensive mining operations exploited the Northeastern coal seams of Northumberland and Durham, far removed, from our initial investigations in the regions around Manchester. Fourth, since we anticipated the focus of extractive industry cost accounting would be on expense control, the logical first step in nascent costing, we did not expect to find those manifestations of a more sophisticated development—accurate product costing, overhead allocation, process and labour control, special decision making, etc. Finally, and perhaps most significantly, we were unaware of the class of managers known as viewers*, whose very existence and function it was to collect statistical data related to mining. These viewers operated as cost accountants, though they were never identified in the literature as such.

This chapter is presented in an effort to rectify our former shortsightedness. We will initially analyse extant coal-mining records from Tyneside (Northumberland and Durham) in an effort to expand the findings of McLean (1997) and Oldroyd (1996). Here the costing activities of the Stella Coal Company will be specifically discussed as one of the most fruitful sources of costing expertise we have seen. Subsequently, we will examine extractive operations in other UK venues where mining was not as closely tied to iron production as the case in South Wales. These locations include the Northwest (Lancashire, Staffordshire, and the West Midlands); Anglesey and North Wales, where the product was copper rather than coal; and Scotland. One difficulty with this organisational schemata lies in the relative surfeit of accounting records extant for Tyneside enterprises compared to the other regions. This imbalance results potentially from two unrelated phenomena—(1) the highly organised nature of Tyneside coal-mining ownership that precipitated the generation of more records for control purposes there, and (2) a differential rate of record destruction that accompanied the nationalisation of the industry under the auspices of the National Coal Board (NCB). Whilst this latter factor is highly speculative, there is anecdotal evidence that in some sectors nationalisation was greeted by a wanton destruction of business records—firm personnel actually threw historical production statistics down abandoned mine shafts.

PITS LOCATION AND TRANSPORT

Since the material in this chapter is organised on a regional basis, it is appropriate to discuss initially the geographic location of the extractive industries during the Industrial Revolution. Apart from tin and copper operations in Cornwall and Anglesey, coal mining was the dominant extractive endeavour and is used to illustrate the industry's regionalism. The richest coal seams were located in the North of England and in Scotland. Coal was extensively mined in Lancashire, the West Riding of Yorkshire, Tyneside (Durham and Northumberland), Shropshire, and Wales (Ashton, 1948). In Scotland, coal seams abounded in the coastal region north of Ayr, Lanarkshire (south of the Clyde), and the Midlothian and East Lothian districts south and east of Edinburgh (Flinn, 1984).

The regionalism of the coal-mining industry, a function of its mineral deposits, also determined concomitantly the location of iron foundries given the transport difficulties associated with the iron industry's most vital raw material. Until the mid-eighteenth century, horse-drawn waggons were the primary transport mechanism for this heavy volume cargo. Waggons and waggonways*, tracks initially made of wood but subsequently of cast iron, were generally owned by mine owners or their lessees, whilst independent contractors provided the horses and did the haulage. This limited transport infrastructure came to be supplemented increasingly through succeeding decades by an expanded canal system which linked mines to navigable rivers. Consequently, collieries located away from rivers and the coast came to prosper, as well as a variety of metal-working establishments further afield from the coal and ironstone sources (Ashton, 1948; Brown, 1991; Flinn, 1984).

TYNESIDE: THE STELLA COAL COMPANY

The largest collection of business records we have seen for a British Industrial Revolution extractive enterprise documents the activities of the Stella Coal Company and is currently housed at the Durham Record Office. The Stella archive was deposited there by the NCB years subsequent to the nationalisation process. Since it was the

NCB's first installment, components of this archive all bear the initial reference number NCB 1, which we will not repeat throughout the case study that follows.

There are many strengths observable in the accounting records of Stella. Its management was extraordinarily concerned with controlling expense outlays for capital projects. We have not seen elsewhere such a volume of tender offers requested for a wide variety of projects. Capital improvements were undertaken only on the basis of detailed estimates, whilst subsequent, actual expenditures were carefully tracked. Perhaps the most endearing feature of this archive is the opportunity it provides for researchers to link *ex ante* cost estimates with *ex post* decision making. These linkages are possible here, unlike at Carron and Boulton & Watt, because the surviving records appear very complete, at least for the 1840s.

It should be stated at the onset, however, that the breadth of the record keeping was limited both chronologically and with regard to the types of activities upon which the managers chose to concentrate their attention. The mine was in operation during the first three decades of the nineteenth century, but the owners (the Dunn family) did not maintain detailed costing records. Durham archivists have ascertained that the mines were closed for some periods in the 1830s because of the expiration of certain key leases. When the mines reopened in 1839, it was under the leadership of Robert Simpson, who had been a colliery viewer in his early professional career. As typical of viewers in the Tyneside region, Simpson was enamoured of statistical record keeping. This propensity was reflected by an outpouring of accounting data of various types in the 1840s.

Researchers of a Foucauldian persuasion, who seek the origins of modern managerialism in accounting systems that order about labourers and establish an industrial discipline, would be gravely disappointed in the Stella archive. Extant pit bills span the first half of the nineteenth century, but the earlier ones for 1806 (SC 247) and 1816 (SC 284) are not materially different from 1848 (SC 153). The later reports appear on printed forms and do include a few more data categories, but they are in no way remarkable. Whilst the pit bills do compare productivity on a fortnightly basis to the period immediately preceding, they do so on an aggregated, rather than an individual basis. The data were there for managers to evaluate individual performance, but there is no indication that either colliers or managers were held accountable. There was at Stella an awareness that the expenses of direct and indirect labour should be separated (SC 283). A segregation was also made, typical for the industry, between labour costs above and below ground. The only document we have seen that truly reflected attention to labour cost control at Stella was an 1840s suggestion for ten redundancies at Towneley Colliery that would collectively save an estimated £6/1/10 per week. In some cases individuals, whose services did not appear vital, were specifically named (SC 465; SC 478).

The most remarkable account book dealing with an expansion of operations we have seen for this or any enterprise during the Industrial Revolution is SC 343, detailing the Emma Pit sinking in the mid-1840s. On pages 1–10 of this volume, John Taylor, a consultant who was also manager of the Alport mines in the Northwest, presented a proposal in 1843 to commence this new winning* at the West Towneley Colliery. His report contains six pages of narrative and four of cost estimates. This estimate is not particularly distinguished or precise as illustrated by the final entry, a 10% allowance for contingencies. Based on an estimated total cost of £6,168/1/4, work was begun in February 1845 and completed in April 1847. A detailed listing of all costs, totalling £9,928/7/9, comprises pages 12–24. There then follow the more distinctive accounting data. On pages 25, 27, and 29 the estimated costs are restated, whilst on the opposite pages (26, 28, and 30), actual costs are provided for comparison. Frequently the estimates and actuals are in close proximity; e.g., estimated cost of rope £145/10/0 and actual cost £143/1/1, contingency estimate £560/14/8 and actual £534/13/8. On pages 31–32, there appears a narrative description for certain discrepencies, such as more engine power for the project was needed than thought, unexpected water had to be pumped out, and harder strata than anticipated caused further delay. On page 33, a statement of 'delay days' is provided. The project took 109 weeks to complete, but for 66 of these (460 days) no work was occurring. A progress statistic of 10 feet per week on average was calculated by dividing the depth of the winning (73 fathoms, 1 foot, 1 inch) by the weeks of progress (43). The report concludes with page 34, reproduced as Figure 11, with a reconciliation of the substantial difference between Mr Taylor's estimate (£6,168/1/4) and the actual cost (£9,782/7/9). Charges which exceeded the estimate are given as £472/8/1½ (details provided earlier), whilst those costs that were not initially estimated at all totalled £3,141/18/3½.

Figure 11: Emma Pit Winning, Stella Coal, 1847

COST OF THE EMMA PIT.

Abstract of Charges not Estimated: for the Emma Pit Winning.

	£	s	d
To Extra Engine Power	758	4	9
" Tubbing	885	0	11½
" Sinking 2 Staples	220	0	0
" Coal and Stone drifting for Standage	149	5	2
" Brick Arching in Stone Drift	21	12	7
" Pumps & Iron Work	400	0	0
" Railway Bars, Chairs &c	236	3	4
" Overman's House & Office	103	1	3
" Water Drain through Newbiggin & Dodds Fields	114	17	3
" Cold Water Pipes to Greenside	166	0	0
" Watching Pit at nights	74	16	6
" Jack Screws	5	5	0
" Scale Weights	7	11	6
Total Sum not Estimated for £	3141	18	3½
Various Charges which exceeded Mr Taylors Estimate, viz. for Coals, Flannel & Leather, and Sinking Charges &c	472	8	1½
Actual Cost 9782. 7. 9 / Estimated do 6168. 1. 4			
Total Extra Cost £	3614	6	5

Here the largest unanticipated expenses were extra engine power (£758/4/9) and tubbing* (£885/0/11½). SC 343 is an impressive example of a differential cost analysis, though it does not stand as testament to Taylor's capabilities at estimation. The analysis was so pivotal to the firm's operations that it was replicated with additional detail in the 1848 memorandum book of M.W. Dunn, who continued in an ownership capacity after Simpson took over management of the mines (SC 345, pp. 169–234). Here there was contained as well the costs of a dwelling and an office building at the new winning (ibid., pp. 236–240), with some expense items included of a most modest amount (2d). The analysis was again recorded in a miscellaneous bundle of documents catalogued SC 622.

The Stella archive is replete with numerous estimates and cost abstracts prepared for capital improvements, though most pale by comparison to the Emma Pit winning. Pollard (1965) did not deny the existence for the period of numerous costings of this ilk, though he did question the dependability of the numbers generated and their relevance to correct business decisions. What distinguished the Stella estimates was the fact that for many projects two prognostications were solicited. For instance, two estimates were made in 1821 for certain components of a 20-horsepower engine that would double its capacity to generate power (SC 471, p. 201). Jonathan Robson estimated the cost at £195/15; Stephen Robinson was less optimistic, suggesting £208/4. Two viewers, John Buddle and James Hall, were requested to make numerous estimates for the firm in the 1820s. Typical was a comparative costing for leading* coals to Derwenthaugh and Lemington from Crawcrook Colliery. Both estimates were for a yearly production level of 26,000 chaldrons* and took into account wayleaves*, horse upkeep, waggon and boat repair, and interest on capital expended for the waggonways, the bridge, and the staith*. Hall concluded that there existed an 8¾d per chaldron advantage in favour of the Derwenthaugh destination. Buddle, though the most famous viewer of his times, compiled a less detailed estimate, but arrived at a similar conclusion (SC 473, pp. 51–53). It is known that Stella followed this advice as there is included in SC 471, pp. 186–190 the calculated expense of a waggonway from Towneley to Derwenthaugh. This accounting is quite interesting even apart from its standing as an example of an *ex post* action. The waggonway was built in four stages, costing £4,534/6/10. The associated expenses were divided into nine categories and maintained on a stage-specific basis. For example, fencing cost £70 for stage one, £40 for stage two, etc. In calculating yearly depreciation on the waggonway, the firm took the rather strange action of recovering 10% for 'money laid out' but only 5% for materials. A per chaldron cost was calculated for each of the four stages.

As typified by this accounting, Stella's management was vitally concerned with coal transport. We have seen previously how James Hall was consulted during the 1820s on these matters. A visual image of one such estimate appears as Figure 12. This 1830 reproduction was the middle page of a three-page analysis of comparative costs associated with utilising either a private or a public railway to lead coals the 5¾ miles from Crawcrook Mill to Benwell Staith. The public routing afforded a significant cost advantage (SC 473, pp. 63–65). In one of Simpson's memo books (SC 478), there is a comparative cost analysis for different kinds of rails used in the construction of railways. It was determined that the ones Stella had been using cost £207/3 per mile more (pp. 1–3). This estimate was revised in 1841 to reflect subsequent prices (pp. 69–72). In the same volume there are recorded the comparative costs for shipping coals at Stockton and Samfrey Bats (p. 32). Subsequently in the memo book, there are two costings comparing relative expenses for 1841 and 1842 for shipping coals on the Tyne and for using Shields as a transshipment venue (pp. 120–123). There also exists an 1848 estimate for laying a railway from Blaydon to the coke ovens (SC 465/14). The company maintained careful records for its fleet of horses, used both in pit work and transport. There is a page of memoranda attached to a monthly report of cash expenditures (SC 93). Here the holdings of horse corn are given, along with the number and locations of the horses. We were somewhat amused by the eminently practical inventory method used for keeping track of the equines—beginning horses + horses bought – horses sold – horses dying = ending horses.

It was previously mentioned that on occasion Stella Coal would solicit multiple estimates for capital investment opportunities. The same process was in place for subcontracting externally various projects. In 1840, five tender offers were received for providing waggon wood and four for ropes (SC 478, p. 11). In 1845, a rash of projects went out for bid. Six different jobs involving masonry work to the engine house resulted in eight offers (SC 480, p. 50). Three steam engine upgrades

Figure 12: Railway Estimate, James Hall, Stella, 1830

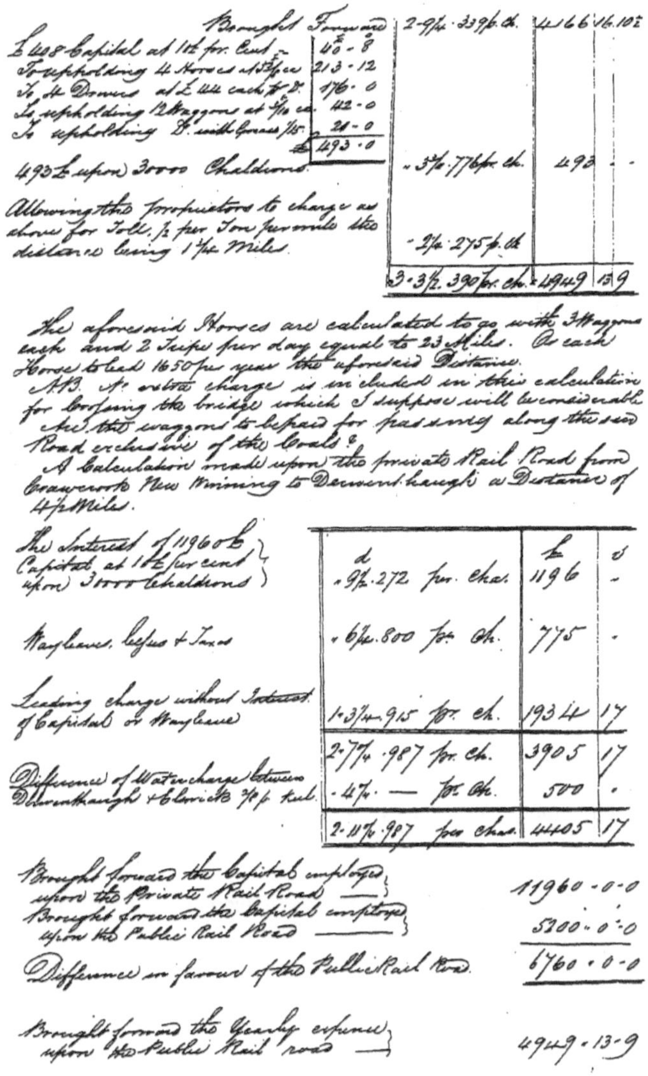

Brought Forward		2-9/4 · 339 p. ch.	4166	16.10½
£408 Capital at 10 per Cent	£ 40 - 8			
To upholding 4 Horses at 53 p. ea.	213 - 12			
To 4 Drivers at £44 each p. D.	176 - 0			
To upholding 12 Waggons at 3/10 ea.	42 - 0			
To upholding D. with Gears 7/5	21 - 0			
	£ 493 - 0			
493£ upon 30000 Chaldrons		- 3⅞ · 776 p. ch.	493	- -
Allowing the proprietors to charge as above for Toll ½ per Ton per mile the distance being 1¾ Miles		- 2¼ · 275 p. ch.		
		3 - 3½ . 390 p. ch.	4949	13 9

The aforesaid Horses are calculated to go with 3 Waggons each and 2 Trips per day equal to 23 Miles. As each Horse to lead 1650 per year the aforesaid Distance.
N.B. No extra charge is included in this calculation for crossing the bridge which I suppose will be considerable and the waggons to be paid for passing along the said Road exclusive of the Coals &c.
A Calculation made upon the private Rail Road from Crawcrook New Winning to Derwent haugh a Distance of 4½ Miles.

	d	£	s
The Interest of 11960£ Capital at 10£ per cent upon 30000 Chaldrons	- 9½ · 272 per Chal.	1196	-
Wayleave, Cesses + Taxes	- 6¼ · 800 p. Ch.	775	-
Leading charge without Interest of Capital or Wayleave	1 - 3¾ - 915 p. ch.	1934	17
	2 - 7¾ · 987 p. Ch.	3905	17
Difference of Water charge between Derwenthaugh + Elswick 4d p. keel	- 4¼ — p. Ch.	500	-
	2 - 11¾ · 987 per Chal.	4405	17

Brought forward the Capital employed upon the Private Rail Road	11960 - 0 - 0
Brought forward the Capital employed upon the Public Rail Road	5200 - 0 - 0
Difference in favour of the Public Rail Road	6760 - 0 - 0
Brought forward the Yearly expense upon the Public Rail road	4949 - 13 - 9

were bid for by seven firms (ibid., p. 70). John Brown gave a price of £1,099/10/0 for a sinking which was far lower than William Caulson's bid of £1,420/10/0 (ibid., p. 80). A contract for nine items involving pumps attracted six offers (ibid., p. 87). Here again, we have evidence suggesting that the firm moved in directions indicated. Low bids were accepted for three of these projects, and in the case of the fourth the lowest bidder was asked for a further reduction of price.

Like many industry leaders in textiles and iron, Stella conducted a number of experiments designed to reduce costs or to redirect production focus. As we saw at Dowlais, Stella contracted with Dr Richardson in 1848 to analyse three types of coal with regard to carbon content, residual ash, and gaseous matter and six coke varieties for carbon, sulphur, and ash (SC 343, pp. 55–56; SC 486, pp. 72–74). The assay was done with sufficient care that Richardson specified which were 'picked samples' and which were truly average. Tests on hemp and patent wire rope are recorded in the early 1840s (SC 478, pp. 56–57). A four-day experiment was undertaken on drawing coals which were put over a screen to contrast the yields of the Towneley and the Stella seams. The Towneley seam provided a higher percentage of best coals (42.647% versus 40.260%). The care of this exercise, measurement to three decimal places, is belied by the arithmetic once again as the Towneley percentages add up to only 99.9% despite the column's averred footing of 100% (ibid., pp. 124–125).

In a seemingly lighter vein, Stella attempted some motive power trials. An 1822 'Comparative Expenses between leading 20 scores of coals with horses and 20 scores by an engine underground to the depth of Towneley pit shaft (220 yards)' was undertaken. It was calculated that the annual cost per horse was £59/18 for the eight horses required (approximately £480), whilst £240 was the annual expense for the engine (SC 471, p. 208). One must wonder, however, about the genesis of these numbers because in a subsequent document (ibid., p. 222), it was reckoned that it cost £39 per year to maintain a pit horse but £43/10 for a waggon horse. Perhaps the higher number reflected a depreciation charge. Lest one be saddened that the ponies did badly in this comparison with an engine, they did much better in an 1845 cost comparison between human and horse power for putting coals (SC 477, pp. 88–89).

Accounting numbers were also deployed as aids in abandonment decisions. In 1844, Simpson recommended the closing of the Towneley

Colliery. Although labour was cheaper there than at any other installation, the costs associated with its non-central location were deemed prohibitive. It was observed that the work force could be moved to Star Gate. To obtain the same amount of coal as before the proposed abandonment, Simpson suggested opening a new seam at Stella Freehold and increasing the number of days worked beyond the then current nine per fortnight. He forecasted an annual savings of £865/9/0, including a 1/9 per score reduction in raising costs, a relocation of five horses, a reduction in rents and royalties, a diminished use of sundry items (ropes, oil, and grease), the redundancy of a waggonway wright, and reduced poor rates (SC 515). In 1849, Simpson did a similar analysis to determine at which pit work should be curtailed, occasioned by the slow sales the firm was facing (SC 516).

One other element of accounting sophistication, not much practised in the extractive industry, was the allocation of common charges. In 1844, bank work costing £16/14/8 was done at Towneley. The cost was allocated on the basis of that year's production volume to the two seams that comprised operations at Towneley. A similar allocation took place for Stella Freehold (SC 260).

The management of Stella Coal was ultimately concerned with controlling the costs of new capital construction for coal extraction and distribution. Its interest in controlling worker and managers was minimal by comparison. Examples of this expenses orientation are evident in a 17-year abstract (1839–1856) of the cost of coals delivered at Stella Staith (SC 343, pp. 61–66). There are 21 data categories detailed, with a bottom-line cost per score of coals calculated to three decimal places. In an 1840 account book, the bookkeeper allocated ten pages to specifying the cost elements for drawing water out of Stella Freehold and putting in a set of pumps (SC 342). One beautifully maintained document was an expense report for leading at Wylam Colliery in which average costs were calculated for the four years ending 1836 (SC 476). Whilst the most appealling feature of this report, presented as Figure 13, may be the artist's hand, the document does include for many of its wayleaves a charge for damage to the ground. The firm was also conscious of environmental restoration of exhausted workings. There exists an 1841 estimate of cost to fill the Holly Pit and to level the Pit Heap in order to return the land to arable (SC 477, p. 1).

Figure 13: Expenses of Leading, Wylam Colliery, 1836

Wylam Colliery

Total Expense of Leading 20.331 Chas. of Coals & Cinders to the Staith at Lemington on the average of 4 Years. ending 1836.

		£	s	d	£	s	d
Cost of Laying 5 Miles 1517 Yards of Railway including depreciation of £11653 at 7½ per Cent					874	0	0
Cost 2 Locomotive Engines & Tender £800							
Interest and depreciation of Capital of £800 at 7½ per Cent		60	0	0			
Upholding one Engine and Tender		65	6	8			
Enginemen's Wages		98	16	0			
Splint Coal Consumed 364 Chas. @ 4/		282	0	0	506	2	8
Labourage on Railway		109	12	2			
Cast Iron Rails for Repairs		41	8	7			
Waggon Wood repairs		27	4	3			
Waggon Wright Wages 125 days @ 3/		18	15	0			
Mason Work 16 do. @ 5/		4	0	0			
Smith Work 1109 Tons @ 7		32	7	0			
Interest of Capital and Depreciation of £1360 @ 6½ per Cent. on Waggons		88	8	0	321	15	0
Poor Rates &c paid on Wayleave on passing through the follow Townships							
Houghton Township for Poor Rates		4	18	0			
Heddon on the Wall do.		11	5	9			
Newburn Township do.		12	7	6			
Newburn Hall do.		10	0	0			
do. do. for High Way Rate		1	10	0			
do. Township do.		1	0	0			
Heddon on the Wall for Church Rate			15	0	41	14	3
Wayleaves							
Miss Simpson a Certain Rent of		33	0	0			
do. 40 fothers of coals	6/	12	0	0	47	0	0
Christopher Blackett Esq. a Certain Rent of					34	0	0
Thomas Walker Esq. do.					68	0	0
Mr Bewick for 20331 Chas of Coals & Coke × 24 ÷ 440 = 1109 Tons							
400 Tons Certain Rent		40	0	0			
709 Tons	3/	106	7	0			
Damage Ground		1	17	6			
10 Waggons of Coals	7/3	3	12	6			
32 do. Best Coals	20/	33	3	0			
22 do. Small	1/9	1	18	6	165	18	6
Carried Forward					2078	12	5

Overall, the Stella Company was particularly notable for its focus upon capital expenditure control, utilising detailed and, at times, multiple estimates, as well as comparisons of estimated and actual costs. Further in evidence was the use of costing analyses for evaluating transport alternatives, subcontractor tenders, and mine expansion and abandonment proposals. In the cases of capital expenditure and operational expansion proposals, we see clear evidence of post-decision monitoring of actual with respect to estimated costs. Process productivity and cost reduction experiments were also undertaken. The dominant concern with capital expenditure control and major operational expansion/contraction decisions stood in marked contrast to the company's relative inattention to labour and its cost control (other than in terms of broad categories of direct and indirect cost).

TYNESIDE: DURHAM

Other business records we have examined at the Durham Record Office reflect the same quality of costing apparent at Stella, though the holdings are scattered over a number of mining operations and over an extended chronological period. The earliest materials we have seen date from the middle of the eighteenth century. A letter of complaint was sent in 1758 from John Gibson to Richard Stephenson, an agent of George Bowes, a lead mine proprietor (D/st/C2/3/77). Bowes was also a prime mover in the Grand Allies, an early Northumberland association of coal-mine owners (see Oldroyd, 1996). This report criticised the mine director, Mr Horne, for failing to raise a sufficient quantity of ore to cover expenses. Gibson went on to demonstrate that the mines in question could be let more profitably for a one-sixth royalty (duty) based on various selling prices at different mines. Gibson also analysed the profit potential at one mine not currently in production, taking into account two distinct ore prices. The first page of this communication is presented as Figure 14.

Another useful volume records monthly expenses at the Birtley Mine of George Humble & Co. for the late 1760s and early 1770s (NCB 2/4). Various mining functions are charged at a standard rate, which in all probability reflects a going piece rate. These standard charges were annually amended, an attention not evident in the Boulton

Figure 14: Letter, Gibson to Stephenson, 1758

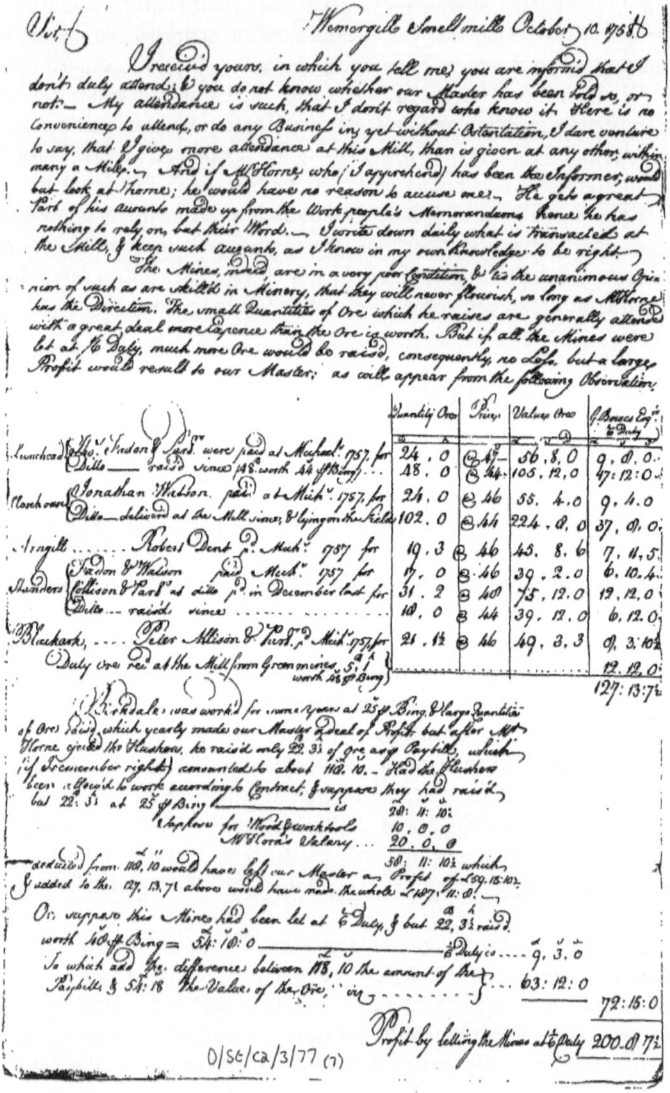

Sir,

Wemergill Smelt mill October 10. 1758.

I received yours, in which you tell me, you are informed that I don't duly attend; & you do not know whether our Master has been told so, or not:— My attendance is such, that I don't regard who know it. Here is no Conveniency to attend, or do any Business in; yet without Ostentation, I dare venture to say, that I give more attendance at this Mill, than is given at any other, within many a Mile.— And if Mr Horne, who (I apprehend) has been the Informer, would but look at home; he would have no reason to accuse me.— He gets a great Part of his accounts made up from the Work people's Memorandums hence he has nothing to rely on, but their Word.— I write down daily what is transacted at the Mill, & keep such accounts, as I know in my own Knowledge to be right.

The Mines, indeed, are in a very poor Condition, & tis the unanimous Opinion of such as are skilled in Minery, that they will never flourish, so long as Mr Horne has the Direction. The small Quantities of Ore which he raises are generally attended with a great deal more Expence than the Ore is worth. But if all the Mines were let at 1/6 Duty, much more Ore would be raised, consequently, no Loss, but a large Profit would result to our Master; as will appear from the following Observation:

		Quantity Ore	Price	Value of Ore	of Bowes Esq. 1/6 Duty
Lunchead	Thos. Fadon & Partners were paid at Michael. 1757, for	24 . 0	@ 47	56 . 8 . 0	9 . 8 . 0
	Ditto —— raised since (48 worth 44 pr Bing)	48 . 0	@ 44	105 . 12 . 0	47 : 12 : 0
Closehouse	Jonathan Watson paid at Mich. 1757, for	24 . 0	@ 46	55 . 4 . 0	9 . 4 . 0
	Ditto — delivered at the Mill since, & lying on the Fields	102 . 0	@ 44	224 . 8 . 0	37 . 8 . 0
Arngill	...... Robert Dent pd. Mich. 1757 for	19 . 3	@ 46	45 . 8 . 6	7 . 11 . 5
Standers	Fadon & Watson paid Mich. 1757 for	17 . 0	@ 46	39 . 2 . 0	6 . 10 . 4
	Collison & Partners at ditto pd. in December last for	31 . 2	@ 48	75 . 12 . 0	12 . 12 . 0
	Ditto ... raised since	18 . 0	@ 44	39 . 12 . 0	6 . 12 . 0
Blackark	.... Peter Allison & Partners pd. Mich. 1757 for	21 . 1½	@ 46	49 . 3 . 3	8 . 3 : 10½
	Duty ore recd at the Mill from Green mines 5 : 1 worth 48 pr Bing				12 . 12 . 0
					127 : 13 : 7½

Kirkdale was worked for some years at 25s pr Bing & large Quantities of Ore raised, which yearly made our Master a deal of Profit: but after Mr Horne joined the Flushers, he raised only 22. 3½ of Ore as pr Paybills, which (if I remember right) amounted to about 118. 10.— Had the Flushers been allowed to work according to Contract, I suppose they had raised but 22 : 3½ at 25s pr Bing —— is 28 : 11 : 10½

Expence for Wood & work tools	10 . 0 . 0
Mr Horne's Salary ...	20 . 0 . 0
	58 : 11 : 10½

deducted from 118, 10 would have left our Master a Profit of £59. 18 : 10½ which & added to the 127. 13. 7½ above would have made the whole £187 : 11 : 8.

Or, suppose this Mine had been let at 1/6 Duty, & but 22, 3½ raised worth 40s pr Bing = 54 : 18 : 0 ———— 1/6 Duty is .... 9 . 3 . 0

To which add the difference between 118, 10 the amount of the Paybills & 54 : 18 the Value of the Ore, is .... 63 : 12 : 0

72 : 15 : 0

Profit by letting the Mines at 1/6 Duty 200 . 8 . 7½

D/St/C2/3/77 (7)

& Watt system forty years later. The rate for hewing*, for example, fluctuated from 1/10 per score in December 1763, to 2/6 in October 1766, and 2/4 in February 1771. Meanwhile, the cost for drawing reflected a similar pattern—8d per score in December 1763, 1/8 in December 1765, and 1/6 in February 1771. It is interesting to note that whilst the fluctuations for these two activities moved up and down in approximate tandem, amendments did not occur at precisely the same point in time. It would seem therefore that the rates were examined on a monthly rather than a yearly basis.

The pit bills, fortnightly production reports, appear to have been more carefully done in the Durham vicinity than elsewhere. There survives a series of pit bills for the Ouston Colliery from 1816 through the 1820s (NCB 12/1). In these documents the cost of each extractive process is provided for each of the 26 pay periods yearly. Then, an annual cost per score is computed for each process. Data on output, total cost, cost per ton*, and stores are maintained for each of the mine's two pits. Common charges, such as engines other than those underground, waggonways, blacksmithing, and sundries are not allocated to the individual pits. Likewise, fortnightly pit bills exist for the Percy Main Colliery, again dating from the 1820s (NCB 2/269). For example, an 1821 production report for the Howden Pit, West Side comprised four huge folio pages, immaculately maintained. A printed form was in use, two decades earlier than the appearance of similar documents in South Wales. Here the daily productivity of individual hewers was recorded, broken down into the types of coal mined. Weights were then multiplied by a piece rate for each variety to give the fortnightly wage for each. The mine overman signed the report as an attestation to its accuracy.

Finally, there is at Durham a collection of papers that once belonged to James Hall, a foremost colliery engineer and an early partner in the Stella Coal Company. There is an estimate of expenses for an unidentified colliery, assuming a vend* of 30,000 tons. The report is distinguished for its utilisation of transfer prices (e.g., the cost of coal used at the lime kilns), its calculation of salvage value on refuse and unusable coals, and its accounting for ground damage (NCB 1/TH/1). There also appears an abstract of the working at the Blackboy Colliery for 1843–1846. Here the cost per chaldron for 14 expense categories was detailed to three decimal places. A build-up for some was also provided as hewing was broken down into 20 components, banking and mechanics into ten each, materials into 50, colliery rents into six, and railway dues into four. The remaining cost categories were not subdivided (NCB 1/TH/6). Thomas Hall, whose relationship to James is not known to us, performed a forecast of the estimated value of production at South Heaton Colliery for the 1½ years remaining in the life of its leases (1834–1835). The expectation of £16,000 annually was 'discounted at 12% risk' to provide an estimate of £19,754/1/6. Another present value exercise also appeared, discounting 40 years' annual profit of £22,000 at 14%. Hall calculated that annuity at £157,885, whilst our reckoning would suggest the figure should have been £156,343 (NCB 1/TH/15, pp. 45–48; another similar analysis appears on pp. 59–61). Finally, various 1834 estimates for production levels in chaldrons were recorded in this memorandum book written in ink (p. 172). Noted in pencil were variances from the actual volume of output. It appears that notice was taken of differences between estimates and actuals, though there are no explanations provided for production shortfalls.

From the Durham area records then, we find some evidence of the maintenance of monthly expense records utilising regularly reviewed, standard chargeout rates. Also in evidence were costings of mining processes and pits prepared on a fortnightly and annual basis, as well as the calculation of production and profit potential estimates for mine leases.

TYNESIDE: NEWCASTLE

Two unique features characterise the coal-mining records in the immediate vicinity of Newcastle. First, there is evidence of efficient cost keeping from the decades immediately preceeding the Industrial Revolution epoch. These early records reflected methods not in evidence elsewhere until much later. Second, the mine owners in the Newcastle area were highly organised in controlling retail coal sales and the mining labour market. Consequently, various types of accounting records related to this purpose are prevalent in the archives here but not elsewhere.

At the Tyne and Wear Record Office, there are two large compendia of mining records which span nearly three-quarters of a century. There is a volume entitled 'Correspondence, Valuations, Reports, etc.', dated 1776–1839 (DX 198/1), and a view book of George Johnson which covers 1828–1848 (NRO ZW1.5). These collections include a substantial quantity of expense estimates and production reports similar to those we have seen for numerous other extractive operations—estimates for working and winning (NRO ZW1.5, pp. 458–460, 489–491; DX 198/1, pp. 38–39, 42, 72, 97, 100, 172, 266, 299, 307, 403, 558, 609, 641, 656–657, 664, 735) and expenses of leading the ore from the mines to the staiths (DX 198/1, pp. 122–123, 551, 609, 613, 641). Though these reports are unremarkable as a group, it might be observed that the recovery of winning costs was spread over production, that an allowance for ground damage was typically recorded, and that common costs were apportioned to multiple seams or installations as a percentage of the vend. We were particularly intrigued by a 1780 costing calculation at Pontopike Colliery (ibid., p. 97), which included a 1½d per ton expense item called 'Making Horses height Through Troubles'. One other record of this genre deserves special mention because of its early date (1738). This document was 'An account of the Expense of Winning at the South end of Heaton by Fixing an engine on the Thistle Pit and lifting the main coal water to the 33 In: etc.'. This costing was for a four-year project and comprised 20 items of expense, totalling £4,459/8/0 (ibid., p. 37).

Other familiar features in these records were estimates for capital improvements to existing operations (ibid., pp. 506–507, 531) and detailed estimates related to transportation (NRO ZW1.5, p. 196; DX 198/1, pp. 127, 217, 613–615, 647–648). Distinctive in this category was a comparison of the estimated and actual cost of laying the Midgeholme Railway in 1827. Mr Stephenson had estimated the cost at £9,330/14/10, whilst actual expenditures to the point of the analysis were £9,245/10/3. Lest the aforementioned Mr Stephenson be given high marks for his spot-on estimation, it was observed that an additional £2,000 was yet to be spent before completion of the project (ibid., p. 217). Though it was infrequent to find estimates and actuals in such close proximity, this comparison was considerably less sophisticated than the Emma Pit winning at Stella, both in terms of the specification of variances and analysis of the differentials.

The Newcastle area mining records contain a number of valuations of collieries undertaken by viewers (ibid., pp. 178–179, 526, 561, 565–566, 575–576, 711–715). These analyses were on occasion restricted to estimated mineral reserves, but were more typically a total valuation of the colliery. There seemed to be a substantial volume of comparative costings of alternative methods for different extractive processes—leading (ibid., p. 105), raising (ibid., pp. 144–145, 688), drawing (ibid., pp. 690–691). There was a corresponding lack of attention to internal comparisons of actual operations. However, two exceptions were an 1827 cost comparison of two seams of High Main Coal (the Hutton pit cost 7/3 per chaldron and Maudlin 8/1¾) (ibid., p. 529) and a more detailed estimate of costs at various pits belonging to the Mount Moor Company in the period 1790–1795 (ibid., pp. 641–645). Here 33 expense categories were costed to the farthing. This analysis reflected a substantial variation in mining costs amongst Swan Pit (seam 1 = 7/1¾ per chaldron, seam 2 = 7/9), Bounder Pit (7/0), Great Pit (6/6¼), and Way Pit (6/7½). An interesting feature was the use of the word 'decay' to connote the depreciation of horses. One cost comparison took on the appearance of a make-or-buy decision. The title conveys that purpose, 'Comparative Cost of Coke made by the Newcastle & Carlisle Railway Co. at their Ovens; with that made by the Blenkinsopp Coal Co. delivery on the line at Greenhead—for 12 months ending 31 December 1842' (NRO ZW1.5, p. 377).

A number of interesting trials and experiments were undertaken and recorded. In 1769, the coal consumption of nine different Smeaton engines belonging to the Long Benton Colliery was charted (DX 198/1, pp. 115–117). An 1836 cost comparison for drawing coals at the Gosforth Pit revealed the superiority of engines (£509/4/0) over horses (£776/15/0) (ibid., pp. 690–691). In 1842, Mr Blackmore measured the amount of coal from five different collieries required for a journey on the Newcastle & Carlisle Railway from Blaydon to Carlisle. Marley Hill coal did the best (1 ton, 17 cwts., 1 quarter), whilst Blenkinsopp was the worst (2 tons, 6 cwts., 2 quarters). However, the test was conducted in terms of volume only as no comparative prices for the coal varieties were reckoned in the analysis (NRO ZW1.5, pp. 216–217).

There are two other aspects of the Tyne and Wear records that deserve special attention. First, as was typical of the Newcastle vicinity, the coal-mine owners were well-organised in determining production quotas. Returns were collected from ten collieries providing information about gross and net production, sales volume and price, distance to market, and maximum production potential. These data became the statistical basis for determining market share. The following quote details the calculative process for 1836 (ibid., pp. 142–143):

> Powers exercised by the Tees Collieries under existing basis; taking as the data the greatest number of scores drawn in one month during 1835; and calculating eleven months to the year; together with the greatest quantity of being raised, according to their returns, with the prices etc.

In similar fashion, R.W. Brandling, chairman of a 'special committee' to investigate Newcastle area collieries in 1837, was able to generate from 35 collieries information regarding production, distribution, and pricing. The number of employees was also required. Interestingly, except for queries regarding shipping expenses, no other cost data were solicited (ibid., pp. 174–175).

We have stated elsewhere what we perceive to be a lack of attention to labour control in the extractive industries. However, the Johnson view book does include some exceptions to that observation. Johnson in the mid-1830s clocked the time required for 'drawing, striking, and putting* into the shaft each iron 60 peck tub' as 1 minute, 15 seconds. This speed would allow for 7 score per hour, 84 per day, according to Johnson's reckoning (ibid., p. 5). In an 1839 analysis of the Thornley Colliery, Johnson calculated that on average each of the 360 active hewers (28 were reckoned sick per day) could produce 10 corves* of 20 pecks per day (ibid., pp. 26–27). A similar average produce of 17 tubs of 22 pecks was observed for operatives at the Cragwood Colliery (ibid., p. 33).

During the 1830s, there was apparently devised a standard list of eighteen questions that comprised viewers' reports of mine operations. Questions 16–18 dealt specifically with production levels. Question 16 required a statement of the greatest quantity of coal that could be drawn daily from the workable pits by the present machinery. Question 17 requested the same information relative to the current establishment of men. Question 18, perhaps amalgamating information from the preceeding two, asked for the greatest amount ever drawn in two successive fortnights and the pertinent dates (ibid., pp. 95–98). This concentration upon maximum production levels appears again and again throughout Newcastle area archives. However, its intent was clearly not to establish workers' responsibility for certain levels of output. It was to provide the basis for the division of the retail coal market.

The holdings of the Northumberland Record Office include the minute book of the Grand Allies, a Tyneside coal owners association, dating from 1727. This pre-industrial volume reflects some interesting accounting methods, and is described in detail in Oldroyd (1996). An early entry is a costing for the raising and leading of one thousand tens* of coal. Included in the total cost of £6/5/2 is a 4/6 allocation for the expense of laying the waggonways and building the staith. There is also an allocated 4s charge for 'Stock in Trade (besides all hazards) £4,000' (NRO 3410/GA/2, p. 15). The minute book also contains a number of comparative costings from the 1730s, including the cost per ton of working Heaton (£6/12/4) and Long Benton (£6/19/4) (p. 98) and the relative profit margins at Long Benton, Gateshead Park, and Salt Meadows (p. 48).

Perhaps the most interesting feature of the Grand Allies' record keeping was the statistical data accumulated to effectuate the division of the retail coal market. There are a number of agreements in evidence from the 1730s reflecting this distribution. The format typically included the agreed-upon vend of different coal varieties for a particular year, followed by additional columns charting actual sales and the negotiated quota for the succeeding year. In one such marketing arrangement, 22 collieries participated. Nineteen of these failed to sell their allotted volume, whilst three exceeded their quotas (p. 80). The allocations changed from year to year, but there is no indication either of the basis for the distribution or any penalty for excess sales.

There are a number of additional pre-industrial records in the Watson collection which hold some interest. For example, there is an estimate for producing coal circa 1750 which included a 4s per ton charge for agents and viewers (WAT 1/5/5). A 1752 'estimate of the expense of cribbing* and planking made upon 2 fathoms or a 12 foot length of tubb of 7 feet diameter' was impressive in its detail (WAT 1/5/7). There survives an 'account of boring' for 1768 at the Urpeth Colliery in which the type of rock encountered at various depths is maintained in fathoms, yards, feet, and inches (WAT 1/5/15).

Some later documents in the Watson archives are reflective of a greater attention to labour-based statistics than we have seen elsewhere in the extractive industries. In WAT 1/5/88 (1830–1831), the average wages of hewers at Cowpen Colliery are segregated into three classes.

These average weekly wage levels are 19/7¾, 17/5½, and 11/10½ respectively for the three operative categories. Unfortunately, there is no information regarding the method by which miners were assigned in this classification scheme. In another document for the same place and time, the yearly earnings for the six best families were given (WAT 1/5/89). Thus, five Reeds earned £211/11/0 and four Doukins' received £135. More importantly, there is evidence in the collection of the magnitude of control the mine owners exercised in the labour market concomitant with their division of retail sales. There exists an immense spreadsheet, dated 1805, on which are logged the numbers of hewers bound to and from each colliery on the Tyne and Blyth (WAT 1/5/31a). There appears in this record as well the formula used in 1805 to determine the number of pitmen that could be bound to each colliery that year. Each was entitled to 95% of its average, actual labour force for the preceeding three years (WAT 1/5/31g). In WAT 1/5/41a, there is a similar record for 1806, but here there is evidence that the owners' association also had the power to establish maximum wage rates.

A surviving minute book of the owners' association from 1805 provides further evidence of communal control (NRO 263). There appear yearly statistics on chaldrons vended and monthly selling prices. For 1812, there is a return for each colliery of the wage rates paid for various categories of labourers. The owners were particularly concerned with binding arrangements, both the numbers of miners employed and the wage maximums. The minute book contains statements from mine agents who apparently violated the rules established by the association.

Figure 15 is the finest example of a costing record we have seen for the Newcastle vicinity. It has been extracted from a Buddle view book (BUD 22, pp. 248–249) and pertains to the Tanfield Moor Colliery. The first part is an 1831 abstract of charges for working and leading coal. It will be noted that underground charges are maintained separately from expenses at the surface. The underground charges, moreover, are pit-specific for the three mines in operation, whilst the surface costs are treated in common. The second portion is a summary of the waggonway leaves the colliery paid to send its coal to the staith at Dunstan, based upon the average quantity transported in the previous five years.

Other records we have seen at Newcastle are typical of the extractive industries generally, but appear collectively to be of lesser sophistication than Durham documents of the same period. There is for

Figure 15: Expense Summaries, Tanfield Moor, 1831

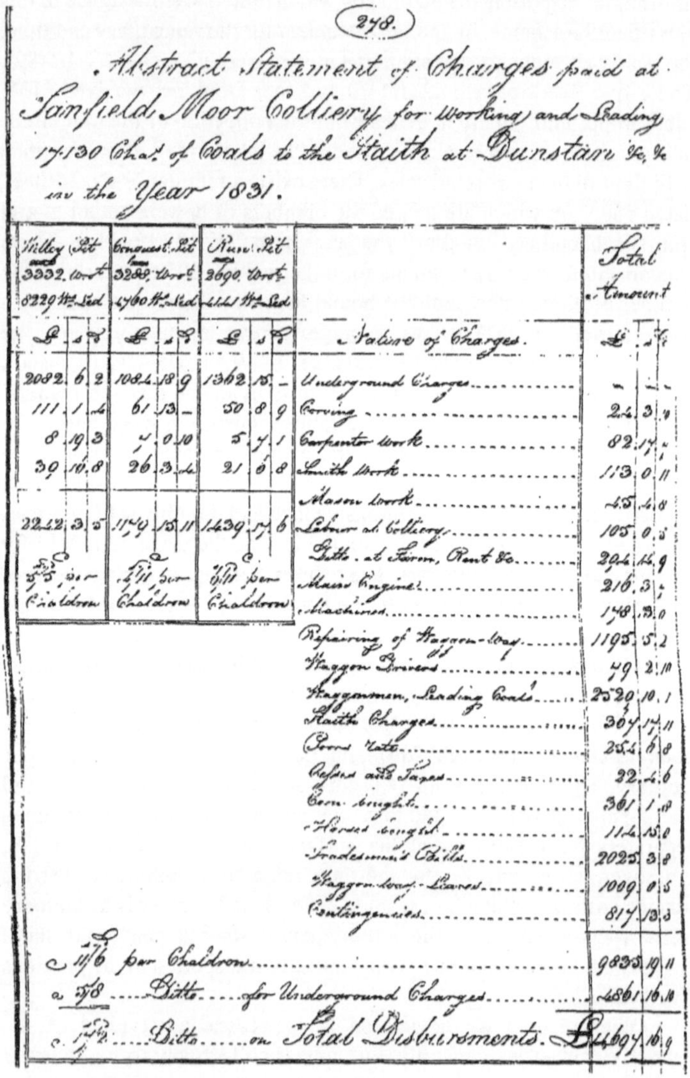

(278.)

Abstract Statement of Charges paid at Tanfield Moor Colliery for Working and Leading 17130 Chas. of Coals to the Staith at Dunston &c. &c. in the Year 1831.

Tilley Pit 3332 Wrot 8229 Wns Led £	s	d	Conquest Pit 3288 Wrot 4760 Wns Led £	s	d	Run Pit 2690 Wrot 4464 Wns Led £	s	d
2082	6	2	1084	18	9	1362	15	–
111	1	4	61	13	–	50	8	9
8	19	3	4	0	10	5	7	1
39	16	8	26	3	4	21	6	8
2242	3	5	1149	15	11	1439	17	6
5/5 per Chaldron			4/11 per Chaldron			6/11 per Chaldron		

Nature of Charges	Total Amount £	s	d
Underground Charges	–	–	–
Corving	24	3	4
Carpenter Work	82	17	7
Smith Work	113	0	11
Mason Work	45	4	8
Labour at Colliery	105	0	5
Ditto at Farm, Rent &c.	204	14	9
Main Engine	216	3	7
Machines	148	13	0
Repairing of Waggon-Way	1195	5	2
Waggon Drivers	79	2	10
Waggonmen, Leading Coals	2520	10	1
Staith Charges	307	17	11
Poors Rate	254	6	8
Cesses and Taxes	22	4	6
Corn bought	361	1	10
Horses bought	114	15	0
Tradesmen's Bills	2025	3	8
Waggon Way Leaves	1009	0	5
Contingencies	817	13	3
c 11/6 per Chaldron	9835	19	11
a 5/8 Ditto for Underground Charges	4861	16	10
c 17/2 Ditto on Total Disbursments. £	14697	16	9

Figure 15: Expense Summaries, Tanfield Moor, 1831

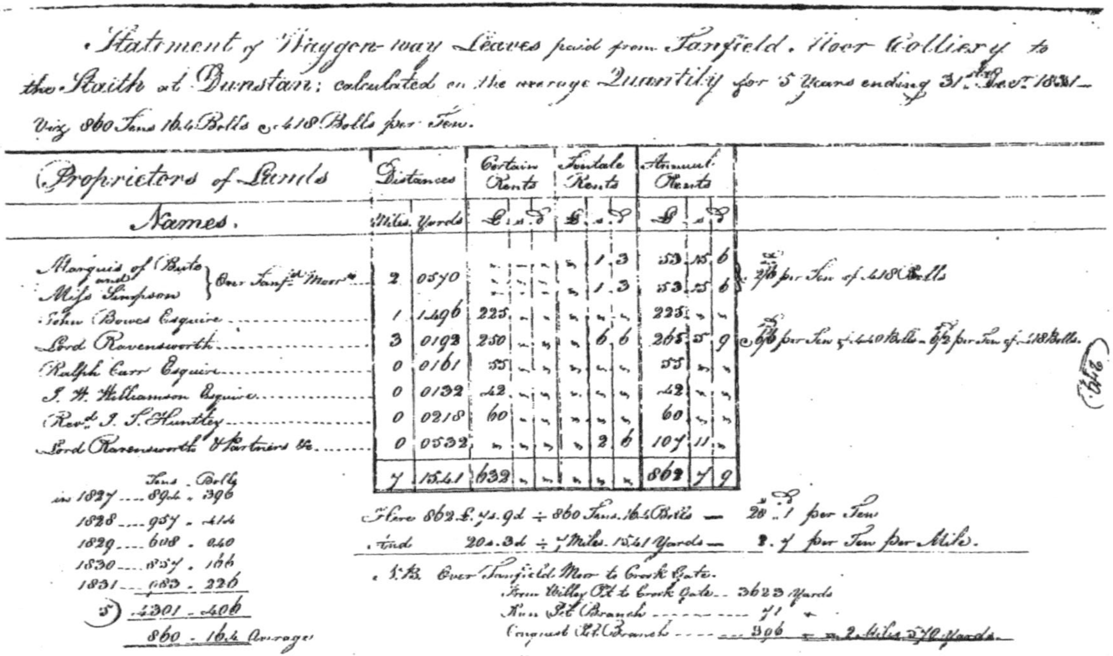
Statement of Waggon-way Leaves paid from Tanfield Moor Colliery to the Staith at Dunstan; calculated on the average Quantity for 5 Years ending 31st Decr 1831 — Viz 860 Tons 16.4 Bolls @ 418 Bolls per Ton.

Proprietors of Lands — Names	Distances Miles	Distances Yards	Certain Rents £	s	d	Tentale Rents £	s	d	Annual Rents £	s	d	
Marquis of Bute (Over Tanfd. Moor*)	2	0570	"	"	"	"	1	3	53	15	6	2½d per Ton of 418 Bolls
and Miss Simpson (Over Tanfd. Moor*)			"	"	"	"	1	3	53	15	6	
John Bowes Esquire	1	1496	225	"	"	"	"	"	225	"	"	
Lord Ravensworth	3	0193	250	"	"	"	6	6	265	5	9	@ 6½d per Ton of 440 Bolls — 6½d per Ton of 418 Bolls.
Ralph Carr Esquire	0	0161	55	"	"	"	"	"	55	"	"	
J. H. Williamson Esquire	0	0132	42	"	"	"	"	"	42	"	"	
Revd. J. S. Huntley	0	0218	60	"	"	"	"	"	60	"	"	
Lord Ravensworth & Partners &c.	0	0532	"	"	"	"	2	6	107	11	"	
	7	1541	632	"	"	"	"	"	862	7	9	

	Tons	Bolls
in 1827	894	396
1828	957	414
1829	608	040
1830	857	166
1831	983	226
5)	4301	406
	860	16.4 Average

Here 862£ 7s 9d ÷ 860 Tons 16.4 Bolls — 20d. 1 per Ton

and 20s. 3d ÷ 7 Miles 1541 Yards — 2. 7 per Ton per Mile.

* N.B. Over Tanfield Moor to Crook Gate.
From Willey Pit to Crook Gate — 3623 Yards
Ann Pit Branch — 71 +
Cragmead Pit Branch — 396 = 2 Miles 570 Yards

(242)

1787 a cost analysis for a proposed new waggonway from Plessey Colliery to the Blyth, skirting the estate of Lord Delaval. A total cost is calculated by multiplying the 6,120 yards of the new waggonway by a standard cost of 3/6 and adding £400 for a bridge. A deduction of 12d per yard for 5,616 yards is subtracted as the distance over which the proposed new road would parallel the existing one. Yearly expenses associated with the extra 504 yards of length are included. The same source also includes a differential analysis for building a reservoir for holding coals, with and without a raised platform (ZRI/35/15).

There is an extant account book for the Cowpen Colliery that spans over two decades, commencing in 1810 (ZRI/35/5). There is a quite rudimentary profit analysis for the enterprise for 1810. The compiler derived a profit of 4/9 per chaldron by subtracting current per chaldron expenses from the previous year's average sales price. One obvious shortcoming in the analysis was the amalgamation of costs from the two seams in operation, divided by two. The bookkeeper was also quick to point out that the anticipated profit had not been realised as the 'books will show' because the estimate was exclusive of any expense for 'decay of materials, fresh winning, or accidents', as well as interest on capital. The accounting appears a bit more advanced two decades later in a comparison of raising costs for 1832 and 1833. It was observed that the 29,375 chaldrons raised in 1832 cost on average 11/1½ (9/6 of underground charges and 1/7½ for incidentals). The next year's production was significantly reduced (17,548 chaldrons), whilst unit costs were much higher at 13/9½ per chaldron (11/3 underground, 2/6½ incidentals). The bookkeeper had two observations to make on these data. First of all, £1,105 could have been saved in 1833 had 13 pit workers been discharged, a course of action indicated by the lower volume of production. This savings included their £45 yearly salary, plus savings on materials they consumed, such as tools, oil, grease, chains, and lamps. Had these redundancies been effectuated, the 1833 cost per chaldron would have been reduced to 12/6½. Second, it was concluded on the basis of these statistics that production should never be allowed to dip below 20,000 chaldrons annually. Reminiscent of Stella Coal, there was also a comparative analysis in an appendix to the 1821 stock taking of expenses associated with keeping a pit horse and a waggon horse. Most of the £10 difference was attributed to the more expensive diet of the waggon horse. The analysis included depreciation of the stock (called wear and tear) at a rate of £3/8/0 annually for pit horses and £5/10/0 for waggon horses. The costs of harnesses, shoeing, and farrier services were not specified but were included in general charges.

Finally, an account book of the Ashington Coal Company (NCB/AS/4) has an interesting story to tell. There is an 1843 report from Francis Turner estimating the cost of winning and probable profit at Black Close, a property of the Duke of Portland. The numbers are badly rounded and the arithmetic is shocking. However, a bottom-line profit of £2,302 was reckoned, representing a 17¾% return on capital. Then, a sensitivity analysis was done which indicated that had sales been £30,000 instead of the actual £17,062/10, the return on capital would have been 20½%. It is unfortunate that this innovative 'what-if' analysis was saddled with lazy costing and poor numeracy. Perhaps the laxness came home to roost in 1855 when Richard Allinson was called in as the accountant to supervise the dissolution of the firm. He wrote (NCB/A5/5, p. 22):

> After a careful review of the foregoing accounts and full consideration of the state in which they came into my hands, I feel it necessary to say, that it appears to me they were not in such form or condition as could be considered proper and satisfactory for the purpose of arriving at a settlement between partners upon a dissolution.

Again, in the Newcastle area, we find considerable evidence of cost estimates related to improvements and proposals for new capital expenditure projects. These analyses included, in some instances, common cost allocations and, more frequently, examples of quite detailed estimates of potential transport costs. Cost comparisons undertaken included costs of alternative extraction methods, engine coal consumption, and drawing coal via engines or horses. Only a limited number of estimated to actual costs comparisons could be located. In the area, however, we did find a greater attention to labour cost control, detailed at the individual level. Valuations of collieries were frequently undertaken, as well as statistical recordings related to production, distribution, pricing, employee numbers, and market share quotas.

LANCASHIRE/STAFFORDSHIRE/WEST MIDLANDS

The word 'inconsistent' comes to mind in describing the cost accounting displayed in surviving mining records for the Northwest of England. Typical of this variability are the records of the Elsecar Old Colliery, a part of the substantial holdings of Earl Fitzwilliam, housed at the Sheffield Archives. A researcher comparing the coal accounts from 1755 (WWMA 1545) to those of 1840 (WWMA 1590) would be delighted to find that the records were exquisitely maintained, but dismayed that there was virtually no change in accounting methodology with the passage of nearly a century. More startling was the contrast apparent in a ledger book, dated 1833 (WWMA 1600). Here the building account reflected neither systemic depreciation nor even periodic write-downs of asset values. There was no effort to identify the components of general charges except for a lump-sum amount, without explanation, that appeared thrice annually in 'sundries'. Yet, the ironstone account contained a stated transfer price, annually amended, but only for the years 1828–1830. For 1827 and 1831–1833, the column was left blank.

It was a more typical pattern, of course, for the standard of accounting to be either competent or primitive depending on the individual enterprise. The 1830s production book of the Ladyshore Coal Company (Bolton Archive Service, ZLA 15/9/21) does track the daily productivity of individual operatives in various parts of the mine, but does so in weights only. Apparently, the firm did not differentiate coal qualities or establish seam-specific piece rates. The Lancashire Public Record Office at Preston contains a memorandum book of a subcontractor at Clivinger Coal (NCC1 18/1) and a 'get book' for George Hargreaves & Co. (NCHa 7/1). These records are very primitive compared to similar documents found in Durham during the same time frame. Also at Preston is the Backbarrow furnace account for 1728–1731 (DOMC 30/1) where outputs were maintained in weights only and were not furnace-specific. The accounting here might be excused, however, because of its early chronology and also because of the provision, as reported previously, of an excellent cure for the bite of a mad dog.

There was also some fairly crude record keeping manifested by West Midlands mining operations. There exist monthly recordings of coal get and expenses for the Spring Head Colliery in the 1830s and the Clewes Moor Colliery in the 1840s (archive of John Foster & Sons, #41 and #42, Leeds University Library). Here no cognisance was taken of any expenses other than prime costs. At the Sheffield Archives in the Arundel Castle collection, there are a number of mining reports of rather poor quality, dating from the 1790s and the first decade of the nineteenth century. The Hesley Colliery (S209) records made no distinction between coal types (hard or small) in establishing piece rates per corve or waggon. A distinction was made at the Handsworth (S208) and Sheffield Collieries (S199), but the record keeping was not sufficiently sophisticated to separate the coal sold from the coal used internally to run the mine machinery. In all mining operations that comprised the Arundel Castle collection, there seemed to be an emphasis upon the financial arrangements rather than the cost accounting. The accounting was a little better at the Listerwick Colliery. In a book identified as the journal, the firm maintained a daily record of the number of loads got in by each individual collier (West Yorkshire Archive Service, Calderdale, SH:2/CM3, 1843). This information was then amalgamated into the 'Coal and Cash Book' in which the disposition of the coal was recorded weekly, as well as the cash flows associated with sales, wages, and sundry expenses (SH:2/CM4/1).

Notwithstanding the dark side of the cost accounting detailed above, certain firms in the Northwest's extractive industry did significantly better. One mining concern whose history runs the course of the British Industrial Revolution was the Bridgewater Collieries, a component of the various enterprises of the Duke of Bridgewater, who is best remembered for the canal that bears his name joining Manchester and Liverpool. There exists a lengthy time series of selling prices per ton of various coal varieties that runs virtually unbroken from 1764 to 1810 (there are no entries for 1793–1799 and 1804–1805). The selling prices provided represent a standard cost of extraction plus profit and are labelled 'Value per ton as estimated at the Sough Mouth for the colliery profit'. That the prices given represent a standard rather than actual production costs is surmised by the consistency of the time series. For instance, there was no variation at all in coal prices from 1764 to 1782 (common was 3/4, sodering 4/2, cannel* 5s, blend 2/6, sleek 1/6, cokes 2s), despite the fact that the prices were dispersed throughout the source document in annal form, along with many other pieces of information (NCBw 6/1, Annual Department Accounts 1763–1790, Manchester Central Library). There was a universal rise in the price quotes in 1783, fluctuations both up and down in 1784 depending on the coal type, and consistency again until 1791 when there was another increase across the board. During the first decade of the nineteenth century, there was annual fluctuation, mostly in an upward direction, until the series ended in 1810. One element of sophistication that can be noted here, as contrasted to the poorer accounting of coal-mining operations in the Sheffield region, was the separation of coal vended (handled through the colliery account) and the coal used internally (charged to the navigation account).

An even more impressive exercise emanating from the same source was the allocation of contingent expenses, an example of which for 1785 is transcribed as Table 7. It will be noted that the data that appear are cross-referenced to other accounting records that have not survived. This document is the best we have seen with regard to the allocation of direct and common expenses. Unfortunately, we are unable to determine how the common expenses were apportioned to the navigation, colliery, and lime accounts. All we do know is that the allocation was not made proportionately to the direct expenses charged.

Finally, there is in the archive a bundle of 161 miscellaneous items pertaining to the later activities of the colliery in the 1830s and 1840s (NCBw 19/1, Bundle 1). Herein included are differential coal prices on a field-specific basis (which did not exist for the 1764–1810 series), reserve estimates for various mineral fields, and piece-rate calculations. There is a wealth of information about the firm's steam engines—comparative data on costs and coal consumption, depths and horsepower measurements, and monthly reports on the state of the engines and boilers. There is also an 1847 estimate of 58 items comprising the cost of sinking two pits. The distinguishing feature not found in other estimates of this genre was an allowance in the event that quicksand was encountered in the winning.

At the Staffordshire Record Office, there are a number of mining records from enterprises involved in the extraction of both coal and copper. There exists for the Ecton Mines a tribute book (D3060/4) and a collection of 6-week 'reckonings' (D3060/2), which are accountings for productivity made pursuant to tribute bargains, both dated from the 1820s. The tribute book details exactly the location of the veins to be harvested. Because of the differential amounts to be paid, it may be

Table 7: Contingent Expenses, Bridgewater Colliery, 1785

Particulars of the Contingent Expense	Books	Pages	Total	Certainly known to belong to the following accounts: Nav	Coll	Lime	Remains still to be proportioned
Materials consisting of Cordage and Sail Canvas, Timber & Boards, Iron & Nails, Scrap Iron, Brass and Cast Metal, Lime for the Works, Slate	34	32	2964/11/5½	1341/17/3	247/6/10	—	1375/7/4½
Whole of Timber Boards from his Grace's Shropshire estate			423/1/6				423/1/6
Making 1914 thousand bricks	20	33	801/13/8				801/13/8
Salaries to clerks	19	53	1483/18/7	543/18/7	197/3/–	40/10/–	702/7/–
Additional wages to boatmen, labour	19	24	131/8/10	119/16/6	11/3/6	–/8/10	
Coal used at Worsley Field, the Forge, Smiths, Shops, etc.	21	49	158/15/11	23/11/11	85/17/–		49/7/–
Petit expenses	22	53	274/11/5½	105/9/0½	23/7/6	1/12/7	144/2/4
							3495/18/10½
The Whole amount of the contingents being £3495/18/10½ is proportioned as follows				1933/13/9½	1512/5/1	50/–/–	
			6238/1/5	4068/7/1	2077/2/11	92/11/5	

assumed that some costing must have been done in determination of the piece rates. However, no build-ups of the rates are provided. The 'reckonings' are simply the quantities mined multiplied by the agreed piece rate and signed for by the recipient. However, deductions are also recorded for candles, powder, working tools, and scrap iron.

There is also at Stafford a series of reports from John Taylor, the manager of the Alport mines, to the proprietors (504B/L357). Taylor communicated with the owners every four months from 1839 to 1850. These reports are not particularly helpful in an accounting sense because they were largely narrative rather than statistical; yet, there are some interesting features. In an 1839 report, Taylor provided a good justification for hiring a trained accountant:

> I must remark further that the bookkeeping on mines is an important branch of the management, and, ought to be communicated to a person thoroughly trained to the business; and that if accounts for such a concern as the Alport Mines will become, be kept as they ought to be, and the duty of receiving and delivering the stones be attended to in a manner which may best insure their economical applications; there is ample employment for a clerk duly qualified and experienced in mining bookkeeping.

Taylor went on to say that it is wrong in principle to allow a mine agent to keep the accounts, an interesting insight into what we of the modern day would regard an independence issue.

The earliest of Taylor's epistles in 1839 contained his estimate for a major drainage project anticipated to cost some £17,551/3/9. The estimate was poorly done, appearing to be comprised of many ballpark guestimates. Numerous tasks were not costed with reference to necessary labour hours or wage rates. In subsequent communications Taylor reported on the progress of the project. In his letter of 21 January 1841, Taylor, without mentioning any numbers, averred that the project was within budget, although certain costs were higher than expected. Whilst the project was never mentioned again, leading an impartial observer to hypothesise that the costs far exceeded budget, it was a rarity to find in the archives any subsequent attention to an initiated action.

The records of the Middleton Colliery cover the period from 1785–1810, a span of years for which there are considerably fewer archival survivals than for the later Industrial Revolution. Housed at the West Yorkshire Archive Service in Leeds, these beautifully maintained documents, like those of the Philips' tape-making enterprise, frustrate the researcher in that the holdings are so sparse for what appears to have been one of the better accounting systems. There does survive a 1785 'estimate of the several expenses attending the New Winning at Beeston Colliery' (MC 233). As was typical with many cost estimates of this type, two of the largest expense items were estimated at a standard cost per yard. Consequently, the pit sinking and the paved road to the winning were costed without particular reference to the composition of the strata at various depths or the terrain to be traversed. What was most unusual about this particular costing was the basing of engine expenses on the length of time projected for the endeavour. Thus, the cost of the steam engine for the sinking was 6/6 for coal and £8/12/6 for operating costs apart from coal, multiplied by the number of weeks. Another interesting aspect was the observation that of the total cost of £3,277/0/4, a modest £67/2/0 could be saved by making the 244,000 bricks required for the venture on the premises.

Two Middleton record books (MC 133; MC 157), dated 1810, are statistical compilation of weekly workings, leadings, and consumption. Comparative statistics were maintained for the two pits on a daily basis. Additionally, one of the pits was worked in two shifts with separate data kept for each. There were differential hewing and drawing cost standards at various venues. At Lady Pit hewing was costed at 2/2 per dozen, whilst at Pockett's Pit the charge was 2/4. Drawing costs were 1½d per dozen at Fanny Pit, but 1¾d at Lady, Pockett's, and Acres. It is unfortunate that there is no time series for these superior production reports so that the frequency with which the standard was amended could be gauged. Other data categories were maintained here that rarely appeared on similar reports at other mines. Running year-to-date totals were provided for the quantities of coal individual transporters carried from the mines. Also, year-to-date sales of coal were recorded, both for credit and 'ready money'.

There is also at Leeds a minute book for John Hainsworth & Sons, dating from 1837 (uncatalogued). The weekly meetings of the owners featured a number of procurement decisions based upon a system of competitive bidding. Also, a number of subcontracting decisions were made on the basis of accounting numbers. However, most distinctive was the considerable discussion on the topic of swinemuck.

Management actually determined that it should be valued using a FIFO cost-flow assumption, a most appropriate example for using FIFO to approximate the physical flow of inventory. Later, the firm decided to subcontract muck provision.

Another example of careful attention being paid to cost accounting issues in the West Midlands was the High Rake Mine near Sheffield, a lead-mining operation. Here the survivals are very sparse but include letters and estimates concerning a steam engine (Sheffield Archives, Bag C, 587/30, 1836–1837) and a minute book (Bag C, 519), dated in the early 1840s. An engine was purchased in 1837, but only after four estimates had been entertained, including one from Boulton & Watt. Management made its decision only after asking numerous questions about the capabilities and dimensions of the machines in the tender offers. Again, in 1842, another engine was procured on the basis of four bids and considerable study. An entire meeting of management in March was dedicated to this decision. In the meeting immediately subsequent, the proprietors expressed great pleasure with the results.

It is clear that in the Northwest of England a great variance in costing activity and detail amongst different mining firms was practised. Some maintained detailed and meticulously prepared costing records, whilst others, even in comparison with general practice in other regions and industries, would have to be regarded as primitive. These shortcomings included the maintaining of operating statistics in physical terms with no costings applied, no attempts at depreciation or cost allocation, and/or the recording only of prime costs. Yet, other firms in this region utilised standard costings, allocated common costs, estimated mineral reserves, and calculated piece rates, whilst maintaining steam engine performance statistics and detailed pit sinking cost estimates.

WALES

The Welsh mining records discussed below are quite diverse in terms of their cost accounting sophistication. Mona Mine enjoyed the luxury of a full-time accountant, Thomas Beer, during whose lengthy tenure with the firm (at least 1821–1839) useful accounting systems were installed. The diverse mining enterprises of the Vivians were quite poorly charted until the 1840s, when some of the methods we have seen developed in the South Wales iron industry were replicated by the firm. Meanwhile, certain production reports in evidence for smaller mining ventures were amongst the most primitive we have seen.

There are a number of explanatory variables for this pattern. First of all, Mona and pieces of the Vivian conglomerate were copper-mining ventures. The enterprise functioned not only to mine the ore, but to smelt it as well. Consequently, there were more integrated processes that required managerial control. Second, the most substantial coal-mining activities of the region were subsidiaries of the large iron concerns. Thus, their cost accounting is considered in Chapter 3 rather than here.

Mona Mine: The records of this Anglesey copper enterprise are well-known to economic historians, having been examined in Pollard's (1965) broad sweep. They are housed at the University of Bangor Library and are concentrated in the period during which Beer served as the firm's accountant, the 1820s and 1830s. In 1835, near the end of his lengthy tenure, Beer composed a statement of the accountant's duties which included four major points (item 1664):

1. accounts were to be regularly abstracted on proper forms and books;
2. accounting information was to be furnished in timely fashion for particular purposes;
3. maps, titles, deeds, leases, etc. were to be collected; and
4. all the above were to be made available to the noble proprietor.

Fortunately, Beer took efforts to expand upon these identified duties so as to include activities more germane to cost accounting.

The earliest records chronologically dealt with the firm's piece-rate structure for mining, known as 'tribute bargains' (items 48–52). Agreements with workmen were signed every two months and established rates per hundredweight for ore on a shaft-specific basis. It is not clear if these accords were struck with individual operatives or subcontractors who represented teams of workers. Inventory was another major concern. In an 1819 smelting department's stock valuation (item 159), differential values were given for work-in-process, reflecting 'metal in various states'. Inventories of ore were valued at historically determined rates, functions of the amount of good metal expected from different ore varieties. Finished goods inventory was maintained at sales price for good metal less 'returning charges' (item 166). Although it is not clearly stated, returning charges apparently referred to the disposition of waste from the smelting process.

Although it is not known exactly when Beer took on the accounting function, there does seem to have been a depreciation method for the smelters in place from 1818, lasting two decades. Each of 16 smelters was depreciated at £60 for 1818–1819 and 1822–1824. For reasons unexplained, only £55 was taken in 1820 and £52 in 1821. Commencing in 1826, now with 18 smelters, there were differential rates. In 1826, ten smelters were depreciated £90 and eight for £60, whilst over the next four years 13 saw carrying value reductions of £100 and five of £60. Perhaps more interesting than this apparently arbitrary pattern of depreciation was the name given to the document itself, 'Abstracts of Dead Capital' (item 167).

It is evident in communications dating from the early 1820s that standard pricing clearly and standard costing in all probability were utilised in copper-mining operations. However, it would appear that industry-wide standards were employed, rather than ones derived from past operations at individual mines. A problem for Mona as an Anglesey copper mine lay in the fact that industry practice was determined by the Cornish branch of the trade. In an 1823 letter, J. Sanderson, the controlling agent of Mona, wrote to J. Treweek, the chief manager, focussing on this issue (item 478):

> We ought not to place such reliance upon the Cornish Standard in our Calculations to regulate Mining operations; and I recommend as a Rule to be generally observed with respect to the produce of Mona Mine that £90 per Ton of Metal in Cake should be taken as the Average Standard—Limiting all your workings by that Standard, except such as are pursued with a reasonable prospect of Discovery, or for other ultimate objects necessary to the Success of the Mines.

An entire letter from Sanderson to Treweek (13 July 1822, item 422) highlighted the competitive nature of copper mining. Sanderson suggested that an analysis be undertaken to see if the substantially more expensive Bushel iron should be utilised in the smelting process instead of Scull iron. Sanderson based this proposal on his having heard that Cornish copper was preferred over the Anglesey product because of the 'property of iron used in precipitation'. It is not known if the analysis was ever done, but the price differentials between the two irons was considerable (in 1828, Bushel cost £70 per ton and Scull only £40).

Another surviving document from 1822 (item 2637), entitled 'Calculated Charges on Refining Copper Slags', is presented as Figure 16. It will be noted that six operations are defined, two each for smelting, roasting, and refining. For each step a standard is established for the coal input, measured both by weight and cost. Labour expense is provided for all operations, but the corresponding time standard is recorded for only the two smelting operations. Additional material and labour charges are added to these two major cost components at the bottom of the calculation. The £2/18/5 per ton figure struck at the bottom is based on the 26 tons of slag originally inputted. Thus, we are left in a quandary about the piece of the document's first line which refers to '29 percent produced'. Clearly, an average cost per ton of output would have been a more valuable accounting number.

Thomas Beer undertook a number of cost comparisons which appear to have been designed in the first instance to evaluate managers rather than to control expenses. Item 2528 is a record of smelting expenses for 1826–1827, incurred respectively in operations run by Mr Morgan and Mr Rees. The expenses are broken down into only two categories—the cost of labour and the average consumption of coal. A cruder comparison also survives for 1828–1829 (item 2266). Here the managers were not named, though there were two managers being compared. There is only a single line to represent expenses, though there is a marked difference in amount. The fact that the details of expense are not enumerated leads us to believe that the purpose of the documents was to demonstrate the malfeasance of one of the managers.

Two other documents from the archive furnish us additional clues that Beer had a fairly keen awareness of basic cost accounting. His notebook for the 1820s (item 3552) includes calculations that might today be called a breakeven analysis. Beer was cognisant of the required yield of good copper that would be required from ore in order to cover the raising and smelting costs. He advised that if the ore from particular veins did not produce sufficient good metal, that the effort be abandoned. He also did calculations on the maximums that the men could be paid to turn a profit respective to differing grades of ore.

Figure 16: Charges on Refining Copper Slags, Mona, 1822

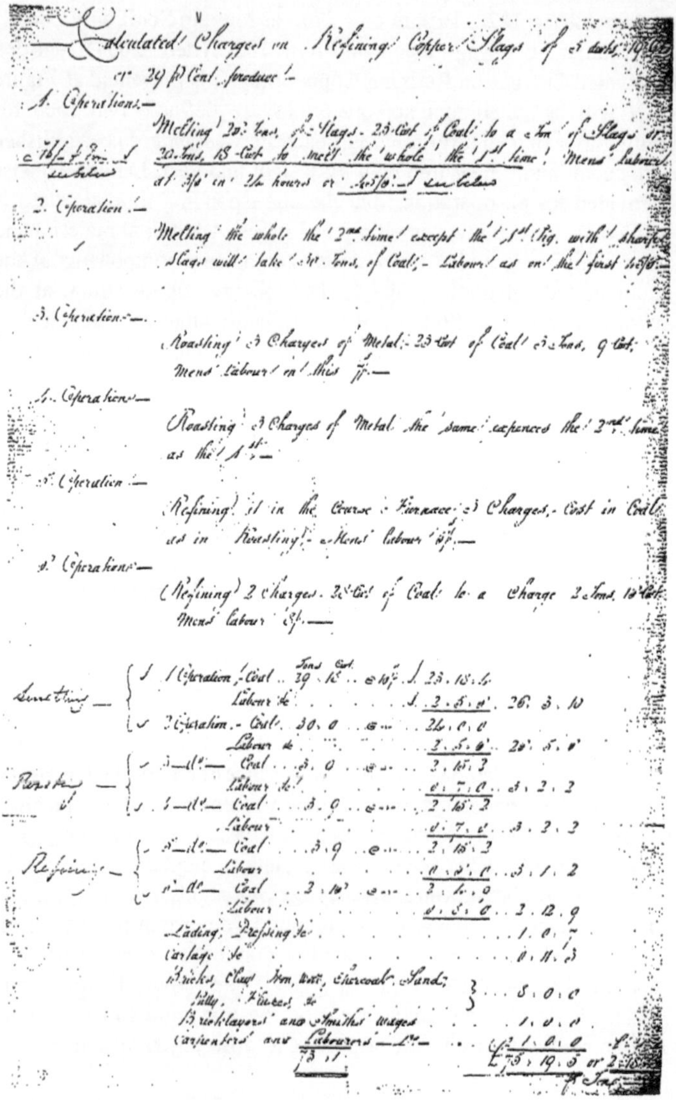

Calculated Charges on Refining Copper Slags of 5 [illegible] 19[illegible] or 29 p Cent. produce.—

1. Operations.—

Melting 20 tons of Slags – 23 Cwt of Coal to a ton of Slags or 20 Tons, 18 Cwt to melt the whole the 1st time. Mens labour at 3/6 in 24 hours or £3.5.0 – see below

2. Operation.—

Melting the whole the 2nd time except the 1st Pig with sharp Slags will take 30 Tons of Coal; – Labour as on the first £3.5.0

3. Operation.—

Roasting 3 Charges of Metal: 23 Cwt of Coal 3 tons, 9 Cwt; Mens labour on this 7/-.—

4. Operation.—

Roasting 3 Charges of Metal the same expences the 2nd time as the 1st.—

5. Operation.—

Refining it in the Course Furnace 3 Charges, Cost in Coal as in Roasting; – Mens labour 8/-.—

6. Operation.—

(Refining) 2 Charges. 28 Cwt of Coal to a Charge 2 Tons, 16 Cwt. Mens labour 5/-.—

		Tons	Cwt			
Smelting	1 Operation – Coal	39	18	@ 10/-	23.18.6	
	Labour &c				3.5.0	26.3.10
	2 Operation – Coal	30	0	@	26.0.0	
	Labour &c				3.5.0	29.5.0
Roasting	3 – do. – Coal	3	9	@	2.15.2	
	Labour &c				0.7.0	3.2.2
	4 – do. – Coal	3	9	@	2.15.2	
	Labour				0.7.0	3.2.2
Refining	5 – do. – Coal	3	9	@	2.15.2	
	Labour				0.8.0	3.1.2
	6 – do. – Coal	2	16	@	2.4.0	
	Labour				0.5.0	2.12.9
	Lading, Pressing &c					1.0.7
	Cartage &c					0.11.3
	Bricks, Clay, Iron, Ore, Charcoal, Sand; Putty, Fluxes &c					8.0.0
	Bricklayers and Smiths wages					1.0.0
	Carpenters and Labourers – do.					£1.0.0
	73 11					£73.19.5 or 2.18 [illegible] Tons

Item 3553 was a comparison of costs for selling a ton of ore at Swansea and Liverpool respectively in 1827–1828. The analysis was not differentially done; rather, there was a soup-to-nuts calculation for both venues. There are several items of interest in this costing. First of all, the application of iron and steel, powder, candles, etc. was made at 'an advance rate'. Whilst we are at a loss to know what this notation means, it was observed that any difference from actual cost would be charged to a sundry account. Apparently, standards were being used for the application of general charges to product. Second, an interest on capital was taken in the costing. Whilst this charge was typical of the period, in this instance there was an interest on capital 'during delays'.

Vivian: The Vivian enterprise encompassed copper, coal, and iron operations in various Welsh locales. Its ample archive is housed at the National Library of Wales in Aberystwyth. Unfortunately, much of the collection proved unhelpful because of its rudimentary accounting and general illegibility. The earliest record worthy of note was smelting charges at Hafod in 1817 (E109). Though this document was not exceptional in the expense items it identified, there were two distinguishing features. There was, first of all, a comparison of costs and savings respective to Anglesey and Cornish ores. Second, there were two columns that compared 1817 costs to 1816, either in a cost 'saved' or 'excess' cost category. There is an 1823 cost-per-ton calculation for the Vivian copper mines (E16), which is mostly illegible but is clearly inferior to similar records at Mona. There is also a document entitled 'Calculation of expenses of reducing copper ore at Mona Smelting House' (E56). What relationship existed between Mona and Vivian is unknown to us.

The various accounting documents notwithstanding, the most significant inclusion in the archive is a diary of H.H. Vivian, dated in the 1840s (E18). The early portion of the volume contains some random cost calculations and logging of expenses at various locales that appear fairly superficial. However, at the end there is a 'Cost of Materials and Iron made, 4 weeks ending 28 July 1849'. This report is similar to the standardised form that was coming into vogue in the South Wales iron industry during the 1840s. The Vivian example, however, was a bit more complex, reflecting perhaps the greater diversity of operations. This greater complexity related to the number and process of transfer prices and cost allocations. As we have seen in Welsh documents previously, the average actual costs per ton of coal (4/6.3), black band (5s), and mine (12/7½) became transfer prices of those raw materials to the productive departments. However, the actual cost of bar iron (£5/2) was not used as the transfer price of bar iron to sheet iron. Rather, a cost of £5/15 was transferred. General charges of £707/9/3 were allocated to five cost centres—coal works (10%), pig iron (10%), bar iron (20%), tin works (30%), copper works (30%). This percentage apportionment does not appear particularly refined by the standard of the times. The number of cost centres was comparatively small; no allocation was made to finers' metal or sheet iron; and a residual amount of £2/19/11 was allotted to the copper works in violation of the stated formula. However, there were further allocations that we have not seen in production reports of this type. The £lll/3/1 expenses of the blast engines were allocated 40% to the blast furnace and 30% each to finers' metal and the charcoal finery. The £377/14/6 cost of mill engines and machinery was apportioned one-third to puddled bars, one-third to bar iron, with no disclosure as to the disposition of the remaining third. Finally, the £444/15/1 accumulated charges of Conveyance and Shipping were allocated to all user departments at the rate of 1/1.3 per ton shipped and/or conveyed.

Sundry: There is a substantial volume of monthly raising reports for Welsh mining operations housed at the National Library. These documents are extremely sketchy and perhaps reflect the reduced accounting requirements of smaller concerns in the extractive industries. These sundry records cover a 30-year time frame and apply to various minerals, but are linked by their rudimentary nature. Objectivity dictates, however, that we report the chaff along with the wheat. Records are extant for the Nant Gwryd slate quarry (1790) (Chirk Castle 8578, 8579, 8595), the Llandidno copper mine (1799–1801) (Vigfair 2594), the Black Pool forge (1805) (Slebach 3403), Edward Rowland & Sons (1811) (coal—Chirk Castle 13774–13804; ironstone—Chirk Castle 13805–13818), Brandy Coal Company (1815–1816) (Chirk Castle 7052–7090), and Jones, Parry, and Far, coal mining (1815) (Chirk Castle 7156–7157).

In this sundry category mention might be made of the role of professional accountancy in at least one Welsh enterprise of the period,

John Nathaniel Miers & Co., a tinplate manufacturer. The firm in 1808 consulted one W. Chapman in London, presumably an accountant. He corrected the books that had been kept 'highly erroneously' since the firm's inception in 1800, putting them on a double-entry system. One of the corrections he made was to introduce the concern to 'depreciation', a term that infrequently appeared during the early stages of the Industrial Revolution (John Jenkins 178).

Thus, in Wales we found some, albeit limited, evidence of a variety of costing activities, including piece-rate records, inventory valuation, smelter depreciation, standard costing, and transfer pricing. There was also some evidence of cost comparisons between managers and ore types (by source), as well as the allocation of engine expenses to cost centres and/or products. Monthly raising reports were particularly notable for the frequency of their appearance in extant firm records.

SCOTLAND

We have seen coal-mining records for two Scottish extractive enterprises—various subsidiaries of the Lothian Coal Company, housed at West Register House, Edinburgh, and the Halbeath (also spelled Hallbeath) Colliery, a small archive located at the University of Glasgow. Though the two collections are separated chronologically by some thirty years, the earlier effort (Halbeath) reflects a significantly greater sophistication in its cost accounting.

There is an output book for the Bryans Colliery, dated 1815–1817 (CB9/30). These weekly production reports logged the output of individual colliers in tubs of great and small coals. Piece rates of 8d for great tubs and 4d for small were paid. These coals were sold for 1/6 and 8d respectively. On 1 May 1815, the selling price of great tubs was reduced 2d without explanation or corresponding decrease in piece rates. The decrease did come, but not until more than a year later, in August 1816. In 1816 as well, a data category for lime coal appeared with the same 4d piece rate as for small coal. More interestingly, beginning in 1816, the names of certain colliers were combined into a single output total. This development would suggest the advent of an internal subcontracting system.

Similar documents for Shaw's Colliery (CB9/8) and Easthouses (CB9/26) suggest their common ancestry as components of Lothian Coal. At Shaw's statistics were kept for each of the two seams in operation. These data could have been used for comparative purposes, though there is no evidence that such was ever the case. At Easthouses there was a greater variety of coals mined. Whilst the selling prices of parrot coal and great coal (lesser) reflected an 8d spread, the piece rates paid were the same. Moreover, the sales price could vary as a function of the pit from whence the coal came, but the contract price paid the hewers never did.

There is also at West Register House one remnant from Fife Coal, an 1839 report on the Denork and Claremount coal fields (CB3/303). Whilst the report does provide estimates of the coal reserves, narratives on the accessibility of various reserves, and suggestions of appropriate royalty rates, the absence of any estimated extraction costs places this analysis at a lower level than others we have seen.

By contrast, the records of the Halbeath Colliery are amongst the most sophisticated mining records in our survey. The earlier of the two volumes that constitute the archive (UGD 194/1) is a minute book. An early entry was an eight-page 'View of Halbeath Coaliery', written by John Wright in 1785 (pp. 15–23). This viewer's report was typical of those common in the Tyneside branch a half-century later. There was narrative about each of the firm's ten coal seams, the state of repair of each fire engine, the hauling capacity of the waggons, and the condition of the waggonways. Wright estimated the coal reserves in each seam, but only according to a standard volume of coal per foot of seam thickness. He did not seek to evaluate qualitative differences amongst the various seams. There is an estimate of 'winning the coaliery' over the next two years. Profit is estimated for working the colliery at a production level of one thousand tons. The cost of sinking pits is allocated to each ton mined.

Wright also has a cost estimate for improving Inverkeithing harbour (pp. 45–50). Here there is a differentiation based on whether the deepening of the channel proposed is 100 or 60 feet wide. There is for 1787 a remarkable collection of minutes, business letters, and calculations (p. 148, *passim*). The firm prepared detailed fortnightly costs of working coal, which were compared to the former period. Thomas Fiswick sent abstracts of expenses and raisings to John

Morrison Jr. These reports were accompanied by extensive commentary comparing actual results to expectations. For instance, 13 November 1787 production was below expectation because of an accident with an engine. This same John Morrison reported to John Campbell on why expenses were vastly higher in Scotland than in England. Unproductive labour was blamed (pp. 313–318).

Impressive as the contents of this minute book were, especially in light of its time frame, a second collection of documents from the early nineteenth century (UGD 194/5) far transcends the earlier material in terms of its costing. There were some interesting financial statements for Cambell & Co., a colliery whose relationship to Halbeath is unknown, for the late 1790s. The firm took depreciation (10%) on pit sinkings rather than allocate the cost to mined tonnage. There is an equivalent of an accumulated depletion account called 'deduct for use'. The firm capitalised rather than expensed repairs. In the 1799 stock taking, there were comparative amounts provided for the 1798 inventory, a touch we have not seen elsewhere.

John Crawford was identified in these papers as Halbeath's accountant. Indeed, his name was appended to notes and explanations that accompanied the firm's balance sheets and profit-and-loss statements. Some sort of an audit was performed on the books in 1799, though the auditor did not sign. The auditor did point out that Halbeath had too much cash on hand and that a loss of £20–£30 interest had been incurred thereby. Another audit, again unsigned, was performed in 1801.

This record also contains for 1802 a comparison of estimated expenses and actual disbursements for a capital project. The accounting numbers were simply set side-by-side without any explanation provided for differential amounts as we have seen at Stella a generation later. Perhaps for the only time in recorded history, the actual expenditures (£1,728) were less than the estimates (£2,024). In 1803, another report was prepared listing further expenditures on a new winning. It seems that the firm continued to track capital expenditures even when projects were essentially completed.

There are two remarkable documents contained in this collection which require elaboration at some length. The first of these was entitled 'Comparative View of the Produce and the Cost of Hallbeath coals for the years 1798 and 1799'. At the top of the record, the preparer gives production totals in tons for great coals, chews, and small coals with a total cost figure for the two years being compared. There is a note to the effect that the deficiency of production for 1799 is something more than a fifth, but that the decline in cost is only 'near 1/12th but it must be recollected that a number of the articles of charge are stationary whatever the produce may be—such as the most of the salaries'. Insights into variable and fixed cost behaviours were pretty rare during this period.

Expenses associated with the mining and marketing of coal is then provided in 31 cost categories, again comparing 1798 and 1799. To the right of these appear nine explanations for certain variances. These observations include such things as the decline in sales commissions in 1799 because of the reduced vend, changes in cost factors between the two years, and charges that should have been made in 1798 which did not hit the books until 1799. The document concludes with a note to the effect that 'the state of 1799 is not only affected by the increase of the cost, but also by the want of the profits that would have arisen from the sale of the deficiency, supposing it had not existed'.

A reproduction of this huge folio page would not fit conveniently into our allotted space. However, Figure 17 provides the expense numbers for the two years plus the explanations. Not included is a reproduction of the 31 data categories.

Another document, not reproduced here because of its substantial size, bears the lengthy title, 'View of the Loss Hallbeath Company will Sustain In the Event of Parliaments Permiting the Importation of Liverpool Salt into Scotland at the Scotch Duty—By such a Measure not only their Salt Works at Inverkeithing, but all the other Salt Works in the Firth will be annihilated, as Liverpool Salt may be Sold after being Imported at a lower price than the Manufacture of Marine Salt Costs'. The loss estimate is divided into three sections. The first lists the 'capital sunk' in the venture that 'will be rendered of little or no value and therefore should be refunded' (£1,415/8/6). Second, annual profits to the Salt Work of £443/15/8 will be lost. This number was calculated as the average for the past five years. However, it was reduced to a net amount (£246/18/2) by the subtraction of 4¼d per ton on an annual utilisation of 3,733 tons of coal that could be sold externally (£66/2/1), salaries of firm management allocated to the salt works (£60), and the 5% interest on the £1,1415/8/6 sunk capital (£70/15/5). Third, annual colliery profits of £135/10/8 would also be lost. The components here are the opportunity to use 3,424 tons of small coal at 6d per ton which

Figure 17: Expenses of Mining and Marketing, Hallbeath, 1799

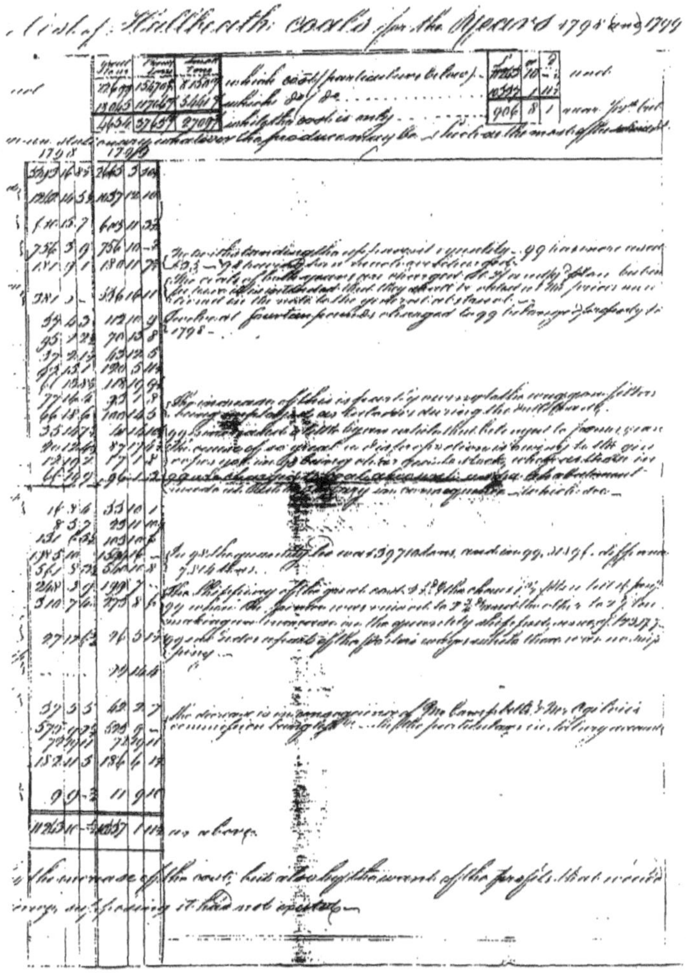

would have to be left underground as no market existed for them (£85/12/0) and the lost wages of colliers best described by the document itself:

> And by leaving these small Coal Underground which are naturally produced from the Great and chews without any extra trouble to the Collier. He will be deprived of a part of his Earning, of course will insist for an equivalent (which cannot justly be denied) by increasing the price paid for Hewing the Great and Chews, equal to the present price paid for Small, which is threepence half penny per ton, will on 3424 Tons amount to £49/18/8.

The losses to the Salt Work (£246/18/2) and the Colliery (£135/10/8) were then multiplied by five years, giving a loss of £1,912/4/2, which was then added to the £1,415/8/6 of sunk capital to provide a 'sum requested to make full Compensation' of £3,327/12/8.

Whilst this computation is impressive in its own right, another remarkable feature was the preparation of a second loss estimate wherein the £70/15/5 loss of interest on sunk capital was dropped from the calculation, but the time frame for lost revenue was extended from five to eight years, giving a bottom-line request for compensation of £3,625/14/0.

Thus, in Scottish mining there was evidence of piece-rate calculations and records once again, along with colliery output records and estimates of reserves. We also find examples of periodic costings (fortnightly) of coal extractions and comparisons of current and prior-period costs, as well as actual versus expected costs of extraction. Comparisons between years were also made for inventories, as well as between estimated and actual expenditures on capital projects.

MINING PRODUCTION

Growth in mining activity and output through the eighteenth and first half of the nineteenth century virtually mirrored that of the metal industries. Coal production grew throughout the eighteenth century due to its displacement of charcoal and an expanded canal system that could service a national market. The subsequent development of railways further stimulated the demand for both coal and iron ore (Brown, 1991; Deane & Cole, 1969; Marshall, 1973).

In extractive industries such as coal mining, progress in terms of technological change was incremental. Indeed, there was very limited opportunity for the application of new machinery in the industry during the eighteenth and early nineteenth centuries. It has been argued that Watt's steam engine was more important economically to iron manufacturers than to the extractive industries for reasons of cost (Ashton, 1948). However, the supply of coal was aided by improvements in geology throughout the eighteenth century as outcroppings became exhausted. Boring for coal helped identify new, previously undiscovered coal seams. Technological developments did assist ore extraction, particularly with regard to the removal of underground accumulations of gas and water (e.g., the Newcomen pumping engines) (Flinn, 1984).

The scale and growth of extractive industry activity is best typified by statistics pertaining to the coal-mining industry during the eighteenth and early nineteenth centuries. Table 8 provides a tabulation of production volume by region between 1700 and 1830.

Northeast England, the West Midlands, South Wales, and Lancashire emerged by 1830 as leaders in output, which totalled ten times the 1700 level. This increase was the result of a relatively steady growth rate across the entire period of approximately 2% per annum. Production almost trebled during the 1750 to 1800 period. Copper mining as well experienced a major expansion between 1748 and 1788. Cornwall was the dominant copper-mining region until 1770 when hegemony passed to the Isle of Anglesey (Deane & Cole, 1969).

WORK PRACTICES

Mines were generally the property of the owners of the land, previously arable, on which they were located. Owners drew rents and royalties from mining operations. Capital investments and operating costs were borne by lessees. Rents most usually took the form of payments based on the amounts of coal or ore removed (Ashton, 1966; Flinn, 1984).

Table 8: Estimated Output of Coal, 1700–1830, by Mining Regions (000s of tons)

Mining region	1700	1750	1775	1800	1815	1830
Scotland	450	715	1,000	2,000	2,500	3,000
Cumberland	25	350	450	500	520	560
Lancashire	80	350	900	1,400	2,800	4,000
North Wales	25	80	110	150	350	600
South Wales	80	140	650	1,700	2,750	4,400
Southwest	150	180	250	445	610	800
East Midlands	75	140	250	750	1,400	1,700
West Midlands	510	820	1,400	2,550	3,990	5,600
Yorkshire	300	500	850	1,100	1,950	2,800
Northeast	1,290	1,955	2,990	4,450	5,395	6,915
Total (tons) (tonnes)*	2,985 3,033	5,230 5,314	8,850 8,992	15,045 15,286	22,265 22,621	30,376 30,861
Annual compounded rate of growth (%)	1.13	2.13	2.15	2.65	2.09	

Source: Flinn (1984), p. 26

In many coal fields working miners formed themselves into companies of 6 to 12 men which undertook excavations under contract to mine lessees (Ashton, 1966). However, work organisation in collieries varied somewhat across regions. In many collieries the lessee or owner actually managed the mining operations personally. In Scotland the colliery was generally supervised by a manager (also known as overseer or oversman). In North Wales, the West Midlands, and Yorkshire, there was a shortage of educated men for carrying out clerical and administrative roles. Consequently, the owner's agent was responsible for accounting and sales, whilst a subcontractor (charter-master*) supervised labour. Whilst managers controlled the daily operations of collieries, as already mentioned in this chapter, viewers provided advice on technical matters and directed such major activities as colliery design, construction, and development. Thus, a professional class of managerial experts gradually developed in the vicinities of the collieries (Flinn, 1984).

As the demand for coal grew in the eighteenth century, wages rose, as did premiums paid to secure new workers. The major problem remained one of securing an adequate supply of labour. Most inventions were aimed at facilitating the process by which the work of experienced miners could be taken over by boys and youths. By the 1780s, miners (pitsmen) achieved sufficiently high wages to allow them to rescue their women and daughters from underground mining work, although young boys continued to work in the mines. Nevertheless, in parts of England and Wales, there continued to be numerous incidences of women working underground (Ashton, 1966).

ECONOMICS OF MINING

Flinn's (1984) study of the British coal industry provides us with further insights into the financing and economics of the industry during the eighteenth and early nineteenth centuries. British mining law conferred upon the owner of land the mining rights to coal that was discovered beneath. Oftentimes coal-mining landowners formed investment partnerships in order to finance the expensive capital requirements for commencing and maintaining mining operations. When capital requirements were greater than the personal financial resources of the group, the partnership was extended to include other classes of individuals, such as lawyers, clergymen, merchants, industrialists, bankers, ship captains, other landowners, and colliery managers. Other sources of these funds for capital expenditure included reinvested mining profits and rents derived from agricultural land. As the scale of mining grew, its capital requirements began to outstrip even the resources of these extended partnerships. Thus, joint-stock mining companies began to appear by the 1820s.

The profitability of mining enterprises tended to fluctuate considerably in the short run and seemed unrelated to trade cycle variations. In the longer term, however, profitability levels were generally maintained at a constantly high level (Flinn, 1984). Local geological conditions and partnership investment circumstances had more impact on individual mine profitability than trade cycles. Profits from a mine were also affected by coal prices, which fluctuated widely as demonstrated in Table 9:

Table 9: Index of Coal Prices, 1700–1830 (1770–1779 = 100)

1700	74.8	1770	98.5
1710	91.8	1780	108.5
1720	80.2	1790	105.5
1730	84.7	1800	122.6
1740	87.4	1810	152.9
1750	80.9	1820	140.3
1760	99.4	1830	127.5

Source: Flinn, 1984, pp. 303–304.

Some indication of mine profitability is provided in Table 10, where Flinn (1984) offered calculations of profit (actual or estimated) as a percentage of 'total costs' for a number of collieries, in particular years between 1717 and 1830 for which records were accessible. These data illustrate the widely divergent profitability of collieries, but at the same time suggest the very handsome returns that could be achieved in some instances. Flinn's calculations must be qualified, as he himself observes, by the vagaries of variant costing practices employed at different mining establishments. He observed that differences included, amongst others, a lack of distinction between capital and current costs, the omission of allowances for depreciation, a lack of precision in measuring capital costs, and differing procedures for accounting for coal internally consumed.

Table 10: Rates of Profit, Selected Collieries, Isolated Years, 1717–1830 (profits as percentages of total costs)

Year	Colliery	Mining region	Actual (A) or estimated (E) profit	Rate of profit
1717	Fenham	NE	E	22.7
1720	Bucksnook	NE	A	3.6
1740	Elswick	NE	E	13.6
1743-8	Cowclose	NE	A	16.8
1752-3	Geo. Weld's	W. Mids.	A	43.3
1773	Bransty	Cumb.	A	30.1
1773	Sheffield Park	Yorks.	A	13.1
1779-92	Ardeers	Scot.	A	21.9
1783-5	Coalpitheath	SW	A	49.2
1783-98	Misk	Scot.	A	4.2
1786	Gateshead Park	NE	E	35.3
1787	Sheriff Hill	NE	E	17.3
1790	St. Anthony's	NE	E	54.0
1795	Pontop Pike	NE	A	30.9
1799-1800	Vane-Tempest collieries	NE	A	39.6
1801	Elvet	NE	E	24.9
1801	Hardy	E. Mids.	A	10.0
1801	Cowpen	NE	E	39.1
1803	West Denton	NE	E	7.8
1803	Willington	NE	E	43.5
1804	Sheriff Hill	NE	E	33.2

Year	Colliery	Mining region	Actual (A) or estimated (E) profit	Rate of profit
1804-9	Heanor	E. Mids.	A	56.5
1806	Felling and Carr's Hill	NE	E	33.3
1807	Heaton	NE	A	34.2
1808	Hewerhill	NE	A	48.0
1811	Alfreton	E. Mids.	E	30.2
1811	Felling	NE	E	30.0
1815	Robert Town	Yorks.	E	0.4
1815	Newbottle	NE	E	26.9
1816	Rothwell Haigh	Yorks.	E	14.4
1816	Flockton	Yorks.	E	54.5
1817-18	Jarrow	NE	A	19.5
1818	Burtonholm	Lancs.	E	52.8
1818-20	Cowpen	NE	A	10.9
1823	Hetton	NE	E	32.1
1824-8	Tanfield Moor	NE	A	32.5
1825-30	Towneley and Whitefield	NE	A	24.3
1826	Wylam	NE	E	12.6
1827	Hetton	NE	E	36.4
1829	Hetton	NE	A	50.2
1830	North Hetton	NE	A	19.2

Source: Flinn (1984), pp. 324–325

ENVIRONMENT AND PRACTICE

The scale and growth of mining activity and output, particularly during the second half of the eighteenth century and early decades of the nineteenth century, almost certainly provided the general background scenario conducive to the maintenance of detailed statistical records of operations and related costs for production, output, distribution, pricing, employee numbers, periodic extractions, raisings, and productivity. We see evidence of these data in the mining records of the Tyneside, Northwest England, and Scottish regions.

Given the restricted sources of finance and the major financial resourcing demands caused by the capital expenditures involved in mining, the attention to mine viability assessments shown in records from the Tyneside, Scottish, and Northwest England regions is understandable. These analyses included estimates of coal/mineral reserves, production and profitability potential of mining leases, and costing calculations for mine expansion and abandonment proposals.

An accumulation of capital based on the financial resources of owners and partners explains the close attention paid to capital expenditure assessment. We find evidence of cost estimates for proposed capital expenditures, pit sinking cost estimates, and estimated versus actual capital expenditure monitoring in all the above-mentioned regions. Given the potential for outdistancing available capital funds, capital expenditures did appear to warrant careful owner scrutiny.

Fluctuating profitability, particularly in the short term, occasioned by such factors as geological variation, fluctuating output prices, and doubtlessly other factors appear to have mandated attention to control of operating costs. We find a variety of approaches to exercising that control, including detailed cost comparisons relating to different ore types, managers, alternative extraction methods, engine coal consumption, motive power sources, and current versus prior-period comparisons of extraction costs and inventory costs. This attention was reflected in the mining records of the Welsh, Tyneside, and Scottish regions. Evidence of standard costing and pricing, as well as actual versus expected extraction costings, was found in mines of all these regions, as well as Northwest England.

With respect to labour, whilst piece-rate calculations and records were identified in the Scottish, Welsh, and Northwest England regions, little evidence (other than in the Tyneside: Newcastle region) of any detailed attention to labour cost control, particularly at the individual worker level, could be found. Given the rising national demand for coal and iron ore, the difficulty in securing new mine workers, and the rising wages of the late eighteenth century, this lack of attention is somewhat curious. In part, this apparent neglect may be explained by the dominant concern of mine owners with financing and controlling the ongoing capital expenditures required by mining operations. Thus, related statistical calculations, record keeping, and associated costings, particularly given the apparent scarcity of personnel with the expertise to carry out such accountings, may have consumed most of the available time for operational control. Hence, labour cost controls, despite the pressure on labour supply, may of necessity have been accorded lesser attention.

Finally, it is worthy of mention that in comparison to the iron industry, mining exhibited somewhat less evidence of attention to detailed cost estimates and comparisons between new and older technology. This pattern probably reflected the slower, more incremental rate of technological change in the mining industry during the period under review.

POSTSCRIPT

As indicated in the introduction to this chapter, we have found a hitherto uncharted wealth of evidence pointing to an active tradition of cost management and control in the Industrial Revolution mining industry. That having been said, it would be remiss of us not to acknowledge the considerable variability in detail, accuracy, and sophistication of cost accounting and cost management records now extant. They vary from what contemporary accountants would regard as extremely primitive to those exhibiting many costing system characteristics that we would recognise and employ today. Particularly notable also is the combination of continuous control information and special decision information generated, as well as the physical operating statistics and financial indicators employed. It suggests an appreciation of the value of a total (financial and operational) control approach only now being rediscovered by contemporary advocates of total quality management.

GLOSSARY

cannel:	a hard variety of coal principally mined in Lancashire
chaldron:	a variable weight, 53 cwt. in Newcastle
charter-master:	a subcontractor who supplied the labour necessary to extract coal and raise it to the surface
corf (corve):	a measure of capacity, varying between 16 and 20 pecks
cribbing:	a temporary wooden lining to a shaft, subsequently replaced by tubbing
hewer (hewing):	a miner who cuts coal from the face
leading:	carriage by horse-drawn cart
putter (putting):	an underground hauler of coal by any form of transport
staith:	a quay for transferring coal from a waggonway to a keel, generally with coal storage facilities
ten:	a variable measure of coal, typically 50 tons approximately
ton:	2,240 lbs.
tonne:	1,000 kilograms
tubbing:	shaft lining made with wood, bricks, stone, or cast iron
vend:	quantity of coal marketed either by individual collieries or by all
viewer:	a mine manager or consultant engineer
waggonway:	a railway for horse-drawn waggons using rectangular wooden (later iron) rails
wayleave:	a right to cross land in another's ownership for the purpose of transporting coal
win (winning):	to prepare a shaft for the extraction of coal

NOTES

1. The first appearance of certain mining industry terms, indicated in the narrative with an asterisk, are defined in the glossary on page 167. Definitions are abstracted from Flinn (1984, pp. 458–462).

6

Carron Company: A Case Study[1]

The case study which follows traces the eighteenth century activities of the Carron Company, a firm that utilised superior cost management during the Industrial Revolution. Compared to other large firms in the iron industry, there are more extant records for Carron, though substantially less than a complete file. Cost accounting researchers are fortunate in that there is a plentiful supply of production reports, mineral field estimates, and minute books—those types of records that are so much more helpful for our purposes than financial accounting survivals. The Carron partners met semi-annually in London (referenced General Court), and those who happened to be in the vicinity of Carron convened monthly at the works (referenced Monthly). The bulk of this archival material is located at West Register House, Edinburgh. Since Carron was absentee-owned during its early years, a flow of correspondence rich in costing data for decision-making purposes passed between Scotland and Birmingham. These letters are contained in the Cadell papers at the National Library of Scotland, Edinburgh. The history of the Carron Company during the Industrial Revolution can be divided into two distinct periods. From the initial founding of the firm in 1759 through 1786, a substantial volume of business records survive. One of the original three founders, William Cadell, was the manager-in-residence at Carron. However, the real power in the firm was Samuel Garbett, a Birmingham inhabitant. The correspondence between the two was lively, though most communications from Cadell have not survived. In 1769, Charles Gascoigne became general manager at Carron, but the information continued to flow because the General Court remained a committed, involved group that was interested in participating in the firm's management.

As the company entered its second phase, Joseph Stainton (1786–1825) and Joseph Dawson (1825–1850) ruled the firm with an iron hand, soliciting virtually no input from the other owners.

Consequently, there developed a serious shortage of those types of records that provide useful information about costing methods and analysis. This declining evidence of managerial accounting is not atypical as many Industrial Revolution enterprises aged, and supports our contention that the dynamic founders may have provided the motivational spark. Sophisticated costing often did not survive them. Also, an early British talent for cost accounting may have been lost during mid-Victorian times due to the dearth of a literature, the decline of British managerial acumen (Elbaum & Lazonick, 1984), and the limiting influence of entrenched family capitalism (Chandler, 1984).

Campbell's definitive firm history of Carron appeared in 1961. Campbell was aware of the firm's accounting methods, though his focus was more oriented toward the physical plant, products, markets, finances, and partnership arrangements. Notwithstanding, we were fortunate to have had this resource as a point of reference.

CARRON'S ECONOMIC AND INDUSTRIAL ENVIRONMENT

Carron Company began operations as a pioneer iron foundry in Scotland in 1759. The company was formed by a Scot, William Cadell, and two Birmingham industrialists, Samuel Garbett and John Roebuck. Carron was the first company to utilise ironstone from central Scotland and the first in Scotland to smelt iron with coke. It was the largest early Scottish operation of its type as evidenced by its physical dimensions. Carron product lines ranged from single-cast iron products (pots and girdles) to ordnance, and included cast iron work for machinery, water pipes, grates, and fireplaces.

The early operation of Carron combined underutilised Scottish mineral resources with English skill and capital. The active founding partners and subsequent early proprietors of the enterprise reflected a general typology of eighteenth century British industrialists—outsiders possessing cash, energy, and organisational talent, but without any particular expertise or experience in the industry they were entering. Roebuck was a medical practitioner in Birmingham with an interest in chemistry. He had opened a laboratory and sulphuric acid plant with Garbett, a prominent merchant and businessman. Cadell was a merchant in Cockenzie who traded iron and timber on the Continent and built his own ships for that purpose (Hamilton, 1928).

Carron Company had severe capitalisation problems in its early years because construction costs far outstripped anticipated amounts. Consequently, between the years 1760 and 1772, five individual partners (original and other subsequent entrants) and two associated private banks suffered bankruptcy or severe financial embarrassment. The company had to resort to desperate financial strategies to maintain liquidity, including private bank loans, drafts, lines of credit, and sundry debts (Campbell, 1961).[2] The continuing financial problems of Carron over the 1760–1778 period were so severe that the company was fortunate to survive at all. This situation was complicated by early technical problems, such as cylinder-boring inaccuracy and ordnance malfunctions. The development of the Carronade cannon during the American War for Independence remedied Carron's long-standing financial difficulties and ensured its future survival.

Eighteenth century English society conferred respectability upon both landowner and merchant. The latter group particularly benefitted from increased involvement in manufacturing activities. A new class of capitalists arose in this period which encouraged inventiveness and business initiative. New industrial discoveries were exploited by businessmen drawn from the middle ranks of society. In partnership with inventors, these businessmen applied their capital, business acumen, and personal networks to promote a British transition from trade to industry (Briggs, 1959). The early proprietors of Carron fitted this mould.

Though born of a pre-existing mercantile network, most of the new industrial enterprises were small and highly localised. Carron Company was an atypically large Scottish industrial undertaking, though self-contained between Stirling and Edinburgh. It marked the commencement of large-scale production in an industry that had previously been pursued only sporadically in Scotland. Even then, it was largely supported by English knowledge and capital (Briggs, 1959; Mackie, 1964).

Carron played an important role in the industrial transformation of Scotland. Natural coal resources were available to support a new technology in iron manufacturing, which included smelting with coke instead of charcoal and the utilisation of hot-air instead of cold-air blast in furnaces, allowing for the use of rich Scottish blackband iron ore.

Whilst most Carron Company land was held for building purposes before 1786, the firm purchased land subsequently to ensure supplies of raw materials and to avoid disputes with landowners over mining damage (Campbell, 1961, 1980). A new link was forged between the fortunes of the coal and iron industries. The iron industry needed to be close to its raw materials and massed along the coal fields. The relationship between coal and iron was further cemented by the development of steam as the motive power in factories. This liaison heralded a period of considerable technological change in smelting, the puddling process for making bar iron, and steam power. Carron became the founding firm of the Scottish iron industry by virtue of its situation at a location where water power, coal, and iron were available together.

Securing adequate labour was also difficult for eighteenth century industry. The problem was evident in coal mining, for example, where the enforcement of the Scottish collier's serfdom did not cease finally until 1799. Carron responded to labour shortages by resorting to English miners at its own Quarole and Kinnaird coal fields (Campbell, 1961). Carron also endured inefficient labour, both in mines and furnaces. At one point in its early years, output only increased after the dismissal of certain inept furnace keepers (Campbell, 1961, 1980). Such problems presented eighteenth century industrialists the challenges of accumulating fixed capital, speeding production and distribution, securing adequate working capital, and managing both men and machines. A wide range of new management skills was necessary for success (Briggs, 1959).

The iron industry grew in prominence with a massive rise in pig iron exports in the second half of the eighteenth century. The Napoleonic Wars of 1792–1802 occasioned a period of prosperity, with high levels of ordnance production at Woolwich, Enfield, and Carron. Iron sales were also stimulated by import limitations on iron supplies from Sweden and the Baltic, as well as by the growing number of commercial uses of iron (ibid.). As a specialist iron producer, Carron faced different marketing conditions from generalist producers of coal or iron. The specialist market was characterised by product differentiation, which ran the risk that a market could suddenly be lost if the differentiated product was superseded in quality or type (Campbell, 1980). In Carron's case the founding partners were willing to experiment with new methods and technologies and thereby gained notoriety in Europe for innovation. By 1786, with this reputation established, experimentation declined. Carron's production of ordnance and shot became highly profitable during the American and Napoleonic Wars, as well as through peacetime sales to the East India Company and foreign governments (Campbell, 1961).

COST MANAGEMENT AT CARRON BEFORE 1800

The Carron Company records reveal plentiful examples of cost management, mostly centred in the 1759–1786 period during which time Cadell, Garbett, and Gascoigne were at the helm. From its first year of operations, the firm was committed to conscientious record keeping as evidenced by a page from the Quarole coal account (GD 58/14/1), presented as Figure 18. Carron's financial statements were in disarray during these early years, despite the bountiful data on departmental costs. The firm's founders had great difficulty coping adequately with depreciation, inventory valuation, and the owners' capital accounts. Consequently, an interesting paradox arose. Prior to 1786, the Carron records reflected correct instincts about cost accounting methodology, but they failed utterly to integrate costing with acceptable financial reporting. This shortcoming of Industrial Revolution accounting has been highlighted by subsequent observers (Chatfield, 1977; Garcke & Fells, 1887). As the financial reporting improved post-1786, evidence of this costing sophistication disappeared, but perhaps only as a function of the paucity of surviving records during the administrations of Stainton and Dawson.

EXPENSE CONTROL

Consistent with the financial exigencies Carron Company experienced in its early years, its business records and partnership correspondence evidence an acute concern over the need to control operating expenses. It was a company convention, dating from 1764, that any capital improvement of 10s or more required approval by a partner, and one in excess of £20 had to be submitted for estimates and considered by all partners (General Court, GD 58/2/1/1, p. 89). In 1764,

Figure 18: Quarole Coal Account, Carron, 1759

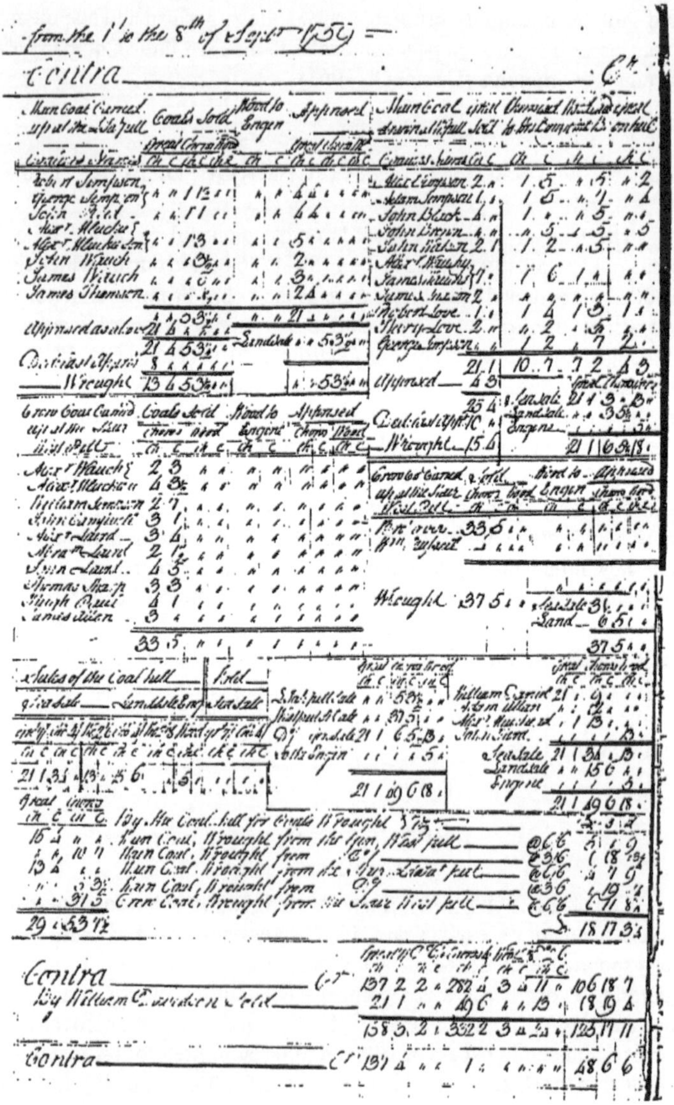

a General Court meeting of the Carron partners resolved to avoid every oncost (indirect) expense not absolutely necessary (ibid., p. 157). Such concerns were reiterated by Cadell in a letter to Garbett, dated 14 October 1767: '...I do most heartily wish to see the utmost attention and economy established in every part of this undertaking...' (Cadell, ACC 5381, Box 28, Folder 1). Referring to the paucity of the firm's capital investment, Cadell again wrote to Garbett on 16 March 1768, calling for every expense to be monitored with the 'utmost parsimony' due to the company's capital deficiency (ibid.). This early concern with levels of expenditures was further demonstrated by the presentation to a 1763 General Court meeting of a detailed set of manufacturing costs for all products (General Court, GD 58/2/1/1, pp. 73–78). Additional available statistics appear to have prompted a letter of 4 July 1766 from Garbett to Cadell, drawing attention to the high levels of metal waste in the air furnaces (Cadell, ACC 5381, Box 28, Folder 1). An expense book for the Quarole Colliery for 1770–1772 (GD 58/14/2) contained receipts signed by recipients of cash with details of how the expense was incurred, alongside a classification of the expenditures into such categories as cost of coal carriage; repairs to houses; repairs to waggons; and oncosts of the raised coal with respect to pits and levels, fire engine, and incidentals. At times there is evidence that Carron's management moved forcefully to institute control mechanisms over expenditures. General Court resolution No. 799 (1778) mandated the use of pay tickets, a control device to track labour costs for all work done at Carron's manufactories and collieries (General Court, GD 58/2/2/1/, p. 165). There were several references in the accounts to deductions from wages for the production of defective output or the failure to account adequately for raw materials disbursed (GD 58/14/2).

RESPONSIBILITY MANAGEMENT

Carron Company pursued a policy of attributing responsibility for cost management to individual managers and departments at a very early stage in its history. In 1765, separate accounts were established for the blacksmith's operation and the plating forge in order to evaluate anchor and anvil production more accurately (General Court, GD 58/2/1/1/, p. 171). Reference to this area of the business occurred again in October 1778 when resolution No. 798 of the General Court requested Gascoigne and a manager named Ambrose Tibbats to investigate and report back on the operations of the plating forge since it had been exhibiting unsatisfactory levels of profit (General Court, GD 58/2/2/1, p. 165). In a letter dated 8 May 1766, Garbett urged Cadell to place the different branches of the business completely on the shoulders of their superintendents for better or worse, 'glory or ignominy', as a function of branch performance (Cadell, ACC 5381, Box 28, Folder 1). Resolution No. 509 (1771) of the General Court went even further, mandating position and performance statements for each department head (General Court, GD 58/6/4/2).

That such intentions were acted upon is suggested by an exchange of letters between Cadell and Garbett noting production shortfalls in the period 1766–1767 and holding the relevant manager, one Mr Mathews, responsible for 'shocking management' (Cadell, ACC 5381, Box 28, Folder 1). In 1769, a representation to the General Court urged the appointment of a powerful general manager at Carron so as to examine more forcefully the causes and effects of unprofitable branches of the firm's operation (GD 58/4/1/1, p. 11). Again, in 1771, there was reference to an examination of every individual branch of trade that had apparently been undertaken, although no results were disclosed (General Court, GD 58/2/1/1, pp. 396–397).

Even in the earliest years, responsibilities were clearly delineated at Carron. Cadell took charge of mineral and raw material supply; Tibbats controlled the air furnaces; and Thomas Roebuck, brother of John, supervised manufacturing generally. Roebuck tabulated the performance of different branches, especially the furnaces, and then planned output (Campbell, 1961). Each department head had to demonstrate profitability in order for operations to continue. Periodic evaluations of this type resulted in the discontinuation of the nail trade and its sale to the Cadell family (ibid.).

OVERHEAD ALLOCATION

The resolutions of the General Court over the 1763–1774 period included a number of clear directives with regard to the treatment of overhead costs. A 1763 pronouncement required that the costs of all goods produced at Carron should include applied overhead (General Court, GD 58/2/1/1, pp. 63, 73–78). In 1771, the minutes contained data on apparent losses showing in the accounts of the air furnaces and the plating forge caused by an excessive allocation of general overhead costs. Accordingly, £1,485/10/10 from the air furnaces and £5,000 from the plating forge were charged to the blast furnace account (ibid., p. 398). This large-scale adjustment is disconcerting because it may have represented a cosmetic effort on the part of management to mask operating losses. Alternatively, it may have reflected a significant misestimation of the allocation base. However, the point must be underscored that *ex post* calculations were being made during a period when the bulk of decisions based on accounting numbers were *ex ante*.

Direct evidence of the distribution of overhead costs based on a predetermined formula is forthcoming from an allocation process utilised in 1763. Overhead (called 'general charges'), estimated at £2,000, was allocated to departments in the following proportions: blast furnaces 18/32; air furnaces 3/32; forge 4/32; plating and balling forges 2/32; slit mill 3/32; filling goods, grinding mill, and finishing goods 1/32; and nailery 1/32 (ibid., p. 63). The basis of this apportionment was not disclosed in the minutes. However, it is clear from numbers Cadell generated for the budgeting of revenues and expenses for the various departments the year before that the allocation was not linked to revenues, expenses, or profits.

Six years later the General Court decided to restrict the variety of expenses charged to the overhead account by specifying that there would be no further inclusion in 'general charges' of rents, water expenses, construction charges, interest on capital, repairs, and salaries. Unfortunately, the records are silent as to which expenses continued to be allocated or why the decision was made to charge specific departments actual costs when items such as rent, water, and repairs are appropriately handled as common costs (Monthly, GD 58/2/3/1, p. 16).

It is therefore clear that a basic system of overhead cost allocation to departments was in place very early in Carron's history. Not only was it considered in departmental performance evaluations, but on some occasions the impact of excessive allocations on department profitability was apparently recognised.

COST COMPARISONS AND TRANSFERS

Examination of Carron's ironstone reports in the years 1770–1772 revealed a detailed system of cost estimates and intracompany charges. The firm's accountant, William Lowes, provided detailed monthly reports that attempted to coordinate output from the fields with furnace consumption. The left-hand side contained Lowes' report, calculations, and suggested charge to the furnaces for ironstone supplied. The right-hand side showed a partner's approval and any instructions:

Expenses of raising, leading, weighing Oncost of 3,232 tons last six months at Banton	£928/6/3½	This calculation is very proper and satisfactory and it is wished that Mr Lowes would continue to
Nearly per ton	5/9	make investigations of the other veins of stones in the same manner. We also wish that Mr
Royalty, Inspection and Surface damages	1/6	Lowes will give us information from time to time of any new fields of Iron Stone that may
Carriage to Carron	4/7½	occur to him, in the course of his enquirys.
It appears this stone should not be charged less than 12/- to the Furnaces.	11/10½	

(signed) Wm. Lowes

Lowes also calculated ironstone reserves in the various fields, providing estimates of how long each would last at current levels of consumption. It was his recommendation that minimally a six-month's supply be maintained in inventory as a contingency measure (GD 58/6/4/1).

A most impressive comparison of costs at various ironstone fields was prepared by John Beaumont, an unidentified analyst, in September 1770. Bottom-line costs at sundry venues were comprised of field-specific costings for raising the ironstone, royalties, inspection, repairs, transport, and weighing. There was also commentary on the quantity of reserves in each location, the quality potential of the different types of ironstone, and the reasons for the substantial price differentials at the various quarries (Cadell, ACC 5381, Box 28, Folder 2).

The ironstone reports (GD 58/2/4/1) also included detailed cost comparisons of producing a ton of metal with differing types of ironstone. Figure 19 is a representation of one such report. Columns 1–3 provide yield data on the weight of ironstone required to produce a ton of iron; column 4 establishes the transfer price to the furnaces; and column 5 the cost per ton of metal, utilising the various types of ore. Though this particular example does not identify specific problems, the Rosyth field was subsequently abandoned as a result of similar comparisons. When expenses at the Banton works became higher than at other fields, an investigatory visit was undertaken by Gascoigne and William Cadell Jr.

In the 1790s, William Benson, the blast furnace supervisor, was transmitting monthly cost comparisons of his operation to the partners. These reports were calculations of cost per ton of good iron at each blast furnace. They were accompanied by notes explaining why production might be down either generally or at a particular blast furnace. Causes cited included bad weather, water level, manpower shortages, equipment breakdowns, downtime for repairs, and differential productive potentials of individual furnaces (GD 58/6/4/4).

These examples of cost comparisons and cost transfers were consistent with the Carron practice of departmental cost management already observed. As early as 1769, some implications were spelled out in a report to the partners entitled 'A Short View of the Affairs of Carron Company'. The author, identified only as Mr Wilson, called for the following practice and objective:

> ...keeping the Co. Transactions in their Books, under such Form, as (upon a comparison with other Works) may be most readily and accurately seen, not only what each of the various Branches turn out, but also in what Parts of these Branches, we are on a footing with our Rivals.
>
> On this Comparison the Gentlemen will be enabled to see the End of each Object in pursuit, discover where our Advantage lyes in our Profitable Articles, and our Loss in the Unfavourable ones; and in the last discern whether such Loss can be removed or not...(GD 58/4/1/1, p. 25)

Figure 19: Ironstone Quantity and Cost Report, Carron, 1772

A Comparative View of the Average Produce of the Ore & Ironstone in Use at Carron, the Quantity of raw & roasted Stone required to make a Ton of Metal of each, & the Expence; likewise the Prices at which the different Mines should be rated to the Furnaces to make Ironstone a saving Account

	To produce a Ton Metal.			Prices to the Furnaces.	Expence of a Ton of Metal from each.
	Average Produce per Cent.	roasted. T. H. Q.	raw. T. H. Q.		
West Glen Banton 1 & 2	51	1.19..	2.18.2	£ .. 12.6	£1.16.6
East Glen Ditto Veins 1.2.3 6.7.8 & 9.	40	2.10..	3.15..	.. 12.6	2.6.10
Bonnyhill	55	1.16..	2.14..	.. 13.6	1.16.5
Brightons & Madistone	42	2.7..	3.10.2	.. 11.6	2.0.6
Dysarts Veins & Niccol No. 5	36	2.15..	4.2.2	.. 11..	2.5.4
Pitfirrane	50	2.. ..	3..	.. 10.6	1.11.6
Castleranky Veins	34	2.18..	4.7..	.. 9.6	2.1.4
Rosyth	38	2.12..	3.18..	.. 8..	1.10.2
Limekilns Ball Stone	31	3.4..	4.16..	.. 9..	2.3.2
Pitreavie Ditto	37	2.14..	4.1..	.. 9..	1.16.5
West Plain	49	2.. 3	3.1..	.. 6.3	.. 19..
Stone gathered on the Coast	36	2.15..	4.2.2	.. 6..	1.4.9
Lancashire Ore	56	.. ..	1.15..	1.5..	2.3.9

COSTS FOR DECISION MAKING

Costs were frequently compiled for a wide range of management actions at Carron, most notably for product line decisions. The company withdrew from the anchor trade in 1769 because sales did not cover the £4 paid weekly to anchor workers, even though this production afforded the company the opportunity to use its poorer quality iron (Monthly, GD 58/2/3/1, p. 7). In the same year Mr Mathews calculated that every ton of charcoal iron made at the forge cost 16/10 and was inferior to Russian iron that could be purchased for 14/10 per ton (ibid., p. 15). Accordingly, he advised that Carron discontinue charcoal forging. In his 1769 missive to the partners, Mr Wilson recommended that air furnaces be discontinued in favour of blast furnaces, arguing that:

> I am humbly of opinion that every Article cast at them, which possibly can be cast from the Blast however they may swell up the Profit of the Air Furnaces, are to the Company a Loss, of the difference between what they could be cast for at the Blast Furnaces and are cast for at the Air Furnaces—waste of metal and Reputation of the Quality of the Good included (GD 58/4/1/1/, p. 54).

As we have seen, the nail trade was aborted on the basis of an unfavourable cost evaluation. In 1770, the partners passed a resolution to undertake cost analyses of the plating forge and blacksmith branches to determine whether they should be abandoned (General Court, GD 58/2/1/1, p. 270). The next year each division of the company was scrutinised similarly (ibid., pp. 396–397). Unfortunately, the minutes do not reveal the results of these investigations.

A variety of decisions appear to have been made on the basis of cost information. The 1763 minute book reported John Roebuck's estimates of how the use of particular varieties of coals would impact production (ibid., pp. 44–45). The firm in 1769 subcontracted road repairs at Carron on the basis of cost estimates (Monthly, GD 58/2/3/1, p. 23). In the early 1770s, Lowes compared two managers of ironstone quarrying based on their respective output costs (GD 58/6/4/1). (Bailey's operation cost 11/7 per ton, whilst Roper's was considerably more efficient at 8/6.) In 1786, a decision was made to repair a blacking kiln based on a cost/benefit analysis (Monthly, GD 58/2/3/3, pp. 37–38). In 1789, the partners were presented with a proposal to blow-out and repair No. 2 blast furnace, based on a report prepared by the general manager (ibid., pp. 185–186).

Late eighteenth century cost decisions were frequently made on the procurement and repair of steam engines. In 1767, the partners exchanged correspondence on the need to purchase a steam engine, although Garbett was hesitant (Cadell, ACC 5381, Box 28, Folder 1). In 1769, analysis revealed an engine's efficiency could be improved for a cost of £60 (Monthly, GD 58/2/3/1, p. 15). This expenditure was approved by the partners. In 1770, a sophisticated costing of the Kinnaird coal field engine included estimated downtime (Cadell, ACC 5381, Box 29, Folder 1).

A detailed technological and cost analysis of the potential for improving the extraction and profitability of Kinnaird coal was prepared in 1768. Based on an experiment conducted in the presence of Cadell, time-and-motion measurements were made on the coal extraction necessary to fill one waggon. Based on the experiment, costs for workmen and other labour inputs were estimated. Waggonloads of output were forecasted from the use of 6 bullocks, 6 days a week. The expenses of labour, bullocks, engine, carriage, rent, and oncosts were totalled and compared with the anticipated revenues from target output. It was calculated that:

1. 2½ yards of coal 30 inches broad produced 1 waggon of Great-Coal.
2. Each pit comprised 3 sets of workmen.
3. Each workman was to turn out 30 yards per day.
4. At these output levels, the total cost of holers, overseers, drivers, pithorses, bottomer, barksman, candles, baskets, ropes, etc., was estimated to be £1/14/0 for 12 waggons.
5. On the basis of 6 bullocks hauling 12 waggons per day each for 6 days, total costs were calculated to be £154/8/0.
6. Subtracting total cost of £154/8/0 from target revenue of £229/15/0 showed a profit of £75/7/0.

The above analysis was declared to 'make Kinnaird a very agreeable objective'. In order to achieve this profit target, a series of input and cost standards was established (Cadell, ACC 5381, Box 28, Folder 1).

Because the cost of coal production was so vital to Carron's profitability, the General Court put to John Beaumont 13 queries which were answered in a 1770 report. The response contained estimates of the coal reserves in various fields, lands belonging not only to the company but to neighbouring owners as well. Beaumont calculated an estimated cost per waggonload of raising a ton of coal in each field. There was also a cost analysis of a proposal to sink the engine pit three fathoms to make deeper coal seams available for raising. Most remarkable, however, was a detailed production analysis comparing costs at current extraction levels to half the usual volume. Expenses considered in the comparison were quite all-encompassing, including royalties, road tolls, surface damage repair, waggon and waggonway repair. The calculation concluded that at current levels of production, the coal-mining operation would enjoy a transfer price gain of £1,051/10, whilst the proposed halving of operations would result in a £303 loss (Cadell, ACC 5381, Box 28, Folder 2). Though the terms were not actually used, this type of analysis reflected an awareness of the differences between fixed and variable costs.

Carron frequently solicited cost estimates from John Smeaton, next to James Watt the most famous engineer of the Industrial Revolution. In 1769 alone, there were projections of expenses associated with a new wheel shaft for No. 3 blast furnace, a new boring mill, and the power requirements to raise water to the furnaces (Monthly, GD 58/2/3/1, p. 26).

BUDGETS, FORECASTS, AND STANDARDS

From its earliest days, Carron utilised standard costs, as well as sporadic forecasting and budgeting attempts, in its management information system. The data we have seen in Figure 19 became the basis for transfer prices and inventory standards. Similarly, Figure 20 is a report of weekly output, raw materials consumed, and wages paid at the five blast furnaces functioning in the 1790s. Once again, the various material inputs are shown at standard cost (GD 58/6/4/4). Price and quantity standards of inputs and outputs were an integral part of Carron management's decision processes. An additional example can be found in a letter of 26 October 1766 when Cadell attributed a shortfall

Figure 20: Blast Furnace Production Report, Carron, 1793

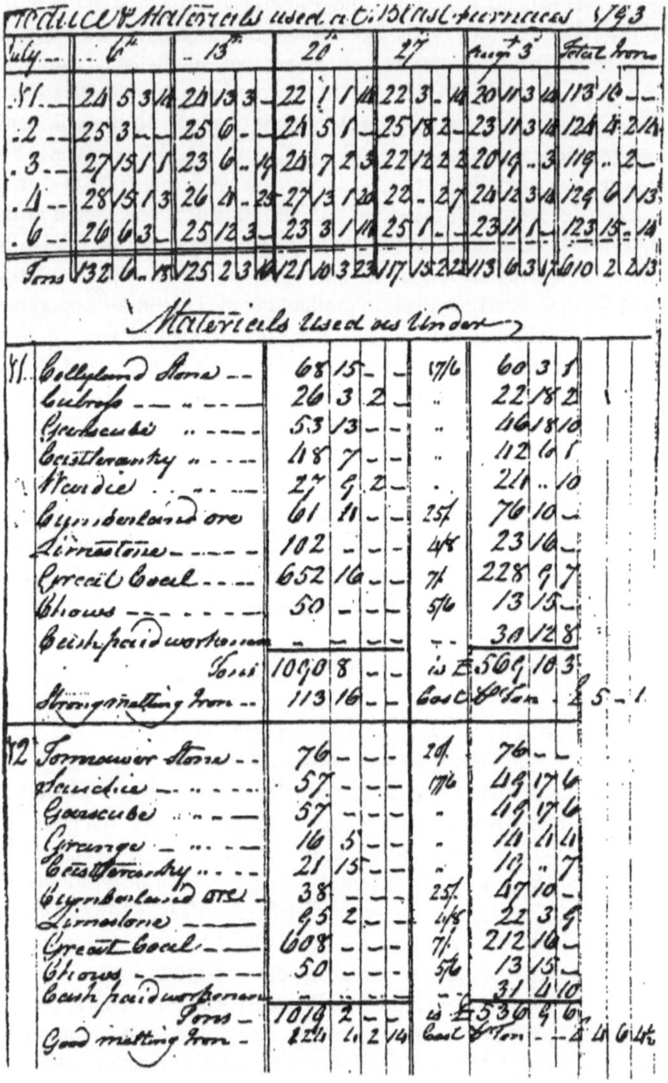

Produce & Materials used at the Blast Furnaces 1793

July	6th				13th				20th				27th				Augt 3				Total Iron			
N1	24	5	3	14	24	13	3	–	22	1	1	14	22	3	–	14	20	11	3	14	113	16	–	–
2	25	3	–	–	25	6	–	–	24	5	1	–	25	18	2	–	23	11	3	14	124	4	2	14
3	27	15	1	1	23	6	–	19	24	7	2	3	22	12	2	2	20	19	–	3	119	–	2	–
4	28	15	1	3	26	4	–	25	27	13	1	20	22	–	2	7	24	12	3	14	129	6	1	13
6	26	6	3	–	25	12	3	–	23	3	1	16	25	1	–	–	23	11	1	–	123	15	–	14
Tons	132	6	–	15	125	2	3	14	121	10	3	23	117	15	2	22	113	6	3	17	610	2	2	13

Materials Used as Under

N1	Collyland Stone	68	15	–	–	17/6	60	3	1	
	Culross	26	3	2	–	..	22	18	2	
	Gerrscube	53	13	–	–	..	46	18	10	
	Castlecarry	48	7	–	–	..	42	6	1	
	Wardie	27	9	2	–	..	24	..	10	
	Cumberland ore	61	11	–	–	25/	76	10	–	
	Limestone	102	–	–	–	4/8	23	16	–	
	Great Coal	652	16	–	–	7/	228	9	7	
	Chows	50	–	–	–	5/6	13	15	–	
	Cash paid workmen	–	–	–	–	–	38	12	8	
	Tons	1090	8	–	–	is £	569	10	3	
	Strong melting Iron	113	16	–	–	Cost	£ Ton			£5 – 1
N2	Tomnower Stone	76	–	–	–	20/	76	–	–	
	Sauchie	57	–	–	–	17/6	49	17	6	
	Garscube	57	–	–	–	–	49	17	6	
	Grange	16	5	–	–	–	14	4	4	
	Castlecarry	21	15	–	–	..	19	..	7	
	Cumberland ore	38	–	–	–	25/	47	10	–	
	Limestone	95	2	–	–	4/8	22	3	9	
	Great Coal	608	–	–	–	7/	212	16	–	
	Chows	50	–	–	–	5/6	13	15	–	
	Cash paid workmen	–	–	–	–	–	31	4	10	
	Tons	1019	2	–	–	is £	536	9	6	
	Good melting Iron	124	4	2	14	Cost	£ Ton	–	–	£4 6 4½

of ten tons and £30 per week in blast furnace output to badly repaired bellows (Cadell, ACC 5381, Box 28, Folder 1). Benson's letter of 22 March 1793 requested the partners to approve an increase in the standard price of pit coal from 6s to 7/1 per ton, chargeable to the furnaces (GD 58/6/4/4). Seventy years after Carron commenced operations, inventory continued to be valued by multiplying tonnage by standard prices (GD 58/8/56).

Evidence is also available of an occasional forecast or budget. A budget was prepared at Carron in 1762. Cadell, who was responsible for the effort, calculated expenses and revenues for each cost centre, though once again there is no information about anticipated production levels or specific revenue/expense components (General Court, GD 58/2/1/1, p. 63). No subsequent attempt to compare budget estimates with actual results was documented in Carron's records, nor could any evidence be located to suggest that budgeting was an annual event. A General Court resolution of February 1763 did request a 13-year projection of income at the Quarole Colliery (ibid., p. 43).

INVENTORY CONTROL

Right from the outset Carron management paid particular attention to inventory control. In 1763, the General Court legislated a monthly examination of each nailer's stock of iron (ibid., p. 54) and a reduction of coal purchases in order to lessen inventory levels (ibid., pp. 33–34). Records in 1764 included a directive to weed out obsolete inventory (ibid., pp. 145–146). Pursuant to a 1771 resolution of the General Court to have job descriptions for department heads, Gascoigne listed instructions for warehouse keeper Ambrose Tibbats: (1) source documents must be kept for all raw materials disbursed to various departments; (2) stockouts should be avoided; (3) stock likely to become obsolete should be eliminated; and (4) finished goods of poor quality should not be accepted from other departments, whilst goods of lesser quality were to be labelled 'half-ware' (General Court, GD 58/6/4/2). Wilson's 1769 analysis of Carron Company called for the proper flow of costs through inventories, with all expenses in the manufacturing part of the business being included before the computation of cost of goods manufactured (GD 58/4/1/1, pp. 38–39). Precedent to that time the expenses of limestone, ironstone, and pit coal depletion had not been transferred to inventory. Campbell (1961) noted the continuity of management's concern over inventory levels, with ongoing efforts to reduce average inventory in warehouses and to stop the accumulation of large quantities of dead stock. Carron actively pursued a policy of careful inventory management and record keeping to facilitate control, undoubtedly prompted by the capital constraints and financial difficulties of its early years.

REFLECTIONS ON CARRON COSTING

Recent significant essays on eighteenth century cost accounting origins have emphasised the importance of achieving an integration of costing with the financial records, as described by Hamilton in 1777 (Edwards, 1989; Mepham, 1988). Edwards (1989) cited Cyfarthfa, the Welsh iron enterprise, as the only firm reported in the literature to date that achieved this degree of sophistication in the eighteenth century, and then not until 1791. Carron's financial statements pre-1786 were a shambles, despite the excellence of the firm's departmental cost collection. Early inventory books, though beautifully maintained, were inconsistent with regard to the items included. Though depreciation was taken in the records as early as 1769, there were major asset write-downs in 1769, 1784, and 1812, indicating the system was functioning on an ad hoc basis. It was not until 25 April 1854 that the General Court resolved to hire a professional accountant (James Brown, Esq of Edinburgh) to determine if the financial accounting books had been properly kept in the past and to spearhead a needed simplification of the system (General Court, GD 58/8/69). However, in some instances Carron did attempt an integration which failed because of the financial reporting shortcomings. The transfer prices developed for the extractive operations did appear in the blast furnace accounts, and those recorded for the furnaces in the 1790s were transferred at standard to inventory. Carron's utilisation of standard costing and departmental allocation of overhead were other cost management techniques which impacted the financial record keeping. Notwithstanding, there is insufficient evidence to claim that anything approaching a mature integration was achieved. We were somewhat hampered in attempts to evaluate this important relationship because the Carron records do not contain many examples of detailed product costings as appear in the archives of other Industrial Revolution firms. There are references to these costings having been requested by the General Court. There was compliance in all likelihood; the calculations just have not survived.

Cost management processes in Carron appear to have been motivated by the firm's early problems with securing adequate partnership capital, attaining profitability, and maintaining liquidity. The vital concern with cost management was evident in the many examples of cost analyses and estimates designed to evaluate the profitability of products and business segments. The directions and forms that Carron cost records and management took reflected key aspects of Carron Company's environment in the second half of the eighteenth century. Whilst the maintenance of profitability would have been an important concern to Carron's management, the attention to expenditure and inventory control was also very much a product of the firm's paucity of capital investment and lack of financing resources. Its system of responsibility accounting and departmental cost management appears at least partly to have been a function of the original partnership combination of inventor (Roebuck) and businessmen new to this particular industry (Garbett and Cadell). Others followed in their footsteps.

Carron quickly became a large-scale, vertically integrated operation involving ironstone fields, collieries, mills, and blast furnaces, ultimately experimenting in and producing a range of specialised products. This complexity, along with a concern to maintain profitable operations in all segments, apparently stimulated the practices of overhead allocation and the interdepartmental charging of coal and ironstone costs from mineral fields to furnaces. The shortage of skilled labour identified by economic historians for that period also afflicted Carron, as did labour inefficiencies. These problems were reflected in the cost records by explanations of shortfalls in output quantity and, at times, quality. References to the need for quality control in the records testify to Carron's position as a specialist producer needing to maintain markets through product differentiation and quality. From the very beginning then, cost management and control were for Carron Company exercises of paramount importance.

In the Carron Company records we have found ample evidence of cost management activity during the early British Industrial Revolution.

Costing was employed extensively in management decision making, ranging from the development of production standards to departmental and product line evaluations. Even more impressive than the variety of uses the Carron owners and managers found for cost data was the detail of certain cost analyses. The 1768 cost estimation for the Kinnaird Colliery provides just such an example.

Accounting historians, in evaluating the managerial accounting of the British Industrial Revolution, must not be deluded by the absence of an accounting literature, an accounting tradition, and an accounting profession. The entrepreneurs of the period, such as the founders of Carron, possessed the economic talent and the foresight to utilise cost management to their competitive advantage.

NOTES

1. This chapter is heavily drawn from R.K. Fleischman and L.D. Parker (1990), 'Managerial Accounting Early in the British Industrial Revolution: The Carron Company, A Case Study', *Accounting and Business Research*, Vol. 20, No. 79: 211–221.

2. The initial capitalisation and early financing of Carron lies beyond the scope of this chapter. Campbell (1958, 1961) provides a complete paper and chapter on these subjects.

7

The Boulton & Watt Case[1]

This chapter is a second case study of a British Industrial Revolution firm whose archive reflects a cost accounting sophistication virtually unparallelled in the period. The Carron Company case study, presented in Chapter 6, provides a Neoclassical analysis, informed by traditional historical methodology, of one leading Industrial Revolution company's managerial accounting activities. It traversed the history of the firm, Carron's economic and industrial environment, and a cross section of its observed costing practices. This chapter provides an historical analysis of another leading Industrial Revolution enterprise, Boulton & Watt (B&W hereafter), addressing its accounting from somewhat differing perspectives and focussing attention particularly on labour and engine standards. In so doing, the discourse illustrates the additional dimensions of historical knowledge that can be to some degree unravelled by corporate case studies of this genre.

This chapter represents a collaborative effort between accounting historians who represent divergent paradigmatic viewpoints—the Neoclassical (Fleischman) and the Foucauldian (Hoskin and Macve). The venture is one of the possibilities the current authors espouse in the essay that constitutes Chapter 9 in this volume—a joint investigation of archival materials in the hopes that the findings will reflect the additive and synergistic value forthcoming from the differing perspectives. Whilst not attempting a reconciliation of views per se, the chapter does aim to identify more clearly some major differences between the approaches; to argue how historical evidence may count in support of one or the other perspectives; to explore how an individual case in accounting history may be understood within each context; and to offer a categorisation of these two approaches that identifies the key issues for further research in understanding the development and significance of early industrial cost management and accounting practices.[2]

SETTING THE SCENE

Studies by Hoskin and Macve (1986, 1988, 1994) have heretofore focussed on the US in the early nineteenth century and, in particular, on developments at the Springfield Armory. They have pointed to the role played by graduates of the US Military Academy at the Armory and on certain early US railroads. They have suggested that pedagogic practices derived from West Point, translated into a business context by these graduates, became the basis for a new, modern 'managerialism'. The point of departure was the control of individuals, achieved through 'a new way of seeing each individual worker in terms of norms and deviations from the norm' (Ezzamel et al., 1990, p. 159). As Hoskin and Macve (1988, p. 41) have noted, such control is a:

> positive power presenting norms of good practice and performance against which each individual's commitment and omissions were constantly evaluated or through which some officially prescribed self-discipline could come to be internalized.

From this perspective, the concept of a 'standard cost', such as standard labour cost per unit, represents the pioneering construction in the business context of target norms of human behaviour. Subsequent practices, such as those of Taylorism's time-and-motion studies, are significant in the construction across industrial culture of 'calculable persons' (Miller & O'Leary, 1987). A crucial aspect of this approach has been the attempt to explore where, when, and how the discourses and practices based on standards of this kind first began to transform the development of management practice—the historical discontinuity when the 'pre-modern' became the 'modern'.

The significance of Hoskin and Macve's attempt to identify the role of the Springfield Armory as crucial lies in their particular identification of disciplinarity as a double power that operates through certain practices (in particular, technologies of writing and learning) to construct forms both of behavioural discipline and of academic disciplinary knowledge. Hence, they stress the role of educational practices in the genesis of managerialism. They especially underscore a link between new practices of writing, examining, and grading under which students were required to learn at West Point from 1817 on, and the subsequent development by those graduates of technologies promoting administrative coordination and human accountability at the Springfield Armory and on the US railroads. Hence, in such newly managerial organisations, certain already existing technologies, such as accounting, could generate a new social and economic power. Hoskin and Macve (1988, p. 68) have thus thrown down the gauntlet to traditional economic rationalists by noting:

> We therefore see accounting not as the "practical" response of men faced with new entrepreneurial and organizational challenges, who "sensibly" devised ways of collecting and processing the data needed to make rational economic decisions—for in that sense no "practical" man would have invented modern accounting practice.[3]

By contrast, the work of Fleischman and his collaborators (Fleischman & Parker, 1990, 1991, 1992; Fleischman et al., 1991; Fleischman & Tyson, 1993) and other researchers (e.g., Edwards, 1989; Edwards & Newell, 1991) has focussed on the British Industrial Revolution as the cradle of modern cost management and cost accounting. The thrust of this research has been to challenge Pollard's (1965, p. 248) oft-quoted observation that 'the practice of using accounts as direct aids to management was not one of the achievements of the British Industrial Revolution'.

These studies have identified a number of examples of sophisticated early developments of cost accounting and cost management practices and techniques, including cost controls, overhead allocation, and the computation of standard costs—all techniques recognisably comparable to modern-day practice. These studies have, at least implicitly, looked for the explanation and significance of these early practices in terms of their economic utility, coupled with the role of dynamic entrepreneurs in assisting cost reduction, maximising profits, exploiting new technologies, and defending against competition.[4]

In comparing these two kinds of study, we see at the root of their major disagreements in historical explanation a difference in the identification and interpretation of one particular historical development, the normalisation of labour standards. From the Foucauldian perspective, the development of physical standards, based primarily on engineering data and used to control physical operations, such as materials usage and machine efficiency, was relatively (although not wholly) unproblematic.

However, the transfer of such performance measurement to human behaviour, to generate norms and standards of human performance, was a development of a different order. There was an intellectual, social, and organisational leap when accounting measurement was first applied to creating labour standards.

The ultimate significance of that departure has perhaps become clear in the way that accounting measures and norms, both internal and external, have now come to permeate organisations from top to bottom, covering both labour and managerial performance. Unlike machines, human beings respond to performance measures by internalising them in forms of self-control. Such a leap, the Foucauldians argue, required the prior development of new practices and discourses in other arenas to create the conditions of possibility wherein it could take place. It was not simply a response to changing economic conditions.

To the 'Neoclassical' economic rationalist, on the other hand, the development of such labour standards is no more problematic than the development of the physical standards. They constitute perhaps an extension of the physical; yet, both are similar in their structure, purpose, and approach, reflecting a rational response to the needs of economic development. That is not to say that Neoclassicists would necessarily regard the articulation and maintenance of labour standards simply as a response to economic conditions, for emergent issues of labour control and industrial relations may well play important contingent roles in the articulation of such standards. However, such contingent factors would still form part of a response, required on overarching, economically rational grounds, to changing real-world demands.

There is therefore a crucial need, if we are to understand the development of modern management accounting practice, for careful and detailed research to establish precisely the relative sophistication at different times and in different places of the costing techniques developed for application to materials, machines, and products (engineering standards) on the one hand, and to human performance (labour standards) on the other. The historical crux lies in comprehending where, when, how, and why the performance measurements, developed through engineering standards, were transferred, through the introduction of labour standards, to establish norms of human performance. This understanding will allow a better evaluation of how this innovation began to influence both individual enterprises and whole industries and developed to become the basis of modern management control.

If it can be shown, by recourse to the detailed historical evidence, that accounting and costing developments in Britain late in the eighteenth and early in the nineteenth century extended to the establishment of human performance norms, this knowledge would render futile the Foucauldian attempts to identify the preconditions for such a development as lying elsewhere, primarily in non-economic settings of the kind located by Hoskin and Macve (e.g., 1988, 1994) in the US in the early nineteenth century. On the other hand, if the crucial development dates from the early nineteenth century US, the traditional Neoclassical view of accounting's historical development as a 'demand response' to the forces of economic development (e.g., Edwards & Newell, 1991, p. 35) would be rendered problematic, for the major achievements of the Industrial Revolution originated in the UK at a time when the US was still an economic backwater.[5]

In this chapter we investigate the possibility that this historical crux occurred at the B&W foundry, one of the classic examples of early British management sophistication. In particular, we will attempt to establish precisely the relative sophistication of the costing techniques developed there for application to human performance—the labour standards.

Of course, we remain aware that individual cases and pieces of evidence cannot be conclusive, and there will almost certainly remain difficulties of identifying and interpreting from the available historical data the precise nature of the developments that took place in the UK and US around the turn of the nineteenth century.[6] But as more studies are undertaken, a careful accumulation of, and attention to, the resulting evidence should at least reduce the scope for misinterpretation of what happened, and when, and thus advance debate on the merits of alternative theoretical approaches to understanding modern accounting's history.

Ultimately, through such a process, there might conceivably even be resolution to what at present appear to be irreconcilable, theoretical differences. In undertaking this project, we did not purposefully seek either reconciliation or debate. Earlier studies (e.g., Dickinson, 1937, 1967; Fleischman & Parker, 1991; Pollard, 1965, 1990; Roll, 1968) have already emphasised the sophistication of the accounting and costing practices developed at B&W. The present authors, from their differing paradigmatic backgrounds, have jointly revisited the archive in order to reassess those existing interpretations and to identify additional material that sheds light on the labour control issue.[7]

The structure of the remainder of the chapter is as follows: the next two sections briefly outline the historical significance and development of the B&W works and the general background of its accounting practices; the following two sections focus on the nature and the relative sophistication of the techniques developed for labour standards and engine standards respectively. The final section assesses the significance of this evidence in advancing the debate between Foucauldian and Neoclassical approaches to accounting history and suggests research priorities for resolving the questions that have emerged in recent years.

BOULTON & WATT: HISTORY AND LITERATURE

The importance of the firm founded by the famed steam engine partnership and perpetuated by their talented scions has been well-documented by economic and accounting historians. Roll's (1968) classic study drew attention to apparently sophisticated scientific management and cost accounting techniques at B&W, but did not presage subsequent study of the British Industrial Revolution as a formative epoch in the development of modern managerial methods. The apparent dismissal of these innovations as the exceptional approach of a single firm was given more concrete expression by Pollard, whose extensive knowledge of the period's business archives led him to the pessimistic conclusion quoted above. At the same time, he did identify B&W as an 'astonishingly fertile pioneer of scientific management practices' (Pollard, 1965, pp. 79, 248), and in a retrospective occasioned by the twenty-fifth anniversary of *The Genesis of Modern Management*, he added a second pioneering company, stating that:

> there has never been any doubt that Wedgwood, together with that other brilliantly-led pioneer firm of Boulton & Watt, was far ahead of the management skills of his contemporaries. No other firm has been found so far which would even remotely approach those two in this field (Pollard, 1990, p. 102).

It will be recalled as well that B&W was accorded the qualitative rating of 'excellent' in all four of the cost accounting activity areas Fleischman and Parker identified in their 1991 study—cost control, overhead accounting, decision making, and standard costing.

Turning to the specifics of the firm's history, the B&W partnership was established in 1775, ostensibly to enjoy the benefits of patents associated with steam engine technology. During the early phase of the firm's history, 1775–1795, the primary focus of operations was not the manufacture of steam engines but consulting engineering—the planning for, and supervision of, the erection of engines. A significant percentage of the engine components was produced elsewhere, typified by the subcontracting of the boring process to John Wilkinson. Engines erected under terms of the B&W patents were improvements over existing Newcomen engines in that their superior pumping capability allowed for the exploitation of deeper ore seams in mines. The firm received royalties calculated at one-third of the saving in coal costs realised from its more efficient engines. This pattern determined the geographical distribution of its engines early-on, as it was in the firm's best interest to market its products to non-coal-mining operations, in regions where coal was expensive and where mines were deep. Hence, Cornish tin and copper mines were the focal point of activities for the first decade.

More importantly, this process of B&W's early revenue collection necessitated elaborate record-keeping systems, not only on its part but by its clients as well. To ensure its fair return, B&W needed monthly data on the productive potential of its engines, actual utilisation, and the coal consumed in the operation. These were recorded in exquisite detail in the early engine books (see Figure 1). Somewhat later, when premiums were commuted to lump-sum payments obviating the need for this elaborate record keeping, B&W accepted shares in its client's mines in lieu of payment.

Commencing in 1782, B&W patented the rotative engine, with the first of the class appearing the next year. The development of this engine essentially changed the nature of business as the firm took a much more active role in making parts at Soho for the engines it erected. The company continued to collect premium payments, but now revenue was based on horsepower units rather than savings on coal consumption.

A major point of departure for the steam engine partnership occurred in 1795 when James Watt Jr and Matthew Robinson Boulton joined the business founded by their fathers. It was in that year that the Soho Foundry commenced operations for the full-scale production of steam engines. The new installation reflected the apogee of scientific management practice in a physical sense with its carefully planned production flow, component and process standardisation, and the subdivision of labour. With the termination of most external subcontracting, accounting innovations could serve an important new purpose in controlling and coordinating the wide variety of labour skills necessary to construct a highly complex commodity (Pollard, 1965).

With the opening of the Soho Foundry, B&W's fortunes came to be guided increasingly by the founders' sons. Watt Jr, in particular, had been trained in management and accounting skills. It was hardly a startling realisation that with the cessation of the patents post-1800, survival of the firm depended on efficiency (Roll, 1968). Techniques were necessary to ensure highly precise workmanship, stock control, and accurate costing of materials and labour processes. Pollard (1965, p. 252) was impressed by B&W in that 'solutions to these problems, consciously adopted, have rightly been compared with the best practices of the twentieth century'.

COST ACCOUNTING AT BOULTON & WATT

The size of the B&W archive reflects both good fortune and the firm's commitment to volume data generation.[8] Accounting information was produced in great quantity to support the management innovations at Soho Foundry. Dickinson (1967, p. 168) wrote with characteristic hyperbole, reiterating Roll (1968):

> There is nothing in the costing, the feeds and speeds, the scientific management of Taylor, Ford, and other experts of the present day that was not found at Soho before 1805. This early engineering works possessed an organization that far excelled that of any other extant establishment and that can bear comparison with that of any works of the present day.

Immoderate as these claims might be, they suggest both the superiority of B&W's cost accounting compared to other British Industrial

Revolution firms and the possibility that certain techniques thought to have been of 1880s origin were anticipated nearly a century earlier.

The bulk of B&W's accounting innovations occurred around the turn of the nineteenth century. The new Soho installation was necessitated by the decision to produce locally components that had previously been externally subcontracted. The quality of work done by subcontractors had been suspect on many occasions, but an even more serious problem had been lengthy time delays (Tann, 1981). Additionally, the firm had encountered great difficulties with the Wilkinsons, culminating in litigation over the pirating of B&W patents (Roll, 1968). There is also evidence to the effect that the entrepreneurs saw value in maintaining for themselves substantial profits traditionally earned by these subcontractors. A new accounting system was accordingly developed to control the new productive processes, with functions now delegated to internal subcontractors.

Instrumental to the advent of the new accounting system was the coming of age of Watt Jr, identified in the literature as being as significant a force behind the success of the firm as the original founders. Dickinson (1937) suggested that there was no aspect of the business that escaped his notice. Tann (1981) recognised Watt Jr as one of a small minority of entrepreneurs of the late eighteenth century with the vision to see the contribution cost accounting could make to business. One of his surviving ledger books, dated 1786–1801 (MI/6/3), contains an annual reconciliation, commencing in 1796, between his numbers and the figures recorded by Pearson, the firm's accountant. For 1797–1798, Watt noted an £81 difference of which he wrote, 'the error probably lies in some of my additions, but I have not time to investigate it'. Notwithstanding, on the very next page three items were recorded that collectively accounted for the discrepancy.

Control of expenditures would be anticipated as a first priority for the initial establishment of a cost accounting system. Sophistication would be indicated by the variety of expenses tracked, particularly indirect costs as distinct from the more obvious prime costs, and the processes by which expenses that collectively comprise overhead ('general charges') were allocated back to profit centres. Also, the utilisation of expense reports for comparative purposes in efforts to establish responsibility management would reflect a higher purpose.

Attention to expenses, as distinct from product costing, was a rather late development at B&W, reflective of Watt Jr's influence. A volume, identified as the Fitting Department Book 1797–1798 (Arch 05/1/386), contains weekly expense reports for various departments exclusive of wages. Distinctive features include a rigid separation of expenses rightfully chargeable to the owners' capital accounts, a segregation of enterprises such as farming and workers' housing, the utilisation of an 'Establishment' account for capital improvements, and an appropriate dichotomisation of raw materials and supplies charged to overhead. The reports maintained expense reports for individual shops of the same function (four lathing and two drilling rooms) which might have been utilised for comparative purposes, though there is no indication that managers were made to answer for the results.

Watt Jr in his ledger (MI/6/3) maintained various categories of general expenses for the engine manufactory, including the charges for procuring cash, postage, insurance, taxes, interest on inventory, presents, and travelling expenses. The salaries of non-direct labourers were also recorded, including the £40 paid annually to Pearson, the accountant. A breakdown of 'general expenses' was annually prepared as a part of the firm's reporting system (MII/7/2).

The B&W archive includes a number of documents prepared periodically reflecting the degree to which expenses were scrutinised. There is a comparative annual expenditure on oil and candles in the engine shops for 1799–1808 in which average yearly expenditures on spermaceti, fish oil, and candles are calculated (Box 48/4). There is a detailed estimate in 1801 for additions to Soho and workers' housing construction (Box 37/8). An 1803 report compared price differentials for the installation of oak and elm planking for floors (Box 48/4). A series of small engine estimates, 1804–1816, reflected an awareness of the impact of transportation charges on selling prices, particularly the savings realised when components were shipped through Liverpool as opposed to other venues (Box 42/1). There are hundreds of bundles, thousands of items, replete with actual and estimated expenses of this genre of which the current authors have only investigated a small sample.

B&W did begin to depreciate its assets relatively early (1806), but in a confused fashion. In an inventory book (Arch 05/1/430), buildings were depreciated at a rate of 10% straight-line, machines and fixtures 15%, and tools/utensils 5%. Meanwhile, in a building and machinery account book (Arch 05/1/181), no depreciation was taken at all before 1815, and only 5% on buildings and 8% on machinery subsequently.

The accounting staff became more coordinated in the 1820s when rates were standardised at 10% for buildings, 15% on machines and fixtures, 15% on patterns, and 10% on 'research and development' items (Arch 05/1/438).

Notwithstanding B&W's concern about costs and its awareness of those indirect charges properly handled as components of overhead, the firm's accountants failed to allocate these costs to profit centres. B&W was not in the vanguard with other Industrial Revolution firms in this regard. Instead, overhead was included in the mark-up on finished goods inventory, which was valued at selling price. Two volumes of moulders' estimates (Arch 05/1/479; Arch 05/1/481) from the 1810s and 1820s provide some insight into inventory valuation. Tools were typically charged at 25% of pre-profit job cost and the risks of the boring function occasionally costed at one-twelfth. This eleventh-hour apportionment of overhead costs explains the pattern evident in B&W's books wherein interdepartmental transfer prices (e.g., foundry to fitting, fitting to stocks) on engine components are lower than the costs included in inventory and in the day book where the disposition of finished product was recorded.

If B&W failed to achieve a high level of sophistication in allocating overhead, the focal point of its accounting system and the basis for its notoriety amongst historians were the articulation of material and labour standards. Here the crucial question, it seems to us, is the extent to which the company set, appraised, and controlled standards of human performance, thus generating labour standards, as well as developed standards of physical performance for its engines. Neither the evidence nor the interpretation of these activities is straightforward.

On the one hand, both human and machine performance were measured in considerable detail across a range of activities, particularly over the 1800–1802 period when the Soho manufactory was extended. It is clear that standards were derived as a means to evaluate the weight of castings produced per man per month, as to establish time-based piece rates in procedures such as turning and boring, and to rate tenders submitted by inside contractors in the manufactory. There is also evidence that the setting of such piece rates increased productivity. On the other hand, this evidence is not necessarily, *ipso facto*, proof that a managerial system was in place and operating.

In this regard it is particularly important to recall the previous discussion on how 'standard' can take on different shades of meaning in both engineering and accounting terminology. A standard may signify little more than an 'average' found, for example, by measuring samples of past activity. Thus, the average cost of batches of a product may be calculated, and again averaged over a number of periods. This amount may then be used as a standard measure of the cost (e.g., for tendering purposes, for internal transfer pricing, or for inventory accounting), even though it may soon cease to reflect actual costs. One might label such calculations as 'positive' (tracking what is) rather than 'normative' (tracking what should be).

In the context of labour, piece rates may be set by averaging observations of actual rates of output over a period or periods and then utilised as a benchmark or standard for future production (perhaps setting a lower standard to provide achievement bonuses or a higher standard if there is believed to be considerable slack in current rates). Here there is an overlap between positive and normative attributes—what has been achieved in the past is a guide to what should be achieved, or surpassed, in the future.

In the engineering context also, the positive and normative meanings may again tend to overlap. The purpose of measuring the level of output from an engine, or the pattern for a component, is normally to control activity by testing for deviations from the standard and taking corrective action where needed. The standards are both positive, descriptive of the capability of the machine, and normative, targeting what should be achieved (allowing for any special conditions of operation). But these parallels between human and engineering standards do not necessarily mean that the labour standards generated at B&W were used managerially, as a means of 'human engineering', exerting constant accountability over performance. Such accountability is typically built upon precision of measure, the fine gradation of hours, minutes, seconds, and even sub-seconds required for a task. It presupposes a regular revision of standards and targets and an integration of activity throughout the work place, whether achieved by hierarchical imposition of order or through the planning of production throughout. A managerial system, in short, will appear to be more than the sum of its parts. At B&W, however, the whole often appears to be rather less than some of its parts, taken individually, might suggest.

LABOUR STANDARDS

B&W, thanks in great part to Roll's early investigation, is renowned in cost accounting history both for its extraordinarily detailed engine books and for its articulation of labour standards based on time studies. However, it now appears to us on re-examining the archive that B&W's labour standards represent only a limited development. In particular, whilst there was an incredible outburst of calculating activity in the 1800–1802 period, there was diminished attention subsequently.

In the early history of the firm, all B&W workers received day wages as befitted an operation that featured little in the way of production. A significant proportion of labour expense was incurred by engine erectors, who spent much of their time in the field, and were thus beyond much direct control by management. Starting with the opening of the Soho Foundry in the mid-1790s, the transition was made to more complex remuneration arrangements, particularly a piece-rate structure. Roll (1968) attributed this development to the greater standardisation of products and specialisation of labour that accompanied the new installation. Roll also observed that circa 1800 some operatives received day rates at the engine manufactory whereas those performing the same function at Soho were paid by the piece.

Time Studies and Piece Rates: The correction of this anomaly was based on the time studies for which the firm is noted. Abraham Storey, Watt Jr, and the younger Boulton were prime movers in this activity at the turn of the century. However, the process did not cease with the initial establishment of the piece-rate system. It continued under the auspices of Haden in the 1810s and Buckle in the 1830s. A typical exercise was a compilation wherein the monthly weights of castings made between October 1799 and June 1800 were reconciled to information from the time book for the four processes involved in making castings. The weight per man per week was then compared to what was the 'average weight supposed by Mr Storey to be made per each man per week'. In three of the four instances, actual production fell short of expectation, but in the case of open-sand casting, weekly output exceeded Storey's norm (Box MII/7/2). These results became the 'basis to the table of premiums'. A premium system was superimposed on existing day rates and represented a 10–16% bonus to the foremen of operative teams for completion of an agreed quantity of output. The premium structure was in place by July 1800, two years in advance of the fully articulated piece-rate scale (Roll, 1968; Tann, 1981). As of 1802, B&W's work force numbered 54 operatives, 20 working for day wages and 34, organised into nine teams for internally subcontracted functions, receiving piece rates (Tann, 1981).

The process for establishing piece-work rates was intricate and lengthy. The first step was observation. Roll (1968) reported a rather simplistic procedure for the establishment of drilling rates in 1801 wherein the performance of a single worker, not a particularly efficient one at that, was observed. Apparently, exogenous factors, such as faulty castings and machinery malfunctions, rendered piece rates determined in this fashion next to worthless. However, documents that the current authors have seen in the archives provided evidence of a more thoughtful time observation process. In Box 37/3, there is an almost illegible document listing 'time of turning' for five product classifications (e.g., pistons and rotative shafts) with a 'proposed standard or average' for each.[9] In some instances, a standard was proposed on the basis of a single trial, but as many as four repetitions were observed for certain categories with quarters of a day as the lowest unit of measurement. In these cases of multiple observations, an average time was struck, but again this average was never denominated for less than a quarter-day. A proposed standard time was then given wherein the standard was usually less than the average observed time. Of 56 individual cases, the standard proposed was less than the average observation on 33 occasions, the same on 18, and higher in only five instances.

A more impressive time study was entitled 'Table of the times of boring cylinders with observations thereon 1800' (Box 37/3). Here a surface area was calculated for 16 sizes of air pumps. The accounts were then consulted to calculate the average actual time to produce the pumps. A ratio between the surface area and the actual days was derived and expected days formulated on that basis. However, the ratio was deemed inadequate because the facing of the cylinder and other parts of the operation did not appear in direct ratio to the surface area. A more exact approach was suggested wherein estimated expected days were derived by adding 72 to the surface area and dividing that result by 30.

Tenders for Internal Subcontracting: In 1802, Thomas Mousley received an internal subcontract to produce pumps, pipes, and other specified items on a piece-rate basis. This contract was the end product of a complicated process that demonstrated the B&W system at its most sophisticated. B&W solicited bids from the foremen of various operative teams on the items in question. For instance, Box 45/19 contains no fewer than four bids for moulding shafts from Croft, Williams, Middleton, and Meadows. To test the bids, interviews were held. Box 45/20 contains details of how an agreed price for each part was built-up on the basis of interviews with Mousley as to the time required. Notes were taken on Mousley's views. Storey (B&W's inspector) doubted that some of the times could be achieved based on what he had seen (in some cases more time was allowed). Then the costs were worked out, with a deduction of one-eighth (written in different coloured ink) being made 'for piece work' to get the price finally agreed.

The build-up of the 6s piece-rate standard for cold water pumps is typical of the process (Box 45/20). It was agreed between Mousley and Storey that 'a moulder can do one in a day, or six per week'. Weekly pay plus premium for Mousley and his two helpers was 34s, or 5/8 per pump. The cost of chipping, getting out, and weighing was 4d per cwt., or 1/1 for a pump weighing 3 cwt., 1 qtr.

From the 5/8, the standard one-eighth (9d) was subtracted to convert to the proposed piece rate, giving 4/9 (sic). Thus, the standard was established at 6s (4/9 + 1/1) (sic). Though the arithmetic leaves something to be desired (albeit coming right in the end), the process was typical of similar computations for working barrels, pumps with jackheads, clack seats, and various types of pipes.

With regard to boiler steam pipes, an analysis over five quarters was done on Mousley as a low bidder to gauge his productivity and efficiency (Box 45/19). These quarterly summaries were very detailed with costs based on day-labour rates plus premiums then in effect. A major issue was the incidence of 'wasters', unusable output. Calculations were jointly made on the basis of actual waste and no waste. Most piece-rate proposals from the foremen assumed that B&W and the subcontractor should split the waster cost, but ultimately the final contracts passed full waste cost absorption to the contractors (Tann, 1981). In any event, Mousley's performance was judged to be 'tolerably industrious' during the first and third quarters, and less so otherwise. It was also observed that he had been helped by foundry labourers and chippers without chargebacks.

The five-quarters cost analysis revealed a bottom-line materials and labour cost of 2/1¼ per cwt. for pipes based on day rates. The standard deduction of one-eighth to convert from time rates to piece rates (here taken to be 3d) brought the price to 1/10½ (rounded up). Had there been no wasters, the cost would have been 1/9 per cwt. However, the firm conceded a 1/10½ base for pipes, in essence giving him 1½d gratis, a cost that would have been 'unnecessary had he not lost so many by his ignorance or neglect'. To this sum was added 4½d for foundry labour, chipping, and 'getting out', costs which Mousley would now have to absorb in addition to wasters.

However, it was then observed that a 2/3 per cwt. standard for all pipes would result in cheating, putting 'temptation in his way', because variations in thickness of the pipes would materially impact costs. Thus, a table was constructed wherein rates were established per foot of pipe as a function of differing inside diameters (from 4 to 13 inches). Because all fractions were dropped, the resulting table was as much in B&W's favour as the 2/3 per cwt. cost had been in Mousley's. These pipe piece rates then appeared on the long list of the products subcontracted to Mousley (Box 45/20).

Piece Rates and Productivity: The degree to which the piece rates benefitted B&W can be measured by comparing the final rates to the various proposals. The prices agreed are about one-third below those in Mousley's proposals.[10] The competitive bids submitted by Isaac Croft also survive (Box 45/20). There are 20 items that appeared jointly on Croft's proposal and the final piece rates contracted with Mousley. On only three occasions were the piece rates offered higher than Croft's bids. Typically, the final rates were significantly lower than those Croft was able to offer.

Another detailed study involved the production costs incurred by William Williams and his men in making air pumps, cylinders, and condensers from dry-sand patterns (Box 45/18). Again, production over five quarters was scrutinised. Actual labour expense at day rates was £177/14/4½. Had the same work been done at proposed piece rates, the labour input would have cost £125/11/7, a saving of £52/2/9½. It was observed that by taking castings at the Leeds price of 2s per cwt., the amount would be £5 more than Williams' proposed piece rates.

It might also be observed that in the establishment of these piece rates, B&W did not operate in a vacuum. The company had knowledge of moulders' rates at other firms. Box 45 contains corresponding piece rates for 1802 at Butterley, Low Moor, Gorsecote, and Halifax (Tann, 1981).

Roll (1968) was of the opinion that the institution of the piece-rate system in 1802 was designed to speed up production by individual operatives. An analysis of Samuel Williams' production in the second quarter of 1802 contrasted his earning potential under a new piece-rate proposal with the old day wages plus premium arrangement. The conclusion was 'so that to earn his present wages he must do one cwt. per day more than has yet been done and 1½ cwt. more than he did in the quarter from April to June, 1802'. This diagnostic must have been particularly disconcerting to Williams as his production appeared to have been approximately two cwt. per day (Tann, 1981; Box 45/1).

A lengthy document in Box 45 (Tann, 1981) underscores the productive speed-up that accompanied the final institution of the piece-rate system on 17 July 1802. For each of the moulder teams doing castings, there appears a statement of production over the eight preceding quarters with comparison to the first several months of the new system. There is commentary on each with regard to earning potential under piece rates. The final page of the document, which appears as Figure 21, illustrates the remarkable output increase under the new method. It was not only Samuel Williams who more than doubled his output. The system resulted both in greater productivity for the benefit of the owners and also in increased pay, indicating there had been considerable slack in the previous system.

Revisions to Piece Rates: However, to modern eyes there is a surprising sequel to this apparent breakthrough. The close attention paid to the introduction of piece rates in the 1800–1802 period was not reflected in the decades following. Amendment of the 1802 calculations did not apparently occur until 1808. In that year there appeared a 'revised calculation of cylinders 4 to 6H (horsepower) sliding valve engines' wherein the estimate of the time required to produce a unit of this output was raised from 1½ to 1¾ days. For the first time a 'risk of

Figure 21: Productivity Report, Boulton & Watt, 1802

Comparative View of the Quantity, say of the Weight of Good Castings done in the Various Quarters since the Institution of Premium, including the first Quarter of Piecework

		1800 1 July to 30 Sepr	1800 1 Octr to 31 Decr	1801 1 Jany to 31 March	1801 1 Apl to 30 June	1801 1 July to 30 Sepr	1801 1 Octr to 31 Decr	1802 1 Jany to 31 March	1802 1 Apl to 30 June	Premium & Piecework 1802 1 July to 30 Sepr
Wm Gilpin		229	—	—	—	—	—	—	—	—
Joseph Croft		383	230	468	473	338	253	588	359	937
William Williams		288	257	277	347	354	246	214	197	—
Halligan & Owen		—	—	—	—	—	—	—	—	331
Isaac Croft		222	258	198	240	243	221	239	191	346
Thos Mousley		205	165	183	164	160	97	158	150	230
Ja^{s} Middleton		—	—	—	—	—	125	211	207	407
Wm Meadows		144	231	212	269	152	98	362	217	96
Jos Marsh		251	219	287	206	152	99	140	120	59
Saml Williams		—	—	—	—	—	159	179	191	396
G. Halligan		579	509	627	657	1331	1135	607	—	—
D. Pearsol		—	—	—	—	—	—	552	1180	1363
G. Croft		270	263	325	360	478	392	457	434	531
E. Collier		359	309	393	405	350	175	184	225	730
B. Young		364	390	393	377	322	346	524	414	
Weight P^{r} Q^{r}	Cwts	3294	2831	3363	3498	3880	3346	4412	3885	5426
	Tons	164.14	141.11	168.3	174.18	194.-	167.6	220.12	194.5	271.6

boring' cost, constituting one-twelfth the piece rate, was added (Tann, 1981; Box 45). In that year as well, internal subcontractors agreed that piece rates on certain categories of pipes were too high and accepted a 3d per cwt. reduction retroactive to the previous year (Arch 05/1/451). A more general amendment of material and labour standards occurred in 1810. Interestingly, whilst the revision contained some information about the build-up of material standards, there was no documentation at all to support changes in labour piece rates (ibid.).

The apparent lack of concern with regard to managing labour piece rates was underscored in 1814 when a strike was threatened over pay levels. Watt Jr, in responding to the unrest, pointed out rather cavalierly, 'settlement of the piecework has for several years been made annually at the periods when it was convenient to me' (Tann, 1981, p. 14).

This 'unmanagerial' approach to controlling labour costs appears to have continued over ensuing decades. A huge volume, the Piece Workers' Ledger (1825–1830) (Arch 05/1/443), devotes 40 pages to Edward Seager's productivity over a three year period. Job numbers are typically given for the work he did on specific accounts. His remuneration appears to have been some combination of day rates and piece-rate premiums. His output was recorded in weight, with the job order charged sometimes by the weight only and sometimes by the weight multiplied by a standard rate. Another book from the 1830s, entitled 'Instructions for Assemblying Engines and Estimates' (Arch 05/1/480), contains 35 pages of labour piece rates, but is most inconsistent in providing estimates of the time that specific functions were expected to take.

Imprecision in Calculations: Even in 1802, when piece-rate calculations were a first priority, the time observations upon which rates were based seem to have lacked precision. Box 45 contains a listing of time estimates for various moulder's functions in the manufacture of a 20-horsepower engine. For all tasks requiring more than a single day, the allocated times were in half-day units. Quarter-days were specified for moulding smaller components requiring less than a day. Given the intricacies of other calculations observed at the time, it would, from a modern viewpoint, seem almost inconceivable that hourly estimates were not attempted (Tann, 1981). However, it appears that quarters of a day remained the normal unit of measurement. A rough calculation on a scrap found in the back of the fitting book for 1809–1837 (Arch 05/1/283) has one task measured at three-eighths of a day, but since the final total is rounded to a quarter fraction, not added exactly, it appears that the clerk was not used to working in fractions smaller than one-fourth.[11]

In 1814, Haden did time studies for the turning, cutting, and finishing of wheels of various sizes. In this particular document there are 20 estimates, six of which were done without trial. For the remaining 14, which were based on Haden's own experiment, there was no repeat testing (Box 48/4).

There is some evidence that this apparent laxness may have resulted not from a lack of care or concern, but from the intrusion of factors that made it functionally impossible to assign accurate time estimates. An 1804–1806 document logs the cost of fitting pairs of rotative and connecting wheels. Even when the dimensions of the wheels were the same, the costs could vary wildly. For instance, one pair of wheels of four feet and two feet diameters respectively cost £4/4, whilst another pair of the same exact dimensions cost 16/6 (ibid.). At the same time, such factors seem inadequate to explain the constant and long-standing absence of a concern with tracking and shaping labour time. The limitations of the firm's time records, and perhaps of the piece rates based on these observations, is reflected by a comment that appeared in an 1830s instruction book (Arch 05/1/480, p. 73):

> The exact time put down by Mr Buckle must not always be taken for the real time a job has been in completing, but in many instances and indeed in general the person who makes out the fitting must be governed by his knowledge of the article fitted.

The Contractual Roles of Piece Rates: Nevertheless, labour cost estimates were needed for pricing jobs, and the 'Estimates Book 1819–1826' (Arch 05/1/481), previously referred to, includes for each job the costs for various labour processes, giving the time required and charged out at various standard rates of pay. The effort put into establishing piece rates and tracking labour costs therefore appears to reflect primarily contractual needs, both internal agreements for the production of engine parts and external contracting with customers for the delivery and installation of engines.[12]

Conclusions on B&W's Labour Standards: Whilst the introduction of piece rates itself appears to have achieved a dramatic improvement in productivity, the exercise was a 'one-off' to establish a new system of 'fair prices' that thereafter received only sporadic attention. There does not appear to be any evidence of meticulous control over subsequent productivity, and the piece-rate regime seems essentially that described by Johnson and Kaplan (1987) when they argued that entrepreneurs did not need cost accounting, even when coordinating multiple processes in protofactories, as long as they were paying market prices (a piece rate) for the output of each worker. Similarly, detailed attention to control and efficiency of labour was not needed until manufacturers attempted to take the manufacturing process out of the hands of internal contractors, operating on a piece-rate basis, and to bring the work force under their direct control.

From a Neoclassical (economic rationalist) perspective, therefore, it would have to be argued that external conditions (competition, etc.) and internal conditions (the nature of B&W's technology and factory organisation) had not yet developed to a stage requiring a more sophisticated approach to control of labour efficiency. The productivity increase associated with the introduction of piece rates may have been sufficient to deflect management's attention from more precise standards and more frequent revisions of existing ones that may have served to alienate the labour force. From the Foucauldian perspective, the important observation would be that the piece-rate system at B&W provided incentives to increase productivity, but it did not represent a continuous 'disciplinary gaze'. It was not yet a management system of the modern kind, 'systems that quietly order us about' (Foucault cited in Megill, 1979, p. 493).

ENGINE STANDARDS

The approach to the setting and maintenance of labour standards at B&W compares unfavourably with that adopted for engine standards. Indeed, the most impressive surviving documents in the B&W archive are the dozens of engine books. These huge volumes contain costings of all components for every major steam engine constructed at the Soho Foundry. There is a printed form for each, numbering six pages in length during the late 1790s (Arch 05/1/231) and seven pages during the 1810s and 1820s (Arch 05/1/409). The standard costs of the hundreds of components comprising these engines were painstakingly entered and organised therein.

Engine Trials: The original founders were interested not only in calculating premium payments but in the comparative efficiency of their engines as well. The early archives feature hundreds of pages on the results of engine trials. Performance efficiency remained a concern for the second generation ownership, though there was apparently diminished experimentation. An 1818 notebook of Watt Jr is replete with steamboat engine trials (MI/6/25). A box labelled 'steam engines' contains 'expectations' for all boilers made at Soho in 1824–1825, with particular reference to the coal consumption per cubic foot of water.

Perhaps because the firm had developed sufficient expertise in its products' capabilities, the emphasis came to centre more on product costing. In 1802, Stoner, Pearsol, and Halligan individually analysed the cost and selling price of fly wheels. There was substantial variation in the three estimates of cost. The document is particularly interesting in that on two occasions, in 1807 and again in 1809, newer cost information was pasted over the original calculations (Box 45/19). One of the most sophisticated comparative costings is one from the 1830s wherein a two-page analysis of 'cost of articles to form a 13H engine upon a 10H Framing' is followed by corresponding costs for a 10-horsepower size. There then follows a differential cost analysis, highlighting the variations between the two (Box 42/12).

Costing Imprecision: There is much to admire about the accounting system utilised by B&W in costing the hundreds of components comprising the major engines constructed at Soho. The detail apparent in the huge engine books does impress. The fact that the firm employed transfer prices distinct from selling prices suggests a sophistication absent in most other Industrial Revolution firms. However, the more deeply the researcher investigates these records, the more certain limitations appear.

Details of the New River Company Engine are recorded in an 1824 engine book (Arch 05/1/251), with associated costs abstracted over the typical seven printed pages. 'Fitting' costs total £644/14/5 and constitute a page and a half in the abstract. In the corresponding fitting book (Arch 05/1/283), greater detail is provided about this cost aspect. However, the total in the fitting book is misadded by £185, an error picked up in the engine book but never corrected in the fitting book. A listing of costs also appears in an engine day book (Arch 05/1/259) wherein the material inputs are listed by weights multiplied by a standard charge. These standards appear to be quite imprecise as they are always rounded to the nearest shilling and, on some occasions, to the nearest five shillings. The labour cost is given only as a single-line item without specification.

In tracing items produced in the foundry from the day book (Arch 05/1/272) to the engine book (Arch 05/1/251), it is apparent that the transfer prices to the foundry account were not the same as charged in the final abstract. For instance, for job VT304 (1824), the charge for a connecting rod in a 13 January entry was 12 cwt., 7 lbs. at 16s per cwt., whilst a 29 September entry in the engine book costed the same component at 18s per cwt. Once again, confidence in the precision of these standard costs is undermined by the rounding and the grouping of various component costs at convenient numbers. This concern is confirmed by an 1820s inventory book where selling prices for cast iron goods in fitted state are examined over the decade. Prices in inventory in 1822 did not change until a reassessment was undertaken in 1830. Then, all items that had been charged at 32s per cwt. in 1822 were lowered to 28s, all 20s items were now 16s, and those that had been 18s and 15s were reduced by only one shilling (Arch 05/1/438).

Conclusions on B&W's Engine Standards: The engine standards computations therefore exhibit a high level of attention to detail in terms of the physical properties being measured and experimented with, but a somewhat more cursory treatment of the associated costs. One explanation for this pattern may be that, although the computation of actual or average cost in money terms is technically similar to the computation of actual or average output in physical terms, the logical categories of the two operations are different. Physical efficiency is, by and large, correlated with observable changes in controllable physical conditions, whilst cost, as a measure of economic efficiency, is also affected by often unpredictable and unknown economic factors, both internal and external. A past measure of physical output as a guide to future output is more reliable and useful than a computation of past cost as a guide to future cost. Moreover, the inevitable arbitrariness of allocations of joint costs (Wells, 1978) renders individual product costings themselves arbitrary, and for many economic decisions it is marginal not average costs that are relevant. However, a jobbing contractor like B&W does need cost estimates as a basis for quoting fair prices to customers, and it is this contracting function of accounting that is a particularly important feature of the B&W costings.

From the Neoclassical (economic rationalist) perspective, it would be argued that the major emphasis on technological efficiency, and related but subsidiary emphasis on costs, was an appropriate response to the conditions facing the firm at the time. The differing aspects of development of engine and labour standards may also be understood as reflecting the much greater difficulty of measuring and standardising human efficiency than machines.

Such a view, however, leaves for further interpretation and explanation the subsequent development of, and debate over, full standard costs of production in the late nineteenth century (Solomons, 1968; Wells, 1978). From the Foucauldian perspective, the development of engine standards by B&W, paying greater attention to the physical than to the cost dimension, may also be seen as an essentially unproblematic technological development. Again, as under the Neoclassical view, it is the later nineteenth century focus on the idea that standards can fully measure 'true cost' that needs explanation. From the Foucauldian viewpoint, this later sophistication makes sense, together with the development of systematic labour standards, in the light of the prior introduction of routine practices for recording and grading human performance, practices that had engineered a new power of surveillance, judgement, and performance control within organisations. Cost ascertainment and control would therefore focus, not on cost as an objective engineering datum about a product or process, but on cost as a construct of routine managerial practices. As such, its value lay in its ability to contribute, within more generalised systems of accountability, to the pursuit both of constant internal cost/quality optimisation and of effective external competitive advantage.

CONCLUSIONS

The development of accounting at B&W exhibits two main stages. During the years when the founders were at the helm, the accounting functions, though numerous, did not manifest particularly sophisticated characteristics. The concern with expenditure control was a natural first step for firms in the forefront of Industrial Revolution cost accounting methodology. The record keeping associated with the plethora of engine trials and experiments was at a high level, but was linked more to the engineering than to the cost accounting function. The data categories maintained in the early engine books served the sole purpose of providing support for computing the annual premiums owed to B&W based on coal savings. It would appear that accounting during this formative period was related entirely to purposes of an external economic and, in particular, of a contractual nature.

Conditions changed radically in the last five years of the eighteenth century. The coming of age of the younger Watt had a positive influence on the firm's utilisation of cost accounting, and, like other UK industrial entrepreneurs, he was in the vanguard of accounting developments (Fleischman, 1993). The cessation of external subcontracting and the associated construction of the new Soho Foundry altered the firm's requirements to control and account for the material and labour inputs of its engines.

The nineteenth century accounting experience at B&W was in some respects paradoxical and quixotic. The firm deployed certain cutting-edge accounting techniques (e.g., depreciation and transfer pricing), but did not exploit them in a consistent manner. The company tracked indirect expenses carefully, but failed to allocate general charges to productive departments, a practice evident amongst leading iron manufacturers during the period. We have seen the flourish of activity circa 1800–1802 that resulted in the establishment of labour piece rates and the costing of hundreds of different engine components. Great efforts were seemingly expended in this regard, but the process petered out in later years. This petering-out could be explained, from a Neoclassical viewpoint, as resulting from an essentially economic calculus—the cost/benefit ratio of the effort involved in updating costs and piece rates on a regular basis was not worthwhile. From a

Foucauldian viewpoint, however, it would represent a failure to establish the disciplinary gaze of a management system of surveillance.

So, above all, the B&W archives suggest a marked difference in the attention paid to material and labour standards following their initial introduction. The firm manifested a far greater concern with component costing than with unit labour costs. The engine books continued to be maintained in exquisite detail. The business records contain numerous product costings into the 1830s. Overall, therefore, considerably more detail seemed to accompany material than labour inputs.[13]

The major finding of our reinterpretation of the B&W archives is essentially a revisionist one. Upon close examination, the accounting there did not reflect the sophistication one might have anticipated given the firm's highest rating in the Fleischman and Parker (1991) survey. The accounting techniques may still have been amongst the best that the period had to offer as suggested by the research of Roll (1968) and Pollard (1965, 1990). However, the labour standards were clearly not the sophisticated means of control of human performance that exemplify modern managerial systems of accountability.

Although the crux of alternative approaches to accounting history has been argued to be the development of such modern standards, B&W itself remains a case where the historical interpretations of Neoclassicists and Foucauldians are still possible. The former would look to the conditions of labour organisation and argue that the economic cost/benefit calculus was not yet sufficient to demand such sophistication in control of human performance (or to evaluate them as valuable once invented for other reasons). The latter would argue that it was only when the discursive conditions of possiblity were created by developments in other spheres (such as the educational developments that took place shortly afterwards in the US) that the control of human performance could take place, in otherwise largely similar labour conditions, as, for example, at the Springfield Armory in the 1830s.[14] In respect of this particular case, however, the jury is still out.

On the nature of the labour standards, we have been able, by further examination of the archive, to shed more light on what was previously a considerably confused issue in the literature. Whilst there is clear evidence of the application of a set of normalising practices to 'rate setting' in the time studies of 1800–1802, on the basis of which piece rates and internal subcontracting prices were set, the relative lack of precision and the failure to follow up this experiment are even more striking. The original time calculations were based on evidence of variable quality about time worked and do not have the kind of precision one might anticipate, being recorded not even in hours but in half-day or quarter-day units. Thus, there appears to have been no managerial system of administrative coordination developed to produce feedforward or feedback data on the rates. The initial impression that, given the presence of time trials, time experiments, and detailed production data, there must have been a managerial gaze permeating the factory and controlling the performance of the employees proves on closer inspection to have been far from the case. Our conclusion therefore is that the B&W piece-rate exercise was a one-off to establish a new system of fair prices that thereafter received only sporadic attention.[15] And for even this one-off, the experiments, whilst they might be called time studies of a kind similar to those later undertaken at the Springfield Armory, were nowhere near approaching the rigour of true time-and-motion studies undertaken there in the 1830s that introduced a new managerial discipline of a modern kind (Hoskin & Macve, 1994; cf Tyson, 1990, 1993).

Such revisionist findings are important in the context of the debate over the genesis of modern management practice. As we have discussed, a major difference of interpretation within accounting history between the Neoclassical and Foucauldian schools has centred on how each interprets the development of labour standards. The former see this process as a gradual, continuous, and natural development, led by engineers. (Moral judgements regarding this pattern philosophically divide them and the Marxist/labour-process school.) The stumbling block for such economic rationalists, however, as Wells' work (1978) identified, is that the engineers produced accounting numbers that, although they seemed natural, could lead to economic nonsense. Yet, management might continue to base decision making on these bogus numbers confident that economically rational actions were being undertaken.

The Foucauldian school would regard the scientific approach to control of human performance, exemplified by Taylorism, as a cultural leap that only took place when discourses and practices, first deployed in other arenas, made it possible. It was not natural and inevitable, and it is no surprise that the numbers have always been problematic.

Whilst standardisation and efficiency seem of the essence of mechanisation, translation of these concepts to human activity is much more problematic. To come to treat human performance like that of a machine, functioning as if it is observable, measurable, and controllable in terms of efficiency, is to create a new discourse and a new way of seeing, describing, and controlling the world.

It is, of course, possible to argue that these viewpoints are simply different histories necessarily illustrating different aspects of the emergence of such modern phenomena as managerialism and cost accounting. Consequently, as Stewart (1992) has suggested, it would simply be a case of 'pluralising our past'. However, just because there are different kinds of history with different theoretical perspectives does not mean that all are equally valid. Even in a theoretically sophisticated world, many apparently major differences come down to the evidence. Often, a sufficiently reflective formulation of the key points of difference, coupled with a diligent search of the available evidence, may resolve what are otherwise defined as essentially theoretical differences. Therefore, in weighing the merits of each viewpoint, it is important to try and ascertain just what was achieved, when, where, how, and why.

As in all history, and from whatever viewpoint, time is of the essence (irrespective of what Foucault himself might or might not have said about origins), and a priority for research in accounting history is now to establish the precise sequence of development that led to the widespread adoption of the standards for measuring human performance that constitute modern managerial control. Herein lies the importance of continuing to research as many of these significant early industrial enterprises as possible in the UK and US, and indeed in Europe, around the turn of the nineteenth century.

NOTES

1. The material in this chapter is drawn heavily from R.K. Fleischman, K.W. Hoskin, and R.H. Macve (1995), 'The Boulton & Watt Case: The Crux of Alternative Approaches to Accounting History?', *Accounting and Business Research*, Vol. 25, No. 99: 162–176. The reader is cautioned in advance of reading this chapter that the data are presented within the context of two historiographic paradigms, the Neoclassical and the Foucauldian. If background information on these theories is required, please consult Chapter 9 before proceeding with this chapter. The reader is also advised that the ideas expressed in this chapter do not necessarily represent the views of Professor Parker. The use of the pronoun 'we' herein refers to Fleischman, Hoskin, and Macve.

2. We leave for a later paper the theoretical and factual arguments at issue between the Marxist/labour-process school (e.g., Clegg, 1989; Hopper & Armstrong, 1991; Tinker, 1992) and other historical approaches. The philosophical gulf is deep and wide (e.g., Hoskin, 1994; Neimark, 1990), but both the Marxian/labour-process and the Foucauldian schools share a concern with understanding power and human control. We suggest that the same historical crux—the nature of the development of accounting for human performance—provides the factual foundation that will determine how far each of these positions can be rationally sustained (e.g., Armstrong, 1994a) and will help identify priorities for future research.

3. Tyson (1990, 1993) has responded by recasting the Hoskin/Macve findings into economic rationalist explanations, though questioning certain of their processes of data selection. Hoskin and Macve (1994) have in turn challenged Tyson's interpretation of the relevant archival records.

4. Both sets of authors have also not been silent about shortcomings they see in the historical theorising of rival groups. Ezzamel et al. (1990), in what was essentially a review of *Relevance Lost*, disputed Johnson and Kaplan's description of the historical importance and non-problematic development of cost and management

innovations. One main contention was that evidence of cost accounting is not sufficient in itself to demonstrate its utilisation for management control and decision making. Ezzamel et al. contended that there was an essential difference between Johnson and Kaplan's view that early cost management numbers represented objective, useful information for management decisions, and their own opinion that accounting numbers are inherently problematic. In their view, the focus of interest is not the numbers themselves but rather the processes by which the numbers and related techniques have evolved and are deployed for the surveillance and control not only of workers, but of managers by managers. From the alternative perspective, Fleischman et al. (1996) have questioned the utilisation of a Foucauldian paradigm given the enigmatic and inconsistent nature of Foucault's theory of history, his refusal to search for origins in history, his relative inattention to factories specifically and economics in general, and his failure to mention accounting even though it does appear to fit his disciplinary discourse.

5. A further issue is the timing of US developments. Miller and O'Leary (1987) argued that the significant development occurred with scientific management from the 1880s onwards. Hoskin and Macve (e.g., 1988) argued, on the basis of evidence from the Springfield Armory, that the crucial development occurred in the period 1832–1842, and that scientific management was a later articulation of practices established some 50 years earlier.

6. Moreover, whilst we attach particular importance to the issue of labour standards as the historical crux, resolving the differences between two overall patterns of historical understanding of accounting's development clearly requires consideration of a whole mosaic of events and their explanations over a long period of time (e.g., Fleischman, 1996; Hoskin & Macve, 1994).

7. This re-examination of the archive has enabled us to offer a more detailed and comprehensive evaluation of the material than was reported in Fleischman and Parker's more general survey (1991) or in Hoskin and Macve's observations (1988) on Roll's (1968) conclusions. Roll's study did not extend beyond 1805.

8. Historians are fortunate that a substantial volume of B&W records survives from the late eighteenth and early nineteenth centuries. This archive, along with the Carron Company's records, is the most extensive the current authors have seen for an Industrial Revolution enterprise. The efforts of the archival staff at the Birmingham Central Library, where the firm's manuscripts are housed almost in their entirety, have made these important materials easily accessible to users. As with all archival records, however, it must be remembered that the accidents of survival mean that it is likely that there is also a substantial amount of material that has not survived, and this material, if available, might have altered the overall picture that we have drawn from the evidence available.

9. The document is undated but others in the box are dated circa 1800.

10. Strangely, Mousley's tender is apparently dated 21 July, the day after the discussions at which the agreed prices were determined.

11. The 3/8ths are not included in the intermediate subtotals either, which are each stated as an amount '+3/8'.

12. See also the 1801–1802 estimates cited by Wells (1978, pp. 73, 77, and Appendix 3).

13. It has been observed that material standard prices in inventory did not fluctuate between 1822 and 1830, but it must be recalled that although the period was one of falling prices, B&W was not positioned in a highly competitive industry, such as iron or textiles, where profit margins were continually in focus.

14. In evaluating the developments at Springfield as representing a crucial step forward in terms of measurement of norms of human performance, as compared with B&W (and with the earlier piece-rate regime at Springfield), one could point *inter alia* to the rigour of the experiments first undertaken in 1831, 'watch in hand' to establish 'the exact time necessary for...each particular task' (some tasks being less than a minute in duration and all being timed to the second, or even to

tenths of a second); to the combination of piece-rate payment with a strict time work-discipline to ensure a regulated ten-hour working day; and, of particular importance for the historical significance of these developments, to the strategic role of Springfield as the public sector forcing house for innovations, both technological and managerial, which were then diffused to the private sector arms industry, not least because private sector contractors had to compete with Springfield's costs as the benchmark. Moreover, the developments at Springfield can be located within a nexus of managerial developments traceable to the influence of West Point and its graduates, which was also significant in the history of the US railroads (Hoskin & Macve, 1988, 1994).

15. Another British one-off experiment in costing occurred at Etruria under Wedgwood beginning in the 1770s (Hopwood, 1987; McKendrick, 1970; Pollard, 1990).

8

New Cost Accounting Perspectives On Technological Change In The British Industrial Revolution[1]

Recent studies by economic historians have inspired fundamental rethinkings about the concept of the 'Industrial Revolution'. Dynamic change, now regarded as economy-wide rather than narrowly industrial, occurred over a longer period of time than has traditionally been assumed. Despite these revisionist concepts, historians have maintained the view that technological change and innovation constituted the focal preoccupation of industrial entrepreneurs and their managerial staffs. The choice of technology in these firms was thought to have depended almost entirely on the labour-saving properties of proposed new devices. This belief has largely sprung from Habakkuk's (1962) research in which he argued that entrepreneurs were not familiar with their capital costs due to the rudimentary nature of British Industrial Revolution cost accounting.

Evidence in this volume suggests that cost management practices during this period were not as unsophisticated as has been hitherto presumed. Indeed, cost accounting almost certainly contributed in a positive fashion to the decision-making processes that determined the entrepreneurs' choice of technology.

By way of apology, the current authors acknowledge that the primary source material reported in this chapter appears elsewhere (with references) in this book. However, we risk some repetition in order to marshall adequate archival data to support and supplement secondary sources that specifically address the relationship between cost accounting and technological innovation, a facet of the British Industrial Revolution that some economic historians rate as its most dynamic feature.

A SNAPSHOT OF TECHNOLOGICAL CHANGE

Technological change in the Industrial Revolution is probably most commonly identified with the advent of steam power. Yet, the adaption of steam to most industries was a relatively slow process despite the fact that the pre-industrial and industrial epochs witnessed a parade of new and improved engines. The Savery engine appeared in 1695, followed over the course of a century by the Newcomen engine (1712), Watt's rotative-propulsion engine (1784), and Trevithick's higher pressure engines (1810) (Brown, 1991; von Tunzelmann, 1978). Rotary steam engines only achieved widespread adoption in the 1840s at the point in time when they had become more reliably engineered (Brown, 1991). Since engine prices remained relatively constant during much of the early industrial period, price alone may not have influenced the timing of the transition to higher powered engines. Governing factors may also have included regional coal prices and the relationship between fixed and variable costs in operations (von Tunzelmann, 1978).

Consequently, steam power does not constitute a wholly representative snapshot of technological change during this industrial period. The wider perspective of manufacturing methods and power sources in the cotton industry illustrates an expanded horizon. From a simple handicraft, spinning was significantly changed by the advent of Hargreaves' spinning jenny, which by the 1780s could incorporate 60 to 80 spindles. By that time mules with capacities in excess of 140 spindles could be operated by a single worker (Chapman, 1972; von Tunzelmann, 1978). Powered spinning ultimately triggered technological change in other functional branches, such as weaving, knitting, bleaching, dyeing, and calico printing. It is important to note, however, that most technical change in the cotton industry took forms other than steam power. In fact, steam did not make significant inroads into cotton manufacturing and spinning, in particular, until the 1830s when it began to replace the water wheel. The new power source offered a number of advantages; e.g., the spinning of finer quality yarn and the reduction of labour costs (Brown, 1991; Chapman, 1972; von Tunzelmann, 1978).

With respect to weaving, the first powerlooms were not installed in Manchester mills until around 1800 and, despite the Luddite uprisings in 1812, did not become widespread until the 1820s and 1830s (Marshall, 1973). Regional and local differences produced a rather staggered adoption of powered technology. The woollens industry was quite slow to embrace new technologies relative to cotton, largely due to the greater technical difficulties encountered in applying mechanisation to wool fibres (Brown, 1991; von Tunzelmann, 1978). Thus, technological change in textiles was generally moderate in pace, with certain processes gradually becoming mechanised and others remaining predominantly manual. Mixed approaches, such as centralised spinning and domestic weaving, remained operational through the 1850s, though declining from the 1820s onwards (Brown, 1991; Bythell, 1969; Fleischman, 1985).

In mining also, a similar moderate pace of technological change is observed. Whilst there were various innovations and technologies employed in extracting coal, manual labour predominated through the mid-nineteenth century (Ashton, 1948). The steam engine did ultimately play a role in the extraction of coal, particularly in exploiting deeper ore seams. New technologies were deployed to reduce underground accumulations of gas and water (Flinn, 1966).

Entrepreneurs of the Industrial Revolution period grappled with a wide range of concerns associated with their endeavours. They tapped multiple sources of finance, organised production, selected sites for operations, sought sources of raw materials, adopted and adapted technologies, and created or penetrated new markets (Brown, 1991). Many technological innovations developed naturally from the routine of daily practice, often in the course of commercial operations. Science, technical development, and practical management were closely interrelated (Musson, 1972). Technical change and innovation were oriented towards multiple factors, including the supplanting of labour, the conservation of raw materials, and the more efficient use of capital (Ashton, 1966). These observations suggest grounds for our questioning the conventional wisdom concerning technological choices and the speed of their adoption during the period.

CONVENTIONAL WISDOM REVIEWED

The concept of the 'Industrial Revolution' has changed significantly since the term first entered the English language in Toynbee's (1884) path-breaking history lectures at Balliol College in the early 1880s. For many years, particularly whilst researchers trained in history rather than economics dominated the study of industrialisation in Britain, attention was focussed on the coming of factories and the attendant adoption of steam power, spawning the popular image of the 'dark, satanic mills'. Later, as developmental economists increasingly turned to history for assistance in solving contemporary problems, the concept of economic development was added to the Industrial Revolution agenda. However, studies still concentrated generally on the expansion of the industrial sector and the shift of resources from agricultural pursuits to industrial practices. Moreover, both historians and economists continued to see the Industrial Revolution as a fairly rapid process. Perhaps the most precipitous timetable was Rostow's (1960) claim that it occurred in Britain between 1783 and 1802, the famous image of the 'take-off'. Rostow, however, broadened the view of the Industrial Revolution in that he stressed economic growth as well as economic development.

As economic history has become more quantified, measurements of economic performance have reinforced this belief. It is now generally accepted that the Industrial Revolution featured growth on a broad front, and that non-industrial sectors, such as agriculture and transport, like manufacturing, experienced change and gains in productivity (for a brief discussion see Vamplew, 1983). Growth measurements have also undermined the idea of a major discontinuity either in the middle of the eighteenth century or during its last two decades (Deane & Cole, 1969; Rostow, 1960). Although not yet sanctified as conventional wisdom, it would appear that rates of growth before 1740 have been underestimated (Crafts, 1985) and those after 1780 overestimated (Harley, 1982), suggesting that change was more gradual than previously assumed.

Nevertheless, despite the transition in interpretation from industrial revolution to economic evolution, the British Industrial Revolution, however defined, is still regarded as a watershed in British, if not world, economic history. One other traditional view has survived the re-evaluation—the importance of technology. In the midst of revisionism, it remains a feature of the Industrial Revolution consistently acknowledged as playing a vital role. Toynbee (1884) initially laid great emphasis on the application of steam power to textiles production. Subsequently, historians have added an almost inexhaustible list of other innovations so that by 1948, one eminent economic historian could sympathise with the schoolboy who proclaimed that 'a wave of gadgets swept over England' (Ashton, 1948, p. 59).

Even amongst contemporary historians, technology remains in the forefront. In an otherwise highly iconoclastic collection of essays on the Industrial Revolution era, the writer of a chapter on technical change, though downplaying the idea of a handful of dramatic breakthroughs, maintained that 'it is the variety and pervasiveness of innovation during British industrialization...which will be argued as having been the key to the growth process' (von Tunzelmann, 1981, p. 143). In another compendium on the contribution of the so-called 'new' economic history's quantitative and theoretical approach to Britain's industrialisation process, Mokyr (1985, p. 28) accepted that 'technological progress, in its widest definition, has remained as the basis of the Industrial Revolution'.

The determining factors of particular technology choices have been the subject of considerable debate (Musson, 1972; Saul, 1970; von Tunzelmann, 1981), sparked over a quarter-century ago by Habakkuk's (1962) theoretical *tour de force* which compared and contrasted the nature of nineteenth century American and British technology. He argued that early British industrial entrepreneurs usually sought labour-saving innovations since they perceived labour to be their scarcest factor of production. One reason cited for this concern was an inadequate appreciation of relative factor costs occasioned by the 'extremely rudimentary' accounting methods of the early nineteenth century and, by implication, of earlier periods. More specifically, Habakkuk suggested that 'it is wildly unlikely that, in comparing alternative techniques, anyone ever applied a notional rate of interest equal to the anticipated rate of profit', and that 'in any case early manufacturers neglected to take account of interest except when they had to borrow from outsiders...in effect, they behaved as if their capital cost them nothing' (Habakkuk, 1962, pp. 26–28). This viewpoint was reinforced in Pollard's (1965) seminal work on the history of management during Britain's industrialisation in which he pronounced his verdict that the accounting methodologies of the British Industrial Revolution did not contribute to the genesis of modern managerialism.

Despite a few case studies which cast doubt on these generalisations (McKendrick, 1970; Roll, 1968; Stone, 1973; see also

Edwards, 1989; Jones, 1985), the judgements of these two respected economic historians have held sway in the profession (see, e.g., Hudson, 1977). Accounting historians have also generally accepted the view that effective cost accounting was not a feature of the Industrial Revolution (Chatfield, 1977; Edwards, 1937; Garner, 1954; R.H. Parker, 1969, 1986; Solomons, 1952; Yamey, 1949). The absence of a contemporary industrial accounting literature and a belief that the Industrial Revolution's business environment was insufficiently complex to require sophisticated accounting techniques have established a tradition now being challenged by recent research findings that managerial accounting was being pursued in a wide variety of firms for pricing, process control, and project evaluation (Edwards & Newell, 1991; Fleischman & Parker, 1990, 1991, 1992; Fleischman & Tyson, 1993; Jones, 1985).

This chapter will support these attempts to demonstrate that the period of the Industrial Revolution was not a cost accounting wasteland. Several firms, amongst them some of the more successful, developed costing systems which enabled them to make rational business decisions, including choices from various technological options.

The pages of *Accounting, Organizations and Society* in recent years have featured a concerted effort to expand the vision of accounting historiography (Hopwood, 1987; Hoskin & Macve, 1986, 1988; Loft, 1986). The call has gone out for an extended analysis of the dynamics of accounting change, 'the full range of impacts' accounting has had on organisations (Hopwood, 1987, p. 226). Whilst the emphasis of much recent research has been to chronicle accounting methodological innovations in relation to societal and political factors, elements of economic rationalism have not been ignored. As Hopwood has pointed out, history has not indicated a single 'unitary mobilizing force' (ibid., p. 227). In this chapter, the authors investigate one such economic underpinning of Industrial Revolution cost accounting—its development as an aid to technological decision making.

ARCHIVAL EVIDENCE OF ATTENTION TO TECHNOLOGY

The archival findings reported in Chapters 3, 4, and 5 provide strong grounds for arguing that significant linkages existed between cost accounting and technology issues in the iron, textiles, and extractive industries despite Habakkuk's (1962) opinion to the contrary. At a macro-level of analysis, it would appear intuitively obvious that if sophisticated cost accounting systems were up and running, as we have argued throughout this volume, that these methods would have been deployed to assist decision making with regard to technological innovation. In the case of the iron industry, the magnitude of the initial investment (£50,000 or more) and the need to expand operations in order to meet the new demands of international markets would have mandated this attention. We have seen how Darby and Dowlais used technology to reduce the cost of coal inputs in the iron-making process in order to survive in a highly competitive market. The emergence of the textile trades, particularly cotton, was characterised by a series of new technological inventions (jennies, mules, powerlooms) which revolutionised the productive capacity of the industry. Perhaps of greater importance was the gradual but inevitable introduction of steam power, which freed enterprises from dependence upon running water and enabled many firms to become players in more efficient, urban labour markets. In the case of the extractive industries, steam engines were absolutely necessary for the exploitation of deeper ore seams as shallower sources were exhausted. We have seen how Boulton & Watt, in the firm's early days, was able to penetrate Cornish tin mining for just this reason. Stella Coal Company's 1840 cost analysis for pumping water to win coal seams is a later example of the same technological imperative. In the sections that follow, we will attempt to illustrate on a more micro-level how various Industrial Revolution enterprises employed cost accounting methodology to deal with technology issues. In particular, we will examine (1) the processes involved in procuring new technology, (2) experiments undertaken to decide between technological alternatives, (3) the accounting used to evaluate existing technology, and (4) special decision making related to technology.

Procuring New Technology: Capital investment in new machinery was a decision of vital importance for Industrial Revolution entrepreneurs, not only because of the substantial expense often associated with technological innovation, but also as a function of the relative shortage of capital during the period. Consequently, careful cost estimates frequently accompanied these decisions. We have seen how several firms corresponded with Boulton & Watt, either requesting detailed estimates of cost for their steam engines or attempting to negotiate a reduction of cost. Survivals include correspondence from Davison & Hawkesley (textiles), Samuel Walker & Co. (iron), and Oldknow (textiles). Carron Company (iron) owners were involved in similar discussions in 1767, long before the foundation of the famed steam engine partnership. In the later Industrial Revolution when steam engine procurement decisions remained paramount in the textile trades, another technological adoption of great significance was the mechanisation of the weaving branch. Ashworth, Horrocks, and Philips all analysed the estimated costs and anticipated revenues from large-scale purchase of powerlooms. Moreover, they followed up their procurement decisions with a close scrutiny of powerloom expenses and productivity.

The Carron archive is especially rich in examples of cost accounting utilisation for technological decisions, perhaps a function, in part, of the voluminous business records that have survived and, in part, because of the firm's rule that all capital expenditures of £20 or more required the approval of all partners. This rule was doubtlessly occasioned by Carron's often precarious funding base, with capital improvements typically financed by short-term borrowings. Carron's General Court, pursuant to this directive, required cost data for all capital improvements. John Smeaton provided estimates in 1769 for a new boring mill and a new wheel shaft for a blast furnace. Similarly, there was a rash of repair-or-replace decisions—to blow out or repair a blast furnace, to repair or replace a kiln, to repair a steam engine in 1769.

Textile entrepreneurs were most concerned about technological innovation. John Marshall & Co. was the industry leader in this regard as evidenced by its experimentation with new spinning and hackling equipment. After having decided to purchase new machinery, the firm continued to monitor the progress of its investment. The Gregs attributed their net operating loss in 1829, in part, to the use of older machinery. The Gotts carefully tracked differential costs and productivity of old and new engines between 1833 and 1857, compiling five-year averages for that purpose. The impressive Ashworth analysis in 1842 of the losses incurred as a result of a power deficiency occasioned by low water levels paved the way for a transition from the water wheel to the steam engine as the motive power source.

Later in the Industrial Revolution, steam engine purchase became a prominent investment decision in the mining sector. Stella Coal received two cost estimates for a 20-horsepower engine in 1821. The Bridgewater Colliery purchased new pit engines in the 1830s and 1840s on the basis of cost estimates. In 1845, Stella solicited seven tender offers for three new steam engines of different sizes and capacities. More impressive perhaps were the pains taken by the owners of the High Rake Mine near Sheffield. In 1836–1837, they received four estimates (including one from Boulton & Watt) for a new steam engine. The firm was careful in its questioning of the engine's capabilities and dimensions. Again in 1842, another engine was procured, but only after an entire meeting of management had been expended in studying the four cost estimates submitted.

Technology Options: It was occasionally the case that Industrial Revolution entrepreneurs analysed their productive processes to determine the cost/benefit of alternative technological approaches. For instance, Benjamin Gott was reputed to have spent thousands of pounds weighing the relative advantages of steam versus water dyeing (Heaton, 1931–1932). Gott also undertook a number of experiments to test the expense associated with mechanised processes as distinct from manual approaches. The Strutts in 1809 and 1810 evaluated their 'old way' and 'new way' for bleaching sewing short skeins and the bleaching of sewing dram balls by hand and by water machines. John Marshall's diary in 1821 includes intricate detail for a series of experiments designed to cost wet and dry spinning. The cost of new technology was an integral part of this analysis.

The Stella Coal Company ran an interesting series of experiments to test the relative costs of human, horse, and machine power for the 'leading' and 'putting' of coal. In 1822 at the firm's Towneley installation, engines were demonstrated to be more cost efficient for leading coal. A ponies versus humans test for putting coal was conducted at Stella in 1845. Lest there be any question, the ponies prevailed by a wide margin. A subsequent experiment at the Gosforth Pit in 1836 confirmed the Towneley verdict that steam engines were more cost effective in the mines than horses.

Enterprises involved in coal production were very much concerned with the differential capabilities of their output on a seam-specific basis.

Dowlais had the coal from their various mines analysed with respect to carbon content, combustible properties, residual ash, etc. in 1812. Stella had a number of similar tests conducted in the late 1840s. The relationship between these types of experiments and technology was brought forward in a series of trials Blackmore conducted in 1842 when he gauged the consumption of coal from various mines by replicating railway journeys over a common distance with the same locomotive.

Finally, mention should be made here of the ongoing experimentation in technology at Boulton & Watt. This famous firm was somewhat distinct from those aforementioned as being a maker of technology rather than its consumer. During the firm's early history, there were seemingly endless trials as its products became perfected. Subsequently, the experimentations were less numerous, though there are extant results of boiler and steamboat engine testing in the 1810s and 1820s.

Comparisons of Existing Technology: Having expended large amounts for technology, Industrial Revolution entrepreneurs did not tire of maintaining cost and productivity records on their investments. This pattern was evident in all three of the major industries studied in Chapters 3–5.

The iron founders were particularly concerned that they be provided with cost data on blast furnace inputs and outputs. The most sophisticated were the weekly reports furnished to Carron's management in the 1790s. Evidence of similar reporting appears in the archives of Butterley, Clyde, and Darby. The Crawshay's empire was the most perplexing in that blast furnace comparisons were made at Cyfarthfa and Ynnisfach, but not at Hirwaun. Two leading iron concerns, Darby and Dowlais, were generating data regarding their various steam engines in the 1820s. At Darby the coal consumption and downtime of each engine was tracked, whilst at Dowlais statistics were maintained on coal consumption and horsepower generated.

The textile entrepreneurs were even more active in maintaining records about the performance of their machines. Marshall, it will be recalled, kept daily performance cards on all machines. An 1823 document of some 14 pages in length, though essentially a comparison of the firm's three mills, included a comparison of coal consumed by the firm's various steam engines. Henry Ashworth was particularly active in maintaining comparative statistics about his technology. He calculated output and profit per spindle relative to cotton and coal inputs. He knew with some exactitude the waste expected from the spinning machines and the anticipated downtime of the powerlooms. The Philips' maintained budgeted and actual output for their various looms. At both Strutts and Cardwell, Birley, comparative data were maintained for the relative expenses incurred in the multiple carding and spinning rooms.

In the extractive industries there was likewise careful attention given to technology issues. We have seen the numerous cost calculations that were undertaken for specific mineral fields or ore seams. Once again, control of the mining operations at Carron reflected the greatest care. At Carron certainly, and most probably at other venues, these comparative data were related to technology decisions, such as the venues at which to allocate resources of capital equipment. Particular mineral fields were abandoned not only when their ore supplies became exhausted, but also when the extractive process became comparatively too expensive.

As early as 1785, the Halbeath Colliery was receiving from viewer John Wright periodic reports on the state of repair of its various fire engines. At Mona Mine in the 1820s, expenses of each individual smelter were carefully tracked, especially the volume of coal consumption. In the Tyneside region in the 1830s, a standard list of viewers' queries for analysis of mine operations solicited a considerable amount of information about the state of technology. The viewers seemed vitally interested in the maximum production possible given the technology available. They seemed vastly more concerned about machines than about men.

This interest of the viewers in technology was translated into a plethora of narrative and statistics about steam engines. The Lancashire-based operations of the Duke of Bridgewater generated details on the coal consumption and operating costs of its various steam engines in the 1830s. A decade later the firm was receiving monthly reports on the state of its engines and boilers. Meanwhile, Stella Coal in Tyneside was undertaking technical trials and making narrative reports on its engines.

Technology and Special Decision Making: A number of major decisions certain Industrial Revolution firms faced had very definite repercussions in terms of technology. For example, the vertical integration decisions we have seen undertaken at Crowley, Oldknow, Philips, Strutt, and Wedgwood meant substantial capital investment in technology. On the flip side of the coin, the abandonments of product lines or phases of operations at Carron, Darby, and Wedgwood freed technology for utilisation elsewhere.

It must be admitted that many of the cost analyses associated with these expansions and abandonments have not survived, if they ever existed. We have seen evidence in the cases of Philips, Carron, and Darby, though even here much of the analysis appeared to be descriptive rather than statistical. We also have not seen any statistical grounding for what must have been one of the most significant technology decisions in the whole of the epoch—the transition of Boulton & Watt from external subcontracting to the production of engine components at Soho Foundry.

However, there are several extant documents that convey to us the expectation that decisions related to an expansion or contraction of operations were done with recourse to cost accounting. The special reports at Carron in the early 1770s, dealing with levels of production and a proposed sinking of the Kinnaird steam engine, took into account a number of factors related to technological issues. Likewise, we have seen two soup-to-nuts cost estimates for entire factory installations which include estimates for the machinery to be contained therein. These two were the anticipated cost of the Pearsce factory near Papplewick (1795) and the Gott proposal for a four-storey spinning factory (1831).

SUMMARY AND CONCLUSION

It is our conclusion, based on the archival record chronicled above, that technological innovations were a matter of deep concern to Industrial Revolution entrepreneurs. As was the case with so many of their business activities, they employed cost accounting techniques to aid them in decisions involving the procuring, tracking, and comparing of their technological investments.

During the Industrial Revolution, there were several significant inducement mechanisms giving rise to technological change in British industry. Those factors advanced in the literature include population growth, rising and redistributed incomes, changing tastes, and overseas markets (on the demand side), and resource scarcities and scientific research (on the supply side) (for comments on these developments, see von Tunzelmann, 1981). Important as such macro-level influences might have been in terms of aggregate technological change, what concerned the individual industrialist, who actually made the investment decision, was the effect which the adoption, adaption, or even rejection of a particular technology would have on his profitability.

Traditionally, both economic and accounting historians have visualised such decisions as having taken place with imperfect knowledge. If true, this misinformation could have had serious implications for the enterprise's choice of technology, for as Rosenberg (1985, p. 125), perhaps the doyen of economic historians on technological matters, concluded from a lifetime's work in the field:

> ...an important common denominator running through these historical examples is the persistence with which firms attack what, at any given time, they regard as the most restrictive constraint on their operations.

If the perceptions of entrepreneurs were based on incomplete or inaccurate data, then clearly they could have been sent down an inappropriate technological trail. This chapter, however, has urged that the shortcomings in cost accounting during the Industrial Revolution have been exaggerated and has suggested that the existence of effective cost accounting in several significant enterprises enabled informed decisions on the choice of technology. The evidence it reviews also strongly suggests that historians may have attributed undue primacy to technological innovation in itself as the focal preoccupation of Industrial Revolution entrepreneurs. Rather, we propose that entrepreneurs maintained a dual and integrated focus upon the interrelationship between technological innovation and cost efficiency.

Two intriguing questions remain to be answered. First, could it be that one explanation of why some of the firms cited above developed a competitive edge in their respective industries was their use of managerial accounting procedures to make rational economic decisions on technology and other matters? Second, can it be established that the leaders in successful technological innovation were also those firms which pioneered the use of, or advances in, cost accounting techniques? Economic *and* accounting historians are invited to consider these issues as part of their research agendas.

NOTES

1. A portion of the material contained in this chapter appeared in R.K. Fleischman, L.D. Parker, and W. Vamplew (1991), 'New Cost Accounting Perspectives on Technological Change in the British Industrial Revolution', in O.F. Graves (ed.) (1991), *The Costing Heritage* (Harrisonburg, VA: Academy of Accounting Historians): 11–24.

9

Expanding the Dialogue: Industrial Revolution Costing Historiography[1]

> *A scientist who is interested in maximal empirical content, and who wants to understand as many aspects of his theory as possible, will accordingly adopt a pluralistic methodology, he will compare theories with other theories rather than "experience", "data", or "facts", and he will try to improve rather than discard the views that appear to lose in the competition (Feyerabend, 1978, p. 47).*

Within the past two decades, there has been a widening of horizons for the investigation of accounting history to incorporate social, psychological, cultural, and political parameters to complement more traditional economic explanations of change. This 'new accounting history' has become a focus of conferences held annually at various venues around the globe and several leading accounting journals, most notably *Accounting, Auditing and Accountability Journal* (*AAAJ*), *Accounting, Organizations and Society* (*AOS*), and *Critical Perspectives on Accounting* (*CPA*).

Recently published writing on the history of accounting generally and the development of managerial accounting during early US and UK industrialisation specifically has focussed attention on three major research paradigms or worldviews. For many years the Neoclassical or economic rationalist perspective has dominated as the mainstream, traditional approach. More recently, this privileged position has come under challenge, primarily in *AAAJ*, *AOS*, and *CPA*, from 'critical' theorists whose voices are now being forcefully heard. The schools represented here are the Marxist/labour process, from a tradition older even than Neoclassicism, and the Foucauldian, more recently arrived and a product in the first instance of French postmodernism.

Unfortunately, this emerging trichotomisation of accounting historiography has been typified by a confrontational tone that suggests the potential for a significant communication failure between and amongst contending parties. What we have seen, as one participant elegantly put it, is 'academic antler-clashing' (Hoskin, 1994, p. 59). A rather aggrieved Foucauldian-Marxist contretemps, inaugurated by an exchange of articles in the early 1990s (Hoskin & Macve, 1991; Neimark, 1990), has been extended in a 1994 *CPA* volume dedicated to dialogue between the leading critical approaches (Hoskin, 1994; Neimark, 1994). Likewise, a Foucauldian-Neoclassical debate over accounting developments at the Springfield Armory in *AAAJ* (Hoskin & Macve, 1994; Tyson, 1993) bears a confrontational tone that may inhibit a full appreciation by participants and readers alike of what are valuable and detailed studies. A more contemporary tempest has been brewing as traditionalist historians (Fleischman & Tyson, 1996; Keenan, 1996; Scorgie, 1996) have taken pen in hand to protest broadsides against their methodology launched from a Foucauldian perspective in Miller and Napier (1993). Merino and Mayper (1993) have specifically noted a gulf of hostility between traditional and critical historians that needs to be bridged.

We are not urging that academic research be done without passion; it would be pretty dull stuff otherwise. Nor are we suggesting that the current debates are approaching some crisis point or academic Armageddon. It cannot be denied that hotly debated beliefs often coalesce around issues of significance and can yield constructive advances in understanding longer-term changes in social, economic, and political structures and processes. We will always have our definitional disagreements, contentions over underlying assumptions of the various theoretical frameworks, and questions regarding the data selection processes of rival researchers. Whilst confrontation over these issues can be constructive, we would argue that it is more likely to be destructive and unproductive when the contending parties so passionately cling to their own beliefs that they fail to listen to opposing viewpoints. It might appear to observers that any party's predilection to dismiss alternative viewpoints as valueless would amount to intellectual arrogance.

We are not simply launching here a plea for harmony. There is value in discourse between differing perspectives. Many of the major developments of accounting history, typified by the origins of cost management, are the product of multiple influences. Consequently, monolithic postures fail to provide the explanatory richness these questions require. Each of several paradigms has valuable insights to offer, but each alone is limited to an incomplete analysis (Chua & Degeling, 1993). At the same time, we take very much to heart the warning of Norris (1991, p. 1) that the end product of an overly conciliatory approach might be a pabulum-like substance:

> A few minutes search through the index of any learned journal is enough to show how structuralism has taken hold in the most respectable and cherished quarters of academic study. Old polemics are quietly forgotten because the ground has meanwhile shifted to such an extent that erstwhile opponents find themselves now in a state of peaceful alliance. To trace the history in detail would provide an instructive example of the capacity of Anglo-American academic criticism to absorb and homogenize any new theory that threatens its sovereign claim.

It is a goal of this chapter to provide a more thorough analysis of the prospects for advancing industrial revolution costing historiography through a pluralistic and synergistic approach. Recent interest in this subject has brought a greater variety of perspectives to bear with accompanying increments to our sum of knowledge. The spirit of the new accounting history demands that practitioners of the expanded discipline avoid a monolithic view of the world. The genesis of industrial revolution cost accounting is a field of investigation sufficiently broad to allow for a multiplicity of explanations. We fully acknowledge that the expanded dialogue possibilities we are espousing here are of sufficient magnitude that perhaps we should not be discussing them within the limited context of such a small component of accounting's history. But we must start the process somewhere. First, we consider the dialogue literature as written by philosophers and historians. Second, we review the historiography on industrial revolution costing that has emanated from the three paradigmatic schools and the ensuing critique of each. Subsequently, these frameworks are further investigated with a view to identifying the potential for their more productive coexistence and constructive dialogue. To this end, the chapter is intended to address not only the participants in these theoretical debates, but also those observers who by virtue of differing degrees of interest, perspectives, and familiarity with the issues are not as fully conversant and require therefore a fuller explication of the terrain. Whilst the task of engaging both the uninitiated and the cognoscenti may be somewhat problematical, the philosophy of constructive dialogue espoused requires us to attempt to engage the interest and comprehension of all parties.

DIALOGICAL LITERATURE

Our call for a greater dialogue amongst participants in the historiographic debate over cost accounting origins appears on the surface to be simplistic and non-problematic, but philosophers have not universally agreed that tangible benefits accrue from this communication form. The legacy of dialogue literature, so highly developed by the Greeks, continues strongly today in the hermeneutics of Gadamer and the critical theory of Habermas (Michelfelder & Palmer, 1989). Indeed, hermeneutics has been accepted in the contemporary world as a research paradigm in the social sciences (Habermas, 1990).

Plato, an exponent of dialogue in its spoken form, was wary of the misunderstandings and misinterpretations that could attach to the words themselves in conversation. However, a more substantial goal for dialogue than the correction of comprehension errors is the possibility that 'the exchange of speech and counterspeech, question and answer, can produce consensus' (Dallmayr, 1989, p. 84). Another facet of Platonic dialogue, the famous *eumencis elenchoi*, which Gadamer (1986, p. 331) called its 'unique and lasting relevance', is the opportunity, indeed objective, for strengthening an opponent's discursive position (Forget, 1989).

Hermeneutics, defined in one instance as 'the art of rightly understanding the speech, chiefly in written form, of another' (Frank, 1989, p. 157), is a more modern philosophical system centred on dialogue to achieve understanding of text, now the written word rather than the spoken as had characterised Greek logocentricism. For the hermeneutical approach, the comprehension of what is said or written is of paramount importance (Gadamer, 1989). Dialogue enables understanding and occasionally consensus, though historical truth in any traditional sense is not at issue. Francis (1994, p. 244) wrote:

> Hermeneutic thought is not concerned with questions of absolute knowledge or the method (epistemology) for attaining it. It is instead concerned with the question of what practices achieve an "authentic" or "good" understanding.

When writing of the past, individual prejudices and issues of the present must necessarily intrude, so that historical narratives can only be relative. Habermas (1990, p. 32), though by no means a relativist himself, observed:

> For this reason it is important to see that all rational reconstructions, like other types of knowledge, have only hypothetical status. There is always the possibility that they rest on a false choice of examples, that they are obscuring and distorting correct intuitions, or even more frequently, that they are overgeneralizing individual cases. For these reasons, they require further corroboration.

In a certain sense, this relativist aspect of hermeneutics is Hegelian in inspiration. Hegel (1975) wrote in *Logic* variously, '...truths of philosophy are valueless, and must be treated as baseless hypotheses, or personal convictions' (p. 20); '...no philosophy has been refuted, nay, or can be refuted...every system represents one particular factor or particular stage in the evolution of the Idea' (p. 126); and '...people quarrel about the correctness of proposed definitions; for here everything depends on what perception we started from, and what points of view we had before our eyes in so doing' (p. 286). Notwithstanding, contemporary hermeneutics does not accord Hegel the same formative influence as Plato because of his introversion, an emphasis on the knowing of a consciousness rather than communicative action. Habermas (1990, p. 9) differentiated hermeneutics from both Kantian and Hegelian philosophy:

> Pragmatism and hermeneutics oust the traditional action of the solitary subject that confronts objects and becomes reflective only by turning itself into an object. In its place they put an idea of cognition that is mediated by language and linked to action. Moreover, they emphasize the web of everyday life and communication surrounding "our" cognitive achievements. The latter are intrinsically intersubjective and cooperative.

A variety of philosophers have supported the premise that historical writing is subjective. Hegel saw the historian as 'a part of the process he is studying, has his own place in that process, and can see it only from the point of view which at this present moment he occupies within it' (quoted in Gadamer, 1986, p. 468). Ricoeur (1965, pp. 26, 31; see also Stewart, 1992), in detailing how history is reflective of the historian's subjectivity, labelled the 'judgment of importance' the selection of those events and developments to chronicle. Historical relativism is also a key principle in hermeneutics. Gadamer (1986, p. xx) emphasised how history becomes old-fashioned to succeeding generations as 'people read the sources differently because they are moved by different questions, prejudices and interests'. Gadamer glorified the differences in the social milieux and circumstances of historical observers, whilst fighting against 'the Enlightenment's prejudice against prejudice' (Francis, 1994, p. 240). Similarly, Habermas (1990, p. 27) observed how the value judgements of historians are represented as facts in discourse, 'because the theoretical framework for an empirical analysis of everyday behavior has to be conceptually integrated with the frame of reference within which participants themselves interpret their everyday lives'.

It is but a short step to move from the historian's subjectivity to the dangers of writing to an historical paradigm. Habermas (ibid., p. 31) wrote:

> There is a sense in which any interpretation is a rational interpretation. In the act of understanding, which entails an evaluation of reasons as well, the interpreter cannot avoid appealing to standards of rationality and hence to standards that he himself considers binding on all parties, including the author and his contemporaries...

Of course, the problem is proving that these standards are truly rational. Ricoeur (1965, p. 36) said that the historian 'may turn toward a particular philosophy to try to determine how the whole problematic of an epoch and all influences of the past are contained therein', thereby running the risk of sacrificing a broader understanding available through a multiplicity of worldviews.

It is our contention that, since historical truth is relative, the input of many may contribute additively and synergistically to our knowledge and understanding of the past. Try as they might, historians are not capable of objectivity. Those who aspire to be so are deluded and ignore the 'distorting lens' through which they view the past (Hill, 1986, p. 14). Horkheimer, a founder of the Frankfurt School, believed that every point of view has its place, but that each is limited in its explanatory value. He wrote, 'the uncovering of limitedness and onesidedness in one's own and in other's thought, constitutes an important aspect of the intellectual process' (quoted in Held, 1980, p. 182). Adorno, Horkheimer's colleague, philosophised in opposition to Hegel that reality could not be understood from a single perspective and that only a number of representations, 'a constellation', would serve to approximate that reality (ibid., pp. 204, 212). The message of the Frankfurt School is an open invitation to evaluate contending approximations of reality.

Hermeneutics underscores dialogue as a methodology for the achievement of mutual understanding. Its literature suggests a number of prerequisites for successful dialogue:

— a continuing willingness of participants to permit the dialogue to carry them along toward mutual understanding (Michelfelder & Palmer, 1989);
— a need in dialogue for a common ground and a common language for communication to occur (ibid.);
— a continuing good will amongst the participants in dialogue; e.g., a willingness to transcend one's narrowness to understand the other (ibid.; Gadamer, 1989); a desire to strengthen the remarks of other participants rather than to expose their weaknesses (Gadamer, 1986); a commitment to the proposition that there need be no last word (Risser, 1989);
— an acceptance by participants that 'in principle a rationally motivated agreement must be reachable' (Habermas, 1990, p. 105).

Dialogue puts participants at risk, not only to the rejoinder of others, but also to their own self-doubts. It exposes one's own prejudices. As Gadamer (1986, p. 341; see also Bernasconi, 1989; Gadamer, 1989) said, 'in a dialogue, we do not remain what we are'.

In April 1981, a contretemps took place at the Goethe Institute in Paris between Hans-Georg Gadamer and Jacques Derrida, a foremost proponent of deconstructionism. Derrida and his supporters raised a number of points that collectively questioned the value of dialogue as a primary methodology and art form of hermeneutics:

- The meanings of the language in a dialogue exceed our intentions. Because of the intrusion of other definitions, it is impossible to determine the intended meaning (understanding) from the alternatives (Michelfelder & Palmer, 1989).
- Participants in dialogue are not openly willing to hear what others are saying. Derrida would argue that philosophers in general use language 'protreptically', assuming their own personal prowess to speak authoritatively. Such communication is antipathetical to the Gadamerian dialogical model of good will and openness to others (ibid., p. 17).
- Participants in dialogue can never experience 'the success of confirmation' that one has been perfectly understood (Derrida, 1989, p. 54).
- Good will, a necessary prerequisite for successful dialogue, is rarely uncoerced, arising out of power differentials that exist amongst participants (e.g., young/old, student/teacher, etc.) (Madison, 1989).

Deconstructionists are skeptical that understanding can be a shared experience given the differing backgrounds and 'horizons of understanding' of participants in a dialogue. Those in the hermeneutic tradition respond that understanding is forthcoming (1) from the 'fusion of horizons' wherein the traditions of participants unite their differences in understanding, and (2) from the functioning of the hermeneutical circle which allows participants to confirm, enrich, or alter their pre-dialogue understandings (Shusterman, 1989). Yet, hermeneutics and deconstruction are distinctly similar in their democratic approaches to knowledge. Arrington and Francis (1989, p. 3) observed, 'the purpose of deconstruction, then, is to subvert the attempt to get closure around knowledge production—the attempt to silence other voices by illicitly claiming to possess a superior awareness of "truth"'.

Arrington and Puxty (1991, p. 31) have done useful work on the role of hermeneutics in accounting research, particularly on the impact of Habermas. They observed how hermeneutics in its broadest sense suggested 'a discursive arena in which any conceivable claim about that shape and character can be brought to bear upon accounting in a democratic and rational way'. They appreciated how Habermas' approach sought to avoid 'the theorist's imperialist view' by lessening the complexity of issues that 'paralyze action' (p. 51). Habermas urged a more critical hermeneutics that constrained total democracy of interpretation lest closure be unattainable. Arrington and Puxty did question the Habermasian view that 'consensus was the objective of social discourse' (p. 52). Hermeneutics anticipates a successful outcome from dialogue conducted according to its ground rules. Gadamer, for instance, believed that truth, albeit limited in the hermeneutic sense, was only attainable via this mechanism (Habermas, 1990). Both Gadamer and Habermas subscribed to the idea that the possibility of consensus was antecedent to successful dialogue. Dallmayr (1989, p. 91), commenting on the Gadamer-Derrida exchange, represented as the former's view that consensus possibilities were prerequisite for 'all human solidarity and the viability of society' (quoting Gadamer). Habermas (1990, p. 105) similarly maintained that 'rationally motivated agreement must be reachable'. We would expect less august benefits from dialogue; namely, understanding and strengthening another's positions, the unmasking of one's own prejudices, and the risking of one's own position to external critique and internal self-doubt. Perhaps in subscribing to this more limited purpose, we have come full circle back to Derrida whose opposition to dialogue was not doctrinaire. Derrida felt 'negotiation' a prerequisite for understanding, and that negotiation was not possible without dialogue (Michelfelder & Palmer, 1989).

Common language is a 'critical preliminary condition' for dialogue lest mutual understanding be impossible, given the cross purposes of the participants in the exchange (ibid., 1989, p. 6). Cooper and Tinker (1994, p. 2), in introducing the recent *CPA* volume of Marxist and Foucauldian dialogue, expressed the opinion that the jury was still out as to 'whether these two projects are fundamentally irreconcilable, or whether fruitful debate and collaboration are possible'. Perhaps the future is even more problematic if Neoclassicists are factored into the equation. Shepardson (1989), commenting on the Gadamer-Derrida debate, wondered if hermeneutics and deconstruction had so little common ground that they represented differing languages. It would be easy to argue that Foucauldians, Marxists, and Neoclassicists are incapable of communication because they subscribe so inexorably to the language of their respective paradigms, each emanating from ardent economic and social underpinnings and goals. But, it seems that with a requisite leavening of good will and respect, the obstacles should not be insurmountable as we are all seeking answers (within the limited context identified in this chapter, at least) to similar, or at least not unrelated, questions.

INDUSTRIAL REVOLUTION HISTORIOGRAPHY

As already outlined previously in this volume, pioneering cost accounting texts date the advent of sophisticated costing from Taylor's scientific management in the US, commencing in the 1880s (Garner, 1954; Littleton, 1933; Solomons, 1952; Yamey, 1949). The advance of note at that time was the development of engineered labour standards and variance analysis. Support for this chronology has also been forthcoming from more recent historical surveys (Chatfield, 1977; R.H. Parker, 1969, 1986). Hopper and Armstrong's (1991) study of American labour control mechanisms in the late nineteenth century, Miller and O'Leary's (1987) work linking the development of labour cost standards to the creation of the 'governable person' in the early twentieth century, and Loft's (1986, 1990) examination of World War I munitions contracting in the UK similarly typify findings reflective of this time frame.

Notwithstanding, a substantial volume of contemporary historical research has suggested a revision to periods earlier in both US and UK industrialisation. Chandler (1977) found costing origins in the heyday of American railroading; Johnson (1972) in US textile mills of an 1850s vintage; and Hoskin and Macve (1988, 1994) and Tyson (1990, 1993) at the Springfield Armory in the 1830s and 1840s. Firm-specific studies of British Industrial Revolution enterprises, such as Roll (1968) on Boulton & Watt (see also Fleischman et al., 1995), McKendrick (1970) on Wedgwood, Stone (1973) on the Chorlton Mills, Edwards and Baber (1979) on Dowlais, Fleischman and Parker (1990) on Carron, and Walsh and Stewart (1993) on New Lanark have contributed to a rehabilitation of the epoch in terms of its cost accounting. Maturing accounting methodologies have also been identified in more general investigations of the period's business archives by Jones (1985), Edwards (1989), Edwards and Newell (1991), Fleischman and Parker (1991, 1992), Fleischman et al. (1991), Fleischman and Tyson (1993). A significant proportion of this work contains not only the findings from archival research into business records, but also substantial theorising about the contextual environment within which more sophisticated accounting practices developed.

Both facts and theories are required for the advancement of knowledge. In the practice of science, one cannot proceed without the other (Feyerabend, 1978). The worldview or paradigm of researchers will affect their theories, their selection of facts, and their conclusions (Feyerabend, 1978; Kuhn, 1970; for accounting, see Chua, 1986). Three major schools have emerged in the examination of industrial revolution cost accounting. Neoclassical (economic rationalist), Foucauldian, and Marxist/labour-process perspectives constitute the bulk of the published writing to date.

This schemata reflects a deliberate classificatory decision which bears some further comment by way of qualification. It relies upon published work which some would argue has been used as an instrument of privilege and domination in the academic world. We would contend that through the agency of such journals as *AAAJ*, *AOS*, and *CPA*, the voices of critical theorists have had the opportunity to be heard. In this particular study, alternative classifications could have been employed. For example, Chua (1986) selected three 'world-views' for analysis of accounting research more generally. She labelled these perspectives the mainstream, the interpretive, and the critical. In their review of historical approaches to organisational theories and organisations, Covaleski and Aiken (1986) examined subcategories of two major perspectives, 'early organizational theories' and 'sociological approaches'. The categorisation for this chapter is based on those research approaches that represent the preponderance of industrial revolution historiography to date. We have taken for this purpose the very identifications traditionally adopted by participants in the debate.

Some of the potential problems inherent in any categorisation of research under particular paradigms include the attribution of one classification to studies that in fact draw upon multiple perspectives. Such imposed artificiality admittedly does some injustice to works so classified; e.g., papers identified as economic rationalist that broadly consider social factors and works labelled Foucauldian that in no way abjure the relevance of economic concerns. Further, there is always the possibility that categorisation may contribute to the further hardening of the very differences for which we investigate harmonisation possibilities. Jones (1992) has warned us of the inherent dangers in seeking to reconstruct theoretical positions which are not our own. With these potential pitfalls firmly in mind, we raise the following points with the intent of disclaiming a perceived rigidity in our subsequent analysis of the contending paradigms:

1. There are more similarities amongst the research schools than is commonly acknowledged.
2. There are also strong debates within schools as to the particulars of theories and facts. Consequently, the complexity of each school may necessarily be inadequately represented in this chapter.
3. Differences amongst and within the schools exist for numerous reasons, including but not limited to ideology, methodology, level of analysis, and assumptions about human behaviour and capabilities.

Yet, we are encouraged in this effort by Dobb (1973, p. 5) who wrote:

> Theoretical analysis and generalisation invariably build upon classification...; and what is classification but a drawing of boundaries between discrete objects, which are in turn derived from the structural pattern one senses (or deems to have discovered) in the real world?

NEOCLASSICISM

Neoclassicism or economic rationalism is synonymous with the traditional or mainstream view of accounting's history, its origins and change processes. However, its claim to a rightful place in the new accounting history may also be argued because its methodologies for investigating and analysing organisation theory represent an interdisciplinary and contextualised approach. In terms of accounting history specifically, the economic rationalist position has in more recent times been promoted by the publication of *Relevance Lost* (Johnson & Kaplan, 1987). Though their conclusion that perceived efficiency gains are (or at least should be) the primary driver of accounting change is not universally accepted by scholars, it might be conceded that the popular book 'moved accounting's history centre-stage' (Ezzamel et al., 1990, p. 157).

Traditional explanations have linked cost accounting origins and subsequent developments to the aspirations of entrepreneurs to improve efficiency. Early twentieth century industrialisation has been most frequently identified as the milieu in which complex organisations and management accounting systems initially flourished. Coase's (1937) thesis that firms grow until substitutability at the margin is no longer more efficient than a market transaction has formed a basis for more recent theorising about the development and expansion of these organisational forms and management techniques. Extending Coase's insights, 'transaction cost theory' (Williamson, 1971, 1973, 1975, 1985) and 'agency theory' (Alchian & Demsetz, 1972; Fama, 1980; Jensen & Meckling, 1976) have become components of the economic rationalist viewpoint.

Chandler, employing a time-honoured metaphor, dated the emergence of the modern business enterprise from the point when firms could function more profitably with a managerial hierarchy rather than market mechanisms. At this point the 'visible hand' of managerial decision making replaced the market's 'invisible hand' (Chandler, 1980, pp. 9–11). The information needs of the centralised firm precipitated the transition from bookkeeping to accounting. Chandler (1977) credited managers of the large American railroads during the 1850s and 1860s with devising nearly all the basic techniques of modern accounting. Cost, rather than earnings, became the criterion by which railroad managers controlled and judged their subordinates. Thus, operational rather than financial controls were introduced.

Williamson (1975) extended Chandler's vision from business history to organisational theory. He described conditions under which forms and practices of internal organisations become more efficient than markets. Transaction cost theory was Williamson's essential contribution. The 'main purpose' of capitalism's economic institutions was to economise on transaction costs. It should be noted that transaction costs were distinguished from production costs, a preoccupation in Neoclassical analysis (Williamson, 1985). Williamson (ibid., p. 11), in paying homage to Chandler's influence, wrote that 'the mistaken notion that economic efficiency was substantially independent of internal organizations was no longer tenable after the book [*Strategy and Structure*, 1962] appeared'.

Building upon the economic theory of Coase and Williamson and the economic history of Chandler, Johnson (1981, 1986) has formed the bridge to accounting history. Cost accounting, he has argued, developed as a rational business response to opportunities involving new technologies and markets. Johnson (1991) dated the internalisation and management of market activity within the firm from the late eighteenth century. The concept evolved rapidly as the number of economic exchanges conducted in managed business rather than market settings escalated. Johnson (1972, 1991) examined the emergence of cost accounting at the Lyman cotton mills in the 1850s. There he observed early examples of financial management with the utilisation of accounting to measure the efficiency of various conversion processes and to monitor the performance of individual employees. The development of sophisticated cost accounting in this context differed from the types of organisations investigated by Chandler. Although cost accounting at Lyman was not related to production or technological decision making, the cost system did facilitate operational control.

Fleischman and Parker (1991, 1992) surveyed the climate and accounting of numerous British Industrial Revolution companies. Stemming from an intensity of competition, mature cost accounting techniques were in evidence, particularly in the dominant textile and iron industries. They hypothesised that accounting innovations were designed and introduced by business entrepreneurs in direct reaction to their economic environments.

It should be noted, in conclusion, that the Neoclassical tradition is significantly broader than the economists and historians identified above. However, the Neoclassical economists of the Chicago school, agency theorists, and the accounting positivists of the Rochester school have not concerned themselves with the topic of early cost accounting developments.

NEOCLASSICISM: THE CRITIQUE

The focus of the Neoclassical critique has centred on the charge of 'economic reductionism', a phrase that came into prominence to describe a form of 'vulgar' Marxism now decades in eclipse, if it ever existed at all. Mills (1993, p. 802) discussed the 'economic fallacy' (a 'privileged position' accorded economic activities) in economic positivism and traditional Marxism. Dobb (1973, p. 145) argued, in contrasting Marxism and Neoclassicism, that the expansion of determination to include socio-economic factors (such as the behavioural implications of ownership or non-ownership of the means of production on social classes) expanded the 'boundaries of the subject...differently and more widely than has become customary with an economic theory conceived as the "laws of the market"'.

Though some would regard Neoclassicism's economic determinism as a strength (Englander, 1987), various researchers have mentioned the fundamental issues that remain unaddressed as a result. Loft (1986) judged the work of economic rationalists too narrow in that history's broader social context was never incorporated. DuBoff and Herman (1980) cited as a major defect in Chandler his failure to come to grips with the realities of power in business and managerial behaviour. Capital accumulation (profitability and growth) appears more central from a managerial perspective than efficiency (Neimark & Tinker, 1987). DuBoff and Herman (1980) also challenged Chandler's assumption that the factory system was a response to technological change rather than an institution created to maintain labour discipline. Hoskin and Macve (1988, p. 68), in addition to questioning the link between technology and accounting innovations, doubted whether economically rational managers would have constructed such a system:

> We therefore see accounting not as the "practical" response of men faced with new entrepreneurial and organizational challenges, who "sensibly" devised ways of collecting and processing the data needed to make rational economic decisions—for in that sense no "practical" man would have invented modern accounting practice (the outputs of which are not obviously what is needed for such purposes).

Hoskin and Macve would argue that the accounting numbers generated by these methods would not be relevant for business decision making per se. Rather, the processes of data collection served to communicate to labour the message that its productive efforts were routinised, systematised, and scrutinised (Ezzamel et al., 1990).

Johnson and Kaplan's (1987) work, its importance recognised in some quarters, has been criticised nevertheless on various grounds. Ezzamel et al. (1990) disputed their description of the historical importance and functional development of cost and management innovations. They contended that the mere existence of cost accounting is insufficient evidence to assume its utilisation for management control and decision making. Even Johnson and Kaplan argued that external financial reporting requirements limit internal accounting's response to efficiency considerations, thereby providing evidence of other influences. Johnson and Kaplan (1987) and Fleischman and Parker (1990, 1991) have assumed a link between cost accounting and 'effective management' without more definitive evidence of that relationship. Miller and Napier (1993, p. 639) cautioned against the tendency in Neoclassical literature to use modern 'notions' in discussing and evaluating periods during which contemporary nomenclature and concepts did not exist (see also Stewart, 1992). In a more global observation, Machlup (1967, p. 9) felt that Neoclassicists were misguided in using the theory of the firm 'to explain and predict the behavior of real firms' when, in reality, 'it is designed to explain and predict changes in observed prices...as effects of particular changes in conditions...'.

Clegg (1989, p. 193) doubted certain economic underpinnings of Neoclassicism, suggesting that 'contracts are rarely the reciprocal, conflict-free and equal exchanges that are axiomized in "transaction theory"'. Thus, the Marxist critique of economic rationalism has stressed the labour contracts which constitute so important a part of industrialisation. Tinker and Neimark (1988) not only questioned the neutrality posturing of transaction cost theory, but took Williamson and Chandler to task for failing to recognise the incompatibility between the quest for corporate cost economies and the well-being of employees (see also Neimark & Tinker, 1987). Tinker (1988) portrayed transaction cost and agency theories as ideologies that protected the interests of the status quo. Likewise, Hopper and Armstrong (1991) have expressed doubt as to whether output efficiency can be achieved as a rational economic exchange between workers and the firm as assumed in transaction cost theory. Further, they accused transaction cost theorists of 'rationalising past events through the institutional lenses of the present', treating all organisational relationships as market transactions to the exclusion of social and political factors (ibid., p. 409; see also Walsh & Stewart, 1993).

Overall then, the Neoclassical critique has argued that the focus upon economic relationships has ignored social and political factors. At an organisational and individual level, it has been contended that economic rationalism has failed to take account of managers' pursuit of personal power and status (see Chua, 1986), perhaps a primary explanatory variable for industrial costing systems. In addition to these allegations of ignored factors, critics have questioned the links that economic rationalists have assumed between cost accounting, on the one hand, and technological development and effective management on the other (Knights, 1990).

Neoclassicists additionally stand accused of a variety of non-theoretical sins ranging from closemindedness, reflected by a refusal to engage in constructive dialogue with critical historians, to an alleged domination of accounting research topics, methodologies, and resources. As holders of powerful positions in academe, Neoclassicists have been able to restrict access to traditional, mainstream journals and to define appropriate scholarship for academic personnel decisions and dissertations.

Since the appearance in 1959 of studies sponsored by the Carnegie and Ford foundations, research, particularly in US business schools, has become increasingly constrained by scientific methodologies (Smith et al., 1988; Whitley, 1986, 1988). This trend has been observed in a variety of disciplines—economics (McCloskey, 1983), finance (Whitley, 1986), and accounting (Smith et al., 1988; Whitley, 1988). The end result has been an enshrinement of Neoclassical economics as advanced by the Chicago school and translated into accounting theory by the Rochester school (McCloskey, 1983; Whitley, 1988). Consequently, we are left with a product that has been variously described as positive rather than normative, narrow in focus, ahistorical, abstract, esoteric, and distant from the realities of practice (ibid.; Whitley, 1986). This now mainstream branch of accounting research has never adequately theorised the appropriateness of natural sciences methodology for the social sciences or the possibility of objectivity (neutrality) given the value-laden baggage carried by researchers (McCloskey, 1983; Smith et al., 1988; Whitley, 1988). Smith et al. (1988), in criticising Kaplan's case-study approach, identified numerous factors that have received little or no attention in 'positivist framework' research—political aspects of management, power relationships, organisational past actions, alternative perspectives offered by social sciences' research paradigms (Weberian and Marxist), and the legitimacy (as distinct from the efficiency) of practices.

The charge has also been made that research funding has created a vested interest amongst mainstream academic researchers. Baritz (1965, pp. 203–204) observed how social scientists who migrated from the ivory tower to industry 'became by default accessories to the power politics of American government and industry, while insisting they were innocent of anything of the sort'. Aronowitz and DiFazio (1994, pp. 247, 263) have wondered if the sharing of values between researchers and their benefactors, as well as the active participation of funding recipients in valorising acceptable research, has not undermined the university's claim to be 'a site of critical and disinterested inquiry' (see also Whitley, 1986). Perhaps ironically, Watts and Zimmerman (1979), leading exponents of positivism, have accused accounting researchers of pandering to the self-interests of funding agencies. This theme has also been roundly articulated for UK academic labour process, though here the government, as the representative of capital, has been more specifically identified as the agent limiting research perspectives (Puxty et al., 1994; Willmott, 1996).

FOUCAULDIANISM

The French philosopher, Michel Foucault, has become a central figure for a substantial group of 'contextualisers' researching early developments in managerial accounting history (Napier, 1989, p. 245). Identified by Habermas (1987, p. 287) as 'the theorist of power', the disciplinary paradigm established by Foucault to chronicle the history of asylums, prisons, barracks, schools, and other closed institutions appears in many ways to parallel changes in the factory system. Accounting techniques serve as a vehicle for the normalising 'gaze' required to accommodate micro-level discipline in the factory setting.

One of Foucault's major contributions to the philosophy of history has been his analysis of the interconnections between power and knowledge (Dreyfus & Rabinow, 1982; Foucault, 1979), an 'indissoluble unity' as Habermas (1987, p. 273) put it. Though Foucault 'eschewed large scale theories' (Gane, 1986, p. 123) and was 'suspicious of claims to universal truths' (Foucault, 1984, p. 4), his admiration of Nietzsche bespoke power as a motivating force in his dialectic (Habermas, 1987; Stewart, 1992). With the industrial take-off of the late eighteenth century, an appropriate apparatus of production became necessary (Foucault, 1984). Within the factory setting, a new, more subtle power technology was required. One of the contributions of the emerging bourgeoisie was the development of a new disciplinary form of power, one that was economic and non-sovereign (Foucault, 1980). Indeed, Napier (1989, p. 245) called Foucault's narration of this shift in power from the sovereign to the disciplinary his 'main contribution'.

The new factory discipline simultaneously induced labour force docility and utility. Foucault used the term 'penal accountancy' to describe the process by which all behaviours could be rated on a continuum from good to evil and overall performance quantified. Actions could be assessed with precision via the mechanism of a 'punitive balance sheet' (Foucault, 1979, pp. 180–181). To integrate the individual worker into the factory system, to render him 'an articulated extension' of the machine, the techniques of 'biopower' were employed (Foucault, 1984, pp. 17, 211–212; Gane, 1986; Sheridan, 1980). The promulgation of normative standards of behaviour and the prescription of punishments for deviation reflected the system's consummate control over attitudes as well as physical bodies (Dreyfus & Rabinow, 1982; Foucault, 1979, 1984).

The Foucauldian view of power differs markedly from a more traditional identification of power as an agency of subjugation and repression. Instead, power is construed as an 'omnipresent web of relations', a network which operates from below as well as from above (Thiele, 1986, p. 248). Power in the Foucauldian sense must be distinguished from domination in that it does not function universally to suppress the interests of the subjected. Grey (1994, p. 13) observed that 'since Foucault sees power as not simply repressive but also as productive, it is possible to conceive of power-knowledge regimes which are productive of particular values which are deemed desirable'.

Smart (1983, p. 102) underscored the importance of non-economic parameters of power for understanding and analysing the interconnections between politics and the economy, as well as the rooting of power relationships in the 'social network rather than the economic condition'. In its more economic sense, power enhances the aspirations of labour in the factory environment by providing motivation, order, and regulation to benefit the more common good (Habermas, 1987; Miller, 1987). Normalising standards provide individuals with opportunities to increase their own well-being (Knights, 1990).

One instrumentality for this exercise of power was knowledge obtained through the surveillance of daily functions (Foucault, 1979, 1984). Foucault's paradigmatic observation mechanism to render the individual worker visible was Bentham's model of the Panopticon. Though conceived as an architectural device for a prison or an asylum in the pre-industrial age, panopticism was readily extended to the factory environment. The technique made the exercise of power more efficient through comparisons of the performance of individual operatives (Dreyfus & Rabinow, 1982; Sheridan, 1980; Walsh & Stewart, 1993).

The Foucauldian influence has been a recent arrival in cost accounting historiography. Hoskin and Macve (1988) detailed how cost accounting at the Springfield Armory in the 1830s and 1840s provided a technique of 'hierarchial surveillance' which rendered labour 'calculable' and 'total human accountability' achievable. The structure of control typified what Hoskin and Macve (1986, pp. 41, 49) called 'grammatocentricism', a series of written rules and regulations giving rise to a distinctive discipline.

The search for disciplinary origins has been extended to British Industrial Revolution historiography as well. McKendrick's work on Wedgwood (1970) and Roll's on Boulton & Watt (1968) underscored the great attention paid by these firms to disciplinary innovations designed to control labour practices (Hopwood, 1987). Walsh and Stewart (1993, p. 797) have documented how Robert Owen utilised at New Lanark a reporting structure that became 'the backbone of a regime of surveillance and hierarchy', permitting upper management to monitor the activities of individual workers. Notwithstanding, a body of Foucauldian thought would urge that historical change, such as the birth of managerial accounting, is not necessarily a response to seemingly economic imperatives. Hoskin (1994, p. 78) suggested alternatively that 'material change [occurs] at the level of practices, and so prior to the changes perceived by dialectical materialism'.

Foucault's voluminous writings encompassed fundamental rethinkings over his career. Miller (1987) and Grey (1994) noted substantial changes in Foucault's theories of power circa 1972. Although Foucault is said to have urged the study of discontinuity in history (Foucault, 1980; Gane, 1986), this characterisation became increasingly uncomfortable for him (Dreyfus & Rabinow, 1982; Foucault, 1988; Sheridan, 1980). Foucault was more clear in disavowing a search for origins in history and would not have seen value in the efforts contemporary historians have expended developing a timetable for the advent of sophisticated cost accounting. Variously he proclaimed that historical beginnings were lowly, that knowledge was not the quest for origins, and that a purpose of genealogy was to destroy the primacy of origins (Dreyfus & Rabinow, 1982; Foucault, 1980; Smart, 1983). Many accounting researchers who use his framework have not been interested in the origins of cost accounting per se, but rather have concerned themselves with the more general concepts of power and control, their development and deployment within the context of accounting.

FOUCAULDIANISM: THE CRITIQUE

The bulk of commentary on Foucauldianism has come from Marxists who accuse Foucauldians of 'symbolic reductionism', an ignoring of the materialist basis to reality, occasioned by their pronounced emphasis on language (Neimark, 1990, p. 110). Neimark (1994, p. 92) took Foucauldians to task for failing to establish priorities in their analysis. Since discourse is so all-encompassing, it can refer 'to everything that is said, written or thought in a given era'. Hoskin (1994, p. 67) argued in response that 'discourse is not self-generating, for there are always historically specific practices which form the controlling, selecting, organizing and redistributing procedures that...structure its production'.

Marxist economic historians (Hobsbawm, 1968; Thompson, 1964) have traditionally been concerned with the exploration of working class subjectivity, a point of commonality between the two critical approaches. However, Marxists believe Foucauldians undertheorise material, economic, and political realities (Tinker, 1992). Cooper and Tinker (1994, pp. 2–3) criticised early Foucauldian theorists for a 'lack of attention...to issues of resistance and for the failure of the analysis to incorporate material conditions. Without theorizing these features, researchers cannot articulate effective action to change regimes of power'. Smart (1983, p. 107) would respond to this critique, as he did to Poulantzas' charge that Foucault failed to analyse state power, by arguing that Foucault's focus was 'upon the new mechanisms of power which have penetrated the body and everyday existence'.

Armstrong (1994a, p. 50) praised Foucauldian historiography for questioning 'the facticity and neutrality of accounting information'. However, he questioned Foucault's monolithic view of power, one common to all disciplinary regimes (schools, hospitals, armies, factories), serving universally to enhance human capacities. The work of Knights and Collinson (1987) highlighted the incompatibility of accounting with other disciplinary power structures. Armstrong (1994a, p. 41) noted that worker organisations differ from a Foucauldian 'disciplinary blockade' where labour is continuously subjected to a moral and material ordering. Surveillance and disciplinary norms are ineffectual for controlling labour in the absence of coercion, economic power, and/or negotiated arrangement. Armstrong (ibid., pp. 33,37) found that the Foucauldian paradigm does not fit the pattern of worker resistance to disciplinary regimes, an anticipated outcome when outside influences infiltrate an industrial environment without a 'total institutions' envelopment of the worker.

Armstrong (ibid.) argued that the visual disciplinary gaze of the Panopticon differs in substance from the formal and abstract nature of accounting systems. Chua and Degeling (1993, p. 312) supported both these latter themes by encouraging further research studies into 'how and why the [panoptic] gaze is circumvented or blinded and resistance succeeds'.

There has been relatively little critique of Foucauldianism by historians of the Neoclassical persuasion. However, Tyson (1990, 1993) has cast into terms of economic rationalism the developments at the Springfield Armory in the 1840s which Hoskin and Macve (1988) explained within a Foucauldian context. Whereas Hoskin and Macve described a control process based on a grammatocentric series of accounting-based standards and regulations, Tyson found the accounting innovations a rational response to perceived economic conditions. Tyson (1993, p. 13) carried the critique a step further in subsequent debate with Hoskin and Macve when he identified a major pitfall in writing to a paradigm and then accused the Foucauldians of falling into it:

> Notwithstanding the advantages of accommodation, the Foucauldian histories appear seriously impaired by the need to substantiate a particular social theory. Underlying these and other theory-driven studies may be the belief that facts can never be objective, so why bother to investigate them carefully. However, conducting research from one particular doctrinaire perspective may predispose the search for confirming evidence and prompt its authors to interweave fact and opinion in order to emphasize a singular world view. As a result, it becomes nearly impossible for most readers to disassemble factual evidence and evaluate reasonably the opinions and interpretations put forth.

In summary, the Foucauldian approach has been variously criticised for its emphasis upon language at the expense of materialist reality and for an alleged inadequacy in theorising economic and political factors. Both its claimed neutrality and its somewhat monolithic view of power have also been questioned. Critics have argued that its focus and reliance upon surveillance and discipline are by themselves inadequate for labour control and that it has not allowed for worker resistance to disciplinary regimes.

MARXISM/LABOUR PROCESS

Given a traditional view of Marxist economic determinism, it is possible to envision accounting as a mechanism to aid the capitalist bourgeoisie in maximising its exploitation of the industrial proletariat. Contemporary Marxist accounting historians, though not having lost contact with a Marxist view of class conflict (i.e., conflictual relationships at the point of production), have moved away from economic reductionism into a broader investigation of the social, cultural, and political underpinnings that define industrial relations.

These expanded horizons, auguring a more eclectic and less monolithic brand of Marxism, have resulted from the combined efforts of academics in a variety of disciplines (e.g., accounting, economics, history, sociology). Jones (1972, p. 112) observed a quarter-century ago that Marxist historians had to venture beyond the 'safe pastures of labour history'. Yet, at that same time, Hobsbawm (1972, p. 282) wrote of the Neo-Marxist retreat from 'vulgar' Marxism and its familiar tenets of class struggle, economic interpretation of history, historical laws, and a narrowness of subjects for historical investigation. Neo-Marxist historiography had become, in part, a 'critique of the simple mechanical schemata of an economic-determinist type'. Meek (1976, p. 310) might not have even conceded that this perceived narrowness ever existed, given his opinion that Marx's unique method for studying economics called for 'a restoration of the essential unity between the different social sciences'. Likewise, Hill (1986, p. 5) observed how Marxist-influenced historians assume the 'connections between the culture and the economics of a society'. Notwithstanding, the avoidance of a monolithic interpretation of history remains an agenda item for some contemporary Marxist accounting historians as evidenced by Neimark's (1990) defence against the 'strawman' she accused the Foucauldians of constructing in waging the battle of conceptual frameworks.

It is the obligation of Marxist theorists to update Marx's writings as appropriate to new stages of capitalist development (Meek, 1976; Thompson, 1989). Commencing in 1974 with the appearance of Braverman's *Labor and Monopoly Capital*, the labour-process school has represented one such Marxist revision. Contributors include theorists running the gamut of critical scholarship, including many avowed Marxists. However, since an element of Marxism's vitality has been the tendency of Marxists to challenge foregoing Marxist theory, labour-process historiography is included as a component of the critique.

No Marxist accounting historian, apart from those of the labour-process tradition, has yet presented research results on early industrial cost accounting. The likelihood exists, however, that a Marxist participation in debate over accounting's implications during this period would be forthcoming if archival researchers prove able to uncover greater evidence of its significance in the transition from domestic system to factory (Tinker, 1992). Meanwhile, we might utilise three surrogates to indicate plausible directions—(1) the work of Marx himself, particularly as elaborated in *Capital*; (2) the evaluations of the British Industrial Revolution by Marxist economic historians; and (3) the research of Marxist accounting historians on later-day corporations and their critique of Neoclassical and Foucauldian postures.

Marx himself in *Capital* (1977) presaged the issues and arguments of more recent work by labour-process researchers. Marx catalogued the specific conditions under which capitalism required the formulation and costing of relationships and parts of the production process. The twin goals of profitability and capital accumulation required measurement techniques. In an introduction to the work, Mandel observed that profit maximisation mandates 'exact and minute cost calculations' (Marx, 1977, p. 65). Marx saw that technology, for capitalists, is evaluated based on its productivity, 'measured by the human labour-power it replaces' (p. 513). Capitalists will only use machinery when such use provides a reduction in price (cost), not necessarily when there is a savings in labour. Cost cutting specific to labour arose first through lengthening the work day, resulting in an intensification of work at no extra cost. Thus, the more intense use of labour and machinery reduced costs and increased profits. When laws were passed to restrict the length of the work day, Marx observed that a further escalation of technology ensued. Piece rates were another control mechanism, rendering 'superintendence of labour...to a great extent superfluous' (p. 695). Middlemen could purvey goods to capitalists at a piece rate that was above the rate paid to labour. These observations exhibit the extent to which Marx focussed on costs, particularly as they impacted labour during this early stage of capitalist development.

Marxist economic historians have written extensively about British Industrial Revolution processes. Thompson (1967) studied the Crowley and Wedgwood enterprises as early examples of industrial time discipline, concluding that the essence of the British Industrial Revolution was not technological change, but the exploitation of labour and the resistance thereto. His larger work on the making of the English working class (Thompson, 1964) exemplifies the breadth of Marxist-inspired research. Here Thompson (ibid., p. 11) wrote, 'I am convinced that we cannot understand class unless we see it as a social and cultural formation'. He criticised Hobsbawm (1957–1958), the Marxist spokesman for the 'pessimist' side in the famous debate over Industrial Revolution living standards, for his overly economic focus. Ultimately, exploitation was the agency by which humanity was reduced in status to an instrument, but the forms of exploitation far transcended the economic and varied widely in different historical contexts (Thompson, 1964).

Marxist accounting historians have actively criticised the theorising of their Neoclassical and Foucauldian counterparts. Here the most oft-heard message is the impossibility of neutrality (Neimark, 1990; Tinker, 1991; Tinker et al., 1991). Accounting functions, which economic rationalists take for granted (such as striving for efficiency and cost reduction), have 'conflictual underpinnings' (Tinker & Neimark, 1988; Tinker et al., 1991). Accounting ranges from a method 'to bolster particular interest groups' (Tinker et al., 1982, p. 167) to an 'ideological weapon' in the class struggle over wealth distribution (Tinker et al., 1991, p. 37). Tinker (1991), in his response to Solomons (1991), argued that representational faithfulness in financial reporting is impossible. Likewise, the accounting historian can achieve neither neutrality nor objective reality (Tinker & Neimark, 1988). Since accountants cannot analyse the past or present objectively, contemporary Marxist research has underscored the role accountants might play in enhancing corporate social responsibility (Tinker, 1984, 1985; Tinker & Neimark, 1988).

MARXISM: THE CRITIQUE

In the early 1920s, Lukacs and Korsch, both active Communist Party members, undertook a critical review of orthodox Marxism. In particular, they disputed the positivist and determinist aspects that suggested 'unalterable stages of historical development' and a natural sciences methodology (Held, 1980, pp. 20–21). Here the pattern of Marxists revising Marx to correspond to new stages of capitalism became an essential component of the critical tradition.

Certain economic rationalist analysts, typified by Chandler, have regarded labour essentially as a non-issue in the development of the modern corporation (Littler, 1990). By contrast, Braverman, whose 1974 seminal work has given birth to two decades of a rich and voluminous labour-process literature, underscored the centrality of labour control within the history of industrial organisations. Braverman, as a major Marxist revisionist, narrowed the focus of investigation to the production process, as opposed to Marx's more general concern with the totality of exchange relations between conflicting economic classes (Littler, 1986). Though Braverman chronicled how different methods of labour control were developed at different stages in capitalism—from the domestic system, to internal subcontracting, to piece-rate structures, to Taylorism (Braverman, 1974; Clawson, 1980; K. Thompson, 1984)—his major emphasis was on the monopolistic capitalism phase born when earlier control attempts failed in the competitive environment of the 1880s (Armstrong, 1984; Littler, 1986). Braverman's 'first principle' was to extricate the labour process from control by workers and to place it firmly in the purview of management. This new form of work organisation, 'deskilling', was a major component of the transition from the craft tradition to Taylorism, and featured variously the fragmentation of work, the cheapening of labour through the reassignment of tasks to lesser skilled labour, and the empowerment of a significantly enlarged managerial corps to supervise the work process (Braverman, 1974; Littler, 1986).

The critique of Braverman has widely expanded the horizons of investigation and, in this regard, has resembled the advent of the new accounting history in our discipline. Braverman's perspective on labour control was quite narrow, focussing on a homogeneous, deskilled labour force (Gordon et al., 1982), a 'conspiratorial one-dimensional concept of management' (Knights & Willmott, 1986, p. 4), and the objective (determined or controlled) aspect of labour relations (Knights & Willmott, 1990). Littler (1986, p. 14) critiqued Braverman's rather monolithic view:

> But it is not possible to analyse capitalism, let alone a social transformation, through one essential relation. Class struggle is a crucial pressure towards labour-saving innovations, but this is not the only systematic pressure which capitalists face and on a day-to-day level it might not be the most pressing one.

Gordon et al. (1982) investigated factors (diversity of working class origins, ethnic antagonisms, unionisation, human agency, class alliances) in US labour history which contributed to the segmentation, as distinct from the homogeneity, of the labour force. Thompson (1989) emphasised the stratification and social division of labour, particularly along the lines of sex and race. Meiksins (1994, p. 47) reviewed the work of critics who took Braverman to task for analysing skills that were essentially masculine and 'purely manual, object-manipulating'. Buchanan (1986) accused Braverman of failing to recognise a plethora of managerial motivations apart from the 'capitalist imperative' and the difficulties management has encountered in labour-process control with advancing technology and information systems. Boreham et al. (1986) underscored three further elements of critique: (1) Braverman's failure to explore avenues apart from labour process by which control is brought to bear (see also K. Thompson, 1984); (2) his virtual ignoring of labour resistance and working class consciousness (see also Armstrong, 1986; Clawson, 1980; Gordon et al., 1982; K. Thompson, 1984; P. Thompson, 1984); and (3) the complexity of certain exogenous influences impacting employment structure, such as unemployment levels, regional economic growth, new industries and products, etc.

It was particularly in the work of Burawoy that the multivariate forms of labour process became evident as worker subjectivity (voluntarism) was analysed alongside Braverman's objective action (Knights, 1990). Burawoy (1979) acknowledged that there was a conflict in economic interest between labour and management (the focus of Marx and Braverman), but that there was a consensual aspect as well. Arising out of contemporaneous political and ideological dimensions coexistent with the economic, the interests of capital and labour should not be viewed as necessarily antagonistic (Knights & Willmott, 1990). The dichotomisation of society into two monolithic groups, based only on economic factors, is inadequate because of the exclusion of political and ideological criteria (Littler & Salaman, 1982).

A number of other refinements in labour-process literature have been advanced. Braverman equated Taylorism with capitalist control strategy despite the fact that 'responsible autonomy' and scientific management's 'direct control' may coexist as distinct managerial techniques (Friedman, 1977). Moreover, Taylorism as a control strategy differed markedly between the US and UK experiences as a function of differing industrial cultures and patterns of worker resistance. Other observers have focussed on more linear, chronological developments in labour control processes. Edwards (1979) studied the transition from 'simple, direct' control in late nineteenth and early twentieth century US capitalism to a Weber-like 'bureaucratic' methodology thereafter. In this model the nature of worker reactions and resistance was identified as the dynamic agent of change. Burawoy (1985) established a paradigm of transition from regimes he labelled respectively as 'despotic', 'hegemonic', and 'hegemonic despotic', wherein the most salient feature in the progression was the functioning of the existing political regime.

Notwithstanding this lengthy litany of complaints, labour process today may not be clearly different from the situation Braverman described in the Age of Taylor. Technology has changed, to be sure, but the computer has made management's control over information more efficient. Greenbaum (1994) has pointed out how diversity in today's work force is an ally in management's objective to keep labour divided. Meiksins (1994, p. 54; see also Smith, 1994), in a retrospective occasioned by the twentieth anniversary of Braverman's seminal work, wrote:

> Braverman's analysis can accommodate the often valuable ideas of his critics regarding subjectivity and resistance, economic change, and the complexity of capital-labor relations, precisely because *Labor and Monopoly Capital* is much more than a book about deskilling. Its central achievement was to restore exploitation, class, and class conflict to their central place in the analysis of work under capitalism.

Since the bulk of labour-process literature has emanated from sociology and management theory, the role of accounting has not been specifically addressed until recently. Hopper et al. (1986, p. 110) sounded a keynote toward bridging that gap:

> We particularly emphasise that accounting, through its espousal of particular reporting structures, its pattern of segmental reporting, and modes of calculation, is a significant plank in efforts to manufacture subjectively the compliance of labour. Its presumed neutrality and objectivity reinforce particular understanding of how industry is, and should be managed. The paper takes issue with such presumptions by drawing attention to ideological aspects of accounting, its relationship to particular interests, and its mediation through processes of resistance.

Hopper et al. (1987, pp. 444–445) wrote that the 'historical totality' of capitalism, the 'dynamic' that impacts most social and economic institutions, is the 'search for means of yielding profitable surplus'. The managers of capitalist enterprises have harnessed the aid of accounting to control labour in an ongoing effort to maximise surplus value. Hopper et al. saw the history of accounting theory as evolutionary. Commencing with the 'conventional' view that accounting systems serve a neutral recording function (Chatfield, 1977), the analysis was broadened to include their importance as support mechanisms for firms seeking to achieve efficiency benefits and administer new technologies (Johnson, 1972, 1981). Labour process, the step beyond, envisioned accounting as a disciplinary technique for labour control. Armstrong (1987, pp. 417–419) put the case similarly. He identified three functions comprising the 'global function of capital'—the extraction, the realisation, and the allocation of surplus value. Accounting practices discussed by Pollard (1965) in the eighteenth century and Johnson (1972) in the nineteenth were isolated examples of efforts to implement the first function. Beginning with the slump of the 1880s, certain costing technologies were 'pioneered' to permit the conversion (realisation) of surplus value from productive processes to monetary form. Though this 'costing renaissance' was nascent until the accounting profession was established as an instrument of power, labour process was born.

Hopper and Armstrong (1991) reinterpreted the early American industrial period formerly studied by economic rationalists Johnson and Chandler. Committed to an historical hypothesis that social and economic conflicts arising from existing labour control practices give rise to new techniques, Hopper and Armstrong attempted to demonstrate how cost accounting came of age to accomplish labour intensification. Specifically, they argued that cost accounting functioned to increase the efforts of labour through 'speed ups' on the production line, the extension of the work day, and seasonal layoffs.

There has been a considerable volume of Foucauldian critique of Marxism, some of which Marxist revisionists themselves have also noted. Foucault himself criticised Marxism for its positivism and conviction that its perspective dominated various conflicting interpretations of meaning. Marx's scientific approach, according to Foucault, allowed its adherents 'to escape the figurality of language' and to advance definitive posturing where 'no single order of validating method' should hold sway (Norris, 1991, pp. 86–87).

Smart's (1983) critique was couched primarily in terms of the failure of Marx and his successors to analyse the capitalist state, the force of nationalism, and the comparative evolutions of capitalist and socialist political regimes. Thompson (1989) responded that Marx's limited analysis of the role of the state was a function of his own times when trade union activity was overvalued as an effective mechanism for change. Labour-process theorists have addressed this shortfall in political analysis Smart noted over a decade ago.

BEGINNINGS

This chapter in no way purports to be the first to call for greater harmony amongst participants in paradigmatic debates, though it does focus specifically on the search for cost accounting origins and does review dialogical literature to support this position. Marxist economists a generation ago lay valuable foundations. Dobb (1973, p. 7) wrote about economic theory:

> In choosing one structure in preference to another, the model-builder is not only providing a scaffolding or framework within which human thought can operate, but is laying emphasis upon certain factors and relationships and excluding others or casting them into the shadows, and in doing so he can be judged to be distorting or illuminating reality...

Dobb (ibid., pp. 18–19) went on to elaborate that although these 'general pictures of society' were not objective, timeless, or absolute, they could be 'rationally debated' and that various socio-historical explanations more closely approximated reality for particular events or times. Meek (1976, p. 8), in addressing his historical study of the labour theory of value to Marxists and non-Marxists alike, expressed his hope:

> ...that the book may play a small part in helping to usher in a period of coexistence between the two groups in which accusations of dishonesty and academic incompetence will be replaced by genuine attempts to understand and evaluate one another's point of view, and in which Marxists and non-Marxists will enter into peaceful

competition with one another to see who can provide the most accurate and useful analysis of economic reality.

In an introduction to an *AOS* compendium of articles from the second Manchester Interdisciplinary Perspectives on Accounting Conference, Miller et al. (1991, pp. 395, 400) wrote a charter for what has come to be called critical accounting history. Numbered amongst their basic points was the expansion of accounting history to include a 'pluralization of methodologies' and a 'heterogeneous range of theoretical approaches' that encompasses new disciplines and questions. Miller et al. (ibid., p. 400) argued an eclectic basis for critical accounting history:

> It is inappropriate to specify criteria that would exclude certain types of research on the basis of their methodological protocols or the time period they address. It is also highly inappropriate to specify the methodological protocols that stamp a particular piece of research as a part of the new accounting history.

These sentiments were seconded in Merino and Mayper (1993, p. 245) as an objective was voiced to enhance the dialogue amongst academics doing accounting research, particularly between traditional and critical historians (also between historians and empiricists). They despaired what they labelled 'methodological transference', one aspect of which was 'a lack of communication between two schools due to rhetorical arguments that discount the methods used by competing world views'. They urged the incorporation of ideas from all paradigms, thereby broadening the call of Hogarth (1991) and Mills (1993) for an integration of findings from other social sciences in understanding accounting's history. We need to recognise our interdependence upon other researchers, to 'celebrate diversity', and to 'keep conversations open' (Merino & Mayper, 1993, p. 262).

The March 1994 volume of *CPA* was a valuable step in providing a forum for dialogue between Foucauldians and Marxists. Though the editors expressed reservations about the enduring value of the exercise (Cooper & Tinker, 1994) and despite the combative tone of certain articles appearing therein, the effort represents a valuable step toward the expansion of dialogue we are urging in this chapter.

Other efforts in accounting history have reflected the potential for paradigmatic integration without being showcased in debate form. Hopwood (1987, p. 227) introduced an element of democracy into the study of accountancy's past when he wrote:

> ...no unitary mobilizing force, be it an economic rationality, a social intent or a political will, has been found to be silently embedded within the shifting course of accounting's subsequent path of modification.

This observation was one of the conclusions Hopwood drew from three case studies in which he examined how accounting could serve as a basis for organisational change. One of these studies drew upon the research of McKendrick into Wedgwood's pottery enterprise. Accounting at Wedgwood was born out of the economic exigencies of recessionary times and, in its basic orientation, was structured to observe the firm in economic terms. However, the end result was the creation of a new visibility, an 'accounting eye', which provided new knowledge on which to base price and product volume. This study of an early industrial cost accounting episode exhibited multiple explanations that included both Foucauldian and economic rationalist aspects.

In a footnote Hopwood allowed that an analysis of Boulton & Watt, based upon Roll's research, might reveal in like fashion accounting's role as an agency of change. Fleischman, Hoskin, and Macve (1995), from their respective Neoclassical and Foucauldian perspectives, followed this lead and found evidence in the articulation of material and labour standards elements suggestive of both paradigms. The careful costing of hundreds of engine components may have reflected an accounting based on traditional economic concerns about profit margins and competition. By contrast, the lack of amendment to an intricate piece-rate system established in 1802 may have suggested a symbolic labour control mechanism by which the operatives were made aware of productivity norms and associated managerial surveillance. Though the authors concluded that Boulton & Watt's accounting was a 'one-off' rather than the birth of modern managerialism, they appreciated the synergistic value of a cooperative examination of the archive. Armstrong (1994b, p. 1), perhaps auguring a Marxist/labour-process joint venture of this type, observed that this attempt 'to test their different approaches to the development of cost accounting against the historical record' was an approach 'unreservedly to be welcomed'.

Loft's work (1986, 1990) on UK cost accounting during World War I further typifies the close links that exist between Neoclassicists and Foucauldians, despite the disagreements between Hoskin and Macve (1994) and Tyson (1993) over events at the Springfield Armory. Though Loft paid homage to the influence of Foucault, many economic aspects of her analysis were distinctly non-Foucauldian. Armstrong (1994a, p. 46) noted that Loft's description was more about 'a diffusion of cost accounting technique' than a 'genesis of a new accounting discourse'. She linked cost accounting developments to such non-Foucauldian influences as 'the sovereign power of the state' and, perhaps, economically rational action (Armstrong, 1991). Armstrong (ibid., p. 43) concluded that 'understood as theories of adoption, there seems to be no reason why the economic theories of accounting development should not be able to accommodate a Foucauldian genealogy of technique as an unspecified procedure of search and experiment'. Bhimani (1994, pp. 667–668), in a recent study of three French companies from the early eighteenth century to World War II, found that the prevailing disciplinary system changed from a 'coercive enforcement of production priorities and subversion of individual worker's will' to a more Foucauldian consensus-based form in the nineteenth century. Bhimani attributed this transition to the 'emergence of the economic man', as workers developed a 'sensitivity to economic gain'.

Marxist commentators, though not addressing accounting specifically, have suggested insights which would allow at least for a Marxist/Neoclassical coexistence. Dobb (1973, pp. 20, 26) wrote two decades ago that the 'two rival types of interpretation will coexist and their implications for action and experience conflict, possibly without the true nature of their different visions of reality being brought plainly to view...'. More recently, Elson (1988, pp. 5, 12) observed that the 'deficiencies of central planning' meant that socialists had to concentrate increasingly on market mechanisms as 'the only feasible solution'. 'Socialists should take advantage of the market as an instrument that permits decentralized decision-making and motivates individuals to satisfy the public interest through pursuing their own interests'.

POWER AND CONTROL: A COMMON INTEREST

There are a number of issues in which members of the three paradigmatic schools potentially share a common interest, including individual versus class action, the role of the state, accounting's objectivity/subjectivity, social structure, gender and race, and a multitude of others. However, within the context of early Anglo-American industrialisation, the explicit prominence of power and labour control amongst critical theorists provides a convenient example wherein dialogue is likely to be productive. For economic rationalists, power and the achievement of control over all means of production and the environment in which organisations operate are likewise central, but often implicit. More problematical social aspects of power and control are mostly ignored or reduced by economic rationalists.

Power is the primary focus of interest for Foucauldians. For the other schools, power exists explicitly and implicitly. The nature and effect of power also relate to assumptions about voluntarism and determinism. Therefore, the positioning of power within each paradigm must be more closely examined. The Marxist/labour-process school traditionally views power primarily in the hands of capitalists and embedded in capitalist structures. Control is exerted by capitalists for the purposes of accumulating additional capital and increasing profits, with a central result being the exploitation of labour. Economic rationalists, it can be argued, agree with this view. Williamson's (1985) observations that issues of power are largely ignored or undeveloped in the economic rationalist literature does not mean a specific view of power is lacking. The ability to design and implement controls (with the related subjectivity of labour), as well as to understand and react to changing technology and market conditions, is often considered non-problematic in the theories and analyses of economic rationalists. It can be considered non-problematic because scholars of this persuasion seemingly assume the existence and righteousness of the power of capitalists and attendant capitalist structures. In this regard, economic rationalists have tended to be deterministic. Marxists and early labour-process theorists focus on the problematic nature of this power relation at the point of production. Whilst they observe and elaborate on the tyranny embedded in such a relationship, early scholars also tended to view the relationship as overly deterministic. More recent scholarship has expanded this analysis by exploring the complexities of both capital and labour in attempts, not always successful, to control a wide range of elements and circumstances. Both the ability of labour to resist and its willingness to consent to arrangements of production are now being examined carefully. Foucauldians avoid sides and motives with a view of power embedded in micro-level activities. Their interest is not so much about who has power and who does not, but how power is institutionalised and produced and reproduced through societal relations.

The commonality of interest in power and control does not translate into agreement on definitions or beneficiaries. However, enough attention has been paid to this intersection amongst these scholarly groups to suggest more dialogue would be productive. For example, agreement between Marxist/labour-process historians and Foucauldians was noted by Clegg (1989, p. 232), who attempted to reconcile Foucauldian and Marxist thought by suggesting that disciplinary forms transcend what is required to achieve efficiency:

> The two concepts of discipline and production are inseparable: this is one of the main lessons both of Foucault's concern with "disciplinary power" and the whole "labour process" perspective derived from Marx and Braverman. Methods of production entail methods of discipline.

A view of power that leaves labour as purely constrained, docile subjects of capital is no longer tenable for any of the schools. Power may be most successfully preserved when it is historically embedded in institutions and organisations (Stinchcombe, 1968) and when there is control over awareness (Lukes, 1974). However, the ability of labour and individuals to resist has only recently become a focus of the Marxist/labour-process school (Armstrong, 1991; Knights, 1990; Knights & Willmott, 1990). Furthermore, management cannot be viewed as a unified force intent on controlling and deskilling labour (Burawoy, 1979; Knights & Willmott, 1990). Capitalists and managers react to various environmental changes which precipitate adaptions in production not limited to or necessarily related to direct controls over labour (Knights & Willmott, 1990). On the other hand, the concepts of class struggle and the objectification of the subjectivity of labour have not been acknowledged by economic rationalists.

Smart's (1983) observation that Marxists and Neoclassicists view power in economic terms, as contrasted to the Foucauldians underscoring of the non-economic parameters, does not do justice to the issue. Knights (1990) suggested that power is much more complex than traditionally viewed in labour-process theory, that inclusion of both Marxist and Foucauldian aspects of power are required to progress beyond a simplistic determinism or a 'control-resistance dualism'. In Knights' view, Foucault's vision of power does not replace the Marxist view of capitalist domination, but 'presents a conception of power and subjectivity that facilitates an understanding of how subjects voluntarily engage in practices which reproduce patriarchal and capitalist institutions' (ibid., p. 327; see also Thompson, 1989). All three schools could benefit from a better understanding of the constituent role of accounting in the 'structuration' (Giddens, 1976) of human action and freedom within the constraints of existing societal structures, organisations, and history. Though this realisation would not eliminate differing values (ideologies) of researchers, such analysis would recognise the subjectivity of capitalists and managers, as well as labour, within systems of constraints and opportunities.

The concepts of 'discipline' and 'rational calculation' have become part of the power and control elaborated by all of the schools. For example, Marx (1977, p. 549) discussed the factory code and the 'barrack-like discipline, which is elaborated into a complete system in the factory'. The required interdependence of the work of the factory created a 'continuity, a uniformity, a regularity, an order, and even an intensity of labour, quite different from that found in an independent handicraft or even in simple co-operation' (p. 465). It was the skilled workers who, lacking discipline, could therefore damage the factory system (p. 490).

Weber, with his emphasis on 'rational calculation' as a basic tenet of capitalism (Garnsey, 1984) and the pursuit of profit as the motive behind efforts to rationalise economic conduct (Dandecker, 1990), is a charter member of the Neoclassical tradition. Moreover, Weber's 'bureaucratic inevitability' meant, in the commercial setting, an officialdom that serves consensual interests, a neutral posturing typical of economic rationalism (ibid.; Clawson, 1980). However, this bureaucratic officialdom, and the rational commercial bookkeeping or accounting that came in tandem, existed to promote 'rational discipline' (Miller, 1987, pp. 6–7), 'types of behavior and outlook' (Garnsey, 1984,

p. 45), and 'control of free labour' (Dandecker, 1990, p. 9). Clearly, we have here institutions born out of economic rationalism serving purposes that exhibit Foucauldian characteristics and concerns.

O'Neill (1986, p. 54) analysed Foucault's work in conjunction with that of Weber, Taylor, and the concepts of scientific management. Weber's technical, legal-rational discipline and authority is complemented by the social organisations and power described by Foucault:

> Thus it may be argued that, while Weber saw the direct line from monastic discipline through Luther and Calvin to bureaucracy and scientific management, he did not pay sufficient attention to the circuits of the factory, workhouse and prison in the creation of industrial discipline and social control.

O'Neill also noted that it is in the interest of bureaucratic management to make 'worker discipline, punishment, and rewards appear to flow from naturally established organizational rules and procedures' (ibid., p. 56; see also Lukes, 1974). Though this connection was acknowledged by Hoskin and Macve (1988), they seemed to believe that O'Neill understated the importance of the processes by which disciplinary regulations are disseminated. They noted the contribution of their own work as providing insight into the processes by which conditions were 'created' for the application and success of disciplinary regulation in the industrial setting. The more complex view of power promoted by Knights (1990) would incorporate both viewpoints.

CONCLUSION

If a more complete understanding of accounting's role in history is to come, it will involve a pluralistic approach that includes serious, intellectual research and debate amongst and within various theories, ideologies, and methodologies. It is far too easy for protagonists of particular approaches to dismiss others as missing the mark. Arthur (1993, p. 210) warned us that 'the political attractions of a viewpoint should not blind us to possible limitations in its scope. The benefits received from tossing out one set of prejudices will be considerably attenuated if we simply replace them with another'. Critics may also claim that those who attempt dialogue across approaches may have an incomplete understanding of the basic issues that comprise each school's ideology and/or may be making hopelessly ambitious and unconvincing excursions into social theorising. However, if the studies and reflections upon costing (and accounting) historiography continue as parallel processes that ignore or deny each other's unique potential contribution to our sum of knowledge and understanding, then the philosophies of their founders will be lost to all but their own converts and the party faithful.

What is the alternative? The prospect of mutually respectful coexistence and the grounds for mutually beneficial dialogue amongst the theoretical perspectives expand the horizons for each theoretical grouping to contribute to a greater advance in knowledge than would be possible for any one group operating in isolation. As Follett (1918, 1951) argued, it is not necessary for the participants in the debate to give up treasured beliefs and positions in search of compromise. Integration, in which protagonists' multiple positions are drawn upon, constitutes a more productive way forward in her view. Thus, cost accounting historiography may benefit from an ongoing dialogue in which the unique insights offered by the different participants achieve a synergy that offers a much richer menu of information and understandings about cost accounting history than could be achieved additively. This interaction represents the real potential power of the multi-theoretical approach advocated in this chapter. That some differences of focus and interpretation should remain between theoretical approaches ought not be a cause for concern, but should be embraced (Feyerabend, 1978). Chua and Degeling (1993, pp. 311–312) concluded that '"facts," unlike an oracle, do not speak with the same voice or say the same thing. There are multiple speakers and "facts" may be subject to multiple interpretations'. Such differences will hopefully foster the continuation of further insights and understandings made possible by the unique perspectives adopted by the coexisting theoretical groups. Thus, the pluralistic approach is oriented towards dialogue, synergy, and respect for difference rather than integration, homogenisation, and ultimate dilution of contributions.

The strategies proposed in this chapter are not intended to dilute the uniquely important perspectives offered by the various paradigms in some integrated, but tasteless porridge. Instead, the desired impact of productive coexistence and dialogue ought to be the maintenance of accessibility, exchange, and interchange with friend and foe alike. Indeed, it is hoped that such openness and public clarity of interchange will stimulate new entrants, sharpen perspectives, and expand knowledge.

The means for furthering coexistence and dialogue are potentially varied. One possibility is the initiation of joint projects that bring several different perspectives to bear upon a single research subject. It is hoped that conferences at which participants from different perspectives can meet and engage in ongoing dialogue will increase. This interaction represents an essential vehicle for keeping the lines of communication open. Other possibilities include the production of journal issues or readings texts in which researchers of different persuasions present their research and provide dialogue that explores common grounds and differences. Greater acknowledgement and cross-referencing of research from other traditions, even when a paper has points of major difference, will encourage readers to consult the literature more widely.

It is possible to envision a variety of benefits that may accrue from the pluralistic, synergistic approach to costing history. Particular perspectives may be susceptible to amendment or amplification through greater dialogue with others, or may be deepened and enriched in the course of debate with those of opposing persuasions. Sensitive and mutually respectful debate may eventually reveal issues and variables not previously considered for investigation by any one individual perspective. Finally, we believe that the pluralistic, synergistic approach will most likely improve understanding of the unique features of the different paradigms and facilitate an ease of comparison and contrast.

Specifically with reference to the subjects of cost accounting change and the cost control relationship, the coexistence of hitherto competing theoretical perspectives is not only possible, but necessary. The issues and events intertwined with the emergence and continuation of various forms of cost accounting techniques are complex and many. Therefore, if we are to advance in our understanding of the contextual and historical role of cost accounting in society, it is essential that the different theoretical perspectives maintain their unique concerns in order to foster useful dialogue and debate. The productivity of dialogue regarding such subjects as industrial revolution costing history will be significantly enhanced by a preparedness of each theoretical group to recognise the potential contribution to our sum of knowledge by the other groups of scholars. Recognising the possibility of coexistence and the grounds for empathetic dialogue can be a first step.

NOTES

1. The material in this chapter is drawn extensively from R.K. Fleischman, L.P. Kalbers, and L.D. Parker (1996), 'Expanding the Dialogue: Industrial Revolution Costing Historiography', *Critical Perspectives on Accounting*, Vol. 7, No. 3: 315–337.

10

Conclusion

This extensive study of British Industrial Revolution costing history has yielded an array of insights that challenge our preconceptions concerning the antecedents of contemporary cost management practices. In addition, these perceptions provide us with considerably enhanced understandings of the environmental drivers, roles, technological interfaces, and management impacts of this early period on cost management innovation and development. Based upon an extensive examination of extant archival sources, we have presented a macro-environmental perspective of Industrial Revolution cost accounting and cost management practices. This investigation has disclosed a number of organisations across a variety of industries exhibiting practices varying from the rudimentary to what could, from a contemporary perspective, be considered quite sophisticated. This conclusion has been drawn from a number of lines of enquiry: industry studies (textiles, iron, and mining); firm case studies (Carron Company and Boulton & Watt); an examination of the relationship between costing and technological change; and a consideration of the perspectives yielded by differing theoretical and methodological paradigms. For the accounting and management disciplines, this study contributes a revision of historical knowledge concerning the foundations and contexts of cost accounting and cost management practices.

ENVIRONMENT AND CONTEXT

We are accustomed to viewing the contemporary business environment as one of the most dynamic and rapidly changing scenarios faced by corporate management. Yet, this study suggests that the period of the Industrial Revolution exhibited a similar (if not greater) rate of change in production, technology, power generation, communication, and transport. Still, we must be wary of misperceiving the historical environment under examination. It is not uncommon for historians studying the Industrial Revolution to portray it as a period of sudden and dramatic change and to focus analysis upon technological innovation.

In fact, the rate of change experienced by businesses during the Industrial Revolution could vary as a function of time, industry, region, and technology. Technological change, for example, was oriented towards a variety of factors such as supplanting labour, conserving raw materials, and using scarce capital more efficiently. In many periods and businesses, technological change was incremental, often being of moderate or even slow pace. Causes of variability in the rate of change included such factors as labour and capital shortages, technical barriers, organisational unit size, geographic location, cost/benefit assessments, and raw material availability.

Thus, we caution against drawing premature conclusions concerning the comparability of historical or contemporary business periods, the speed of environmental change during the Industrial Revolution, or the circumstances surrounding particular cost management developments. The cost accounting and management practices and innovations discussed in this study reflect a rich tapestry of initiatives that both reflected and influenced the particular industrial, regional, technological, social, and economic contexts in which they operated.

COST MANAGEMENT PRACTICES AND ROLES

In the records we have examined, the cost accounting and cost management systems in use during the period ranged from the primitive and incomplete to the detailed, innovative, and sophisticated. In leading companies, such as Carron and Boulton & Watt, we found evidence of significant cost management efforts in areas such as expense control, product costing, inventory control, overhead cost allocation, cost comparisons and transfers, cost analyses for special decisions, budgets and standards, and responsibility management. Carron and Boulton & Watt shared common interests in expense control, inventory valuation/control, and standards (though the labour standards developed at Boulton & Watt appear to have been a single isolated occurance). In other respects, the focus of cost accounting and management efforts differed between the two companies.

Difference and variation recur as common themes of cost accounting and cost management systems found in British Industrial Revolution organisations. For example, systems varied according to the widely divergent sizes and structures of firms, their degree of centralisation and decentralisation, the scale of operating plants, and the amount of vertical integration. We also find general differences in the detail and sophistication of cost accounting records and analyses between industries. Similar costing procedures were apparent in the iron and textile industries, but textile industry costing displayed more variability across its constituent firms than was apparent in the iron industry. Along certain dimensions the costing systems employed in the extractive industry appeared to have been more sophisticated than in either iron or textiles. Nevertheless, the archives confront us with a wealth of evidence pointing to an active and well-developed tradition of cost management and control across a spectrum of Industrial Revolution organisations.

Focal areas of cost management activity seemed to relate to the context and concerns of a particular industry. In iron, attention appeared focussed on utilising cost accounting for cost reduction and new technology evaluation. Resource input costing was also featured as a key activity for firms in this industry. In textiles, expense control was often a primary area of attention, though methods varied significantly across firms in the industry (e.g., in the complexity of calculations). Such variation appeared to have been due to firms having units in geographically diverse locations, varying degrees of process mechanisation, and significantly differing firm size. A substantial number of textile concerns marshalled costing information for non-routine decision making, and many (though with less frequency than in the iron industry) undertook product costing exercises. In the extractive industry, much of the cost accounting transcended that found in the textile mills and the iron foundries. Many firms maintained detailed records of operations and their related costs, including statistics relating to periodic extractions, production processes, output, productivity, distribution, and pricing. Of particular note in the extractive industry was the use made by many firms of a combination of continuous control information, special decision information, physical operating statistics, and financial indicators. This approach could in some senses be seen as prescient of approaches to organisational management more recently promoted by Total Quality Management advocates.

Overall, across the period of the Industrial Revolution, we find evidence of the maintenance and usage of both operating and cost statistics, financial and non-financial information, and both quantitative and qualitative data, presentations, and analyses. The archives reveal a full spectrum of cost accounting and management activities, including expense control, cost comparisons, costing for special decisions, product costing (involving some evidence of what today would be recognised as job costing and process costing), overhead cost allocation, inventory control, budgeting, forecasting, rudimentary standard costing, and responsibility accounting.

This array of cost accounting and cost management activities appears to have served as a vital, direct input to what was a priority activity for many managers of Industrial Revolution enterprises—the planning and controlling of resource (materials, labour, and capital) acquisition and usage. That priority was due to the oftentimes dynamic and competitive environment in which they functioned—one which necessitated continual scrutiny and evaluation of operating efficiency, estimation of reserves (minerals, coal, capital), identification of new input sources (labour, fuel), assessments of mine viability, and appraisal of the costs and benefits of adopting new technology. These concerns were ongoing as sources of raw materials periodically or regionally became scarce, as long-term fixed asset commitments required refinancing though short-term loans or further partner contributions, and/or as greater operating efficiencies were mandated to maintain competitive output pricing and satisfactory profit margins.

KEY DRIVERS

Repeatedly we have uncovered evidence of key environmental factors that appear to have been influential in driving entrepreneurs' and managers' cost accounting and cost management activities. Of particular note were the problems, frequently experienced, of financing capital intensive operations through restricted sources of family and partnership contributions and short-term loans. At least during the earlier part of the Industrial Revolution, this state of affairs was due to the lack of a well-developed banking system and capital market. Not only was access to adequate capital a problem, but enterprises battled with the associated difficulty of maintaining liquidity. Indeed, as firms struggled to finance necessary capital expenditures, technology developments, and adequate working capital maintenance, there were many partners in such enterprises whose financial fortunes came to grief by virtue of the major supplementary capital contributions required of them.

Of course, profitability was also a concern for these organisations, their owners and managers. Often the industry in which they operated was highly competitive, in contrast to assumptions invariably made by some unfamiliar with the Industrial Revolution. For example, in the textiles industry, profit margins for many firms were extremely narrow, necessitating close attention to expense control. This concern became an even greater imperative for mill owners in the face of labour shortages and rising wage levels in the later part of the eighteenth century. Attention to competitive pricing and associated cost control was, therefore, an essential ingredient for longer-term organisational survival, let alone prosperity. In addition, profitability, once achieved, could not be relied upon to persist without the ongoing scrutiny and management of operating efficiency, sources of input supply, technological change, product innovation, and developing markets. In fact, on the strength of the available evidence, it is arguable that such enterprises as Carron and Wedgwood exhibited a considerable degree of sophistication in their approaches to the development and management of product innovation, process technology, and marketing strategy.

Thus, overall, the cost management concerns of these early industrial entrepreneurs were a response to a variety of factors, ranging from the threats of labour and capital scarcity to the pressures of competition, the challenges of technological change, and the opportunities for product innovation and new market development. Theirs was in many respects a world of similar complexity, dynamics, and challenge to the contemporary business world to which we are often tempted to attribute unwarranted uniqueness.

THE 'COST MANAGERS'

This text has not delved with any particular detail into the identities and biographies of firm owners and managers within the Industrial Revolution. Nonetheless, it has argued the crucial role played in the development and maintenance of cost accounting and cost management systems by the on-site owners and managers of many firms. The absence of an accounting profession, an accounting literature on the subject, or a costing tradition emanating from accountants or bookkeepers was pronounced and deafening in its silence. Instead, the attribution of innovation and development in approaches to industrial cost management during the period must go to the then owners and managers of the firms themselves. It was they who developed and utilised their own systems, designing them to meet the unique situational contexts faced by their organisations in an ongoing pursuit of cost efficiency and competitive advantage.

Many Industrial Revolution entrepreneurs personally originated cost accounting systems and cost management approaches themselves, whilst directly participating in the day-to-day management (operational and financial) of their firms. They exhibited an underlying preoccupation with the economy and efficiency of operations, often demonstrating at the same time a sophisticated understanding of the impact of product cost and quality on profits.

From a contemporary perspective, what emerges as somewhat surprising is the fact that neither accounting methods nor resulting accounting numbers appear to have been considered highly confidential commercial secrets to be hidden from competitors. Information about the activities and processes of competitors was generally available, even though cost management techniques were 'homegrown' in that individual entrepreneurs designed the information sets needed for managing their own operations. The transfer of accounting knowledge within and across industries of this period remains for further investigation.

A NEW APPRECIATION OF THE PAST

Throughout this extensive study, we have drawn back the veil of history to uncover revised visions of cost accounting and cost management traditions. Whereas the scientific management period (circa 1880–1920) has formerly been credited as the spawning ground of contemporary practices, this study has uncovered a veritable watershed of such techniques amongst British organisations in the 1760–1850 period. It is a rich heritage indeed, not confined to double-entry financial records but embracing the full sweep of financial and operating statistics, quantitative and qualitative information, primary input/output records, and accompanying managerial analyses of causes, trends, and costs/benefits.

The scope and sophistication of costing practices revealed in this period, whilst highly variable, nonetheless present a collage hitherto unrecognised by economic, business, and accounting historians. Indeed, this study chronicles cost management techniques that predate earlier assumed foundations by over a century. The cost management tradition we have uncovered is one that had as its hallmark the coexistence, and in some cases the integration, of operational and financial control information and associated analyses. We sense evidence amongst some entrepreneurs of an approach to organisational planning and control that embraced the intersection between strategic management, management control, and cost management. This combination manifested itself in entrepreneurs' concurrent attention to a dual planning and control focus, a combination of short and longer time horizons for decision analyses, and recurrent and non-routine decision making—all included in an ongoing iterative style of operational and financial management. This approach appears to have been adopted in response to some entrepreneurs' appreciation of the interface between resources (physical, technical, financial, human), operating strategies, and resulting outcomes. In some cases it almost seems to have anticipated certain strategic management methodologies advocated for organisational management today.

Of particular note has been this study's finding that cost/benefit analyses and technological change decisions were, more often than not, vitally interrelated. Economic and social historians of this period have previously considered that Industrial Revolution entrepreneurs focussed upon the adoption of new technology at the first available opportunity. Business development was represented as very much technologically driven. The findings of our archival research suggest that this view may be an oversimplification. Entrepreneurs often undertook detailed cost/benefit analyses prior to making plant and equipment investment commitments or decisions about changing extraction, production, or distribution methodologies. Cost and technology management was conducted simultaneously with cost analyses often informing decisions to defer new technology investment, to undertake particular types of technological change, to invest in particular locations, or to embark on new process approaches at specific times and at predetermined rates of change. Hence, industry in this period appears to have been driven by numerous forces, amongst which both cost efficiency and technology were featured.

The cost management systems in many Industrial Revolution organisations appear to have been oriented towards the maintenance of efficiency, profitability, and liquidity. What is notable are the numerous occasions upon which the archival records reflect a contrast between a certain degree of sophistication (at least by contemporary judgements) in cost accounting and cost management systems and a relatively crude and disorganised state of financial reporting. Often the cost accounting and the financial reporting systems (to the extent that the latter existed) were not in any discernible sense integrated or even interrelated. The superior development of many cost accounting and cost management systems during the Industrial Revolution stands in marked contrast to the subsequent dominant emphasis accorded to external financial reporting systems in twentieth century business organisations.

Two key observations bear reiteration. First, our research has revealed a situational, almost idiosyncratic approach adopted by Industrial Revolution entrepreneurs to the design and development of cost accounting and management systems, They attempted to adapt, design, and control processes to accord with an industry's features, regional conditions, organisational structure, market competition, etc. Whilst some of their methodologies exhibited degrees of similarity, there is sufficient evidence of difference amongst the systems firms employed to support this conclusion. Some degree of transfer of cost management approaches was, however, clearly occurring, and its manner and degree of transfer warrant further investigation by scholars.

The second observation to be reiterated is that the primary source data, forming the very informative and productive basis for this research, have been the letters, notebooks, minutes of meetings, and reports of owners, managers, and supervisors. These data bring us closer to some understanding (albeit subject to the limitations of our ability to see evidence of outcomes) of accounting records in use and management control in action. They help us bridge the chasm occasioned by sole reliance upon financial reports produced for external consumption, affording us insights into the preoccupations, thinking, analyses, discussions, and decisions of those charged with ongoing strategic and operational management. From this perspective, operational planning, cost management, and operational control have emerged as concurrent owner and manager concerns, with interrelationships between these functions often recognised explicitly or implicitly.

FURTHER QUESTIONS

This study represents but an initial foray into the world of Industrial Revolution cost accounting and cost management. Much remains to be investigated. We are well aware, for example, of the importance of railroads in the saga of US accounting history. We have been informed that UK railway records have been assembled at the Kew Gardens Record Office, but as yet we have not examined these archives. We suspect that they will provide valuable historical information, given that we have seen some Scottish railway records which on cursory inspection hold considerable promise of new revelations. Beyond the railways, there still remains a wealth of archives yet to be examined in the UK, including the records of shipbuilding firms, transport enterprises, and a variety of businesses located in and around London.

Similar factors to those attributed to having prompted the decline of the British economy after the Industrial Revolution may ultimately explain a post-Industrial Revolution backsliding in UK cost accounting. By the time of Taylor and Fayol, many of the developments in cost accounting and cost management pioneered by Industrial Revolution entrepreneurs had at least temporarily vanished from view. However, that observation in itself may be a misrepresentation. What is required is a virtual replication of this extended study to be conducted into available company archives for the 1850–1930 period. This investigation may reveal the degree of continuity in cost management practices, any decline or new developments, and probable influences upon observed trends.

Whilst we have not extensively examined the records of small-scale enterprises, we suspect that the degree of sophistication and complexity in cost accounting and cost management systems uncovered in our research may have been a function of the larger size and complexity of those organisations that formed the bulk of our data set. Of course, we do not contend that all large-scale businesses of the period had sophisticated systems. Nevertheless, it remains an open question as to whether smaller firms achieved similar states of costing development as evidenced in the larger firms whose records we have examined more extensively. In attempting to answer this question, the would-be researcher may face the difficulty that even if smaller firms had well-developed sets of records, they may not have been as assiduous in preserving them as their larger counterparts. Hence, adequate sources may be more difficult for the researcher to trace.

Finally, consistent with our discussion in Chapter 9 advocating an expansion of dialogue amongst different theoretical paradigms and research methodologies, we urge researchers of differing schools of thought to enter this archival world as we have done, and to bring their particular perspectives and focal concerns to bear upon the evidence. Whilst a broadened analysis may foster lively scholarly debate amongst competing ideologies, the potential is enhanced for new insights into the underlying nature of events, practices, influences, outcomes, and the interrelationships amongst them. Such pluralism in historical enquiry into this period of cost accounting history will arguably yield a richer menu of information and understandings which will amend, challenge, build upon, and extend the beginnings that we have attempted to offer here.

POSTSCRIPT

As researchers we have learned much from this investigation and hope that in sharing our conclusions, we can enlist others to enter the 'worlds' of Industrial Revolution and post-Industrial Revolution firm management and accounting. There is much remaining to be learned and understood. We see clear indications of some similarities between the environment of the Industrial Revolution and the contemporary business world at the time we commenced this research. Our perspectives of the foundations of contemporary cost accounting and cost management have been considerably revised and doubtlessly await further revision by those researchers who will follow us. We offer the outline and interpretations presented herein as a small contribution to our discipline's appreciation of its heritage and the environments and practices that have informed the cost accounting and cost management developments that we continue to witness today. Such a deeper and more intellectual appreciation of our history, we believe, makes a significant contribution to our ongoing assessment of the suitability and efficacy of developmental paths of accounting policies and practices in the future.

Bibliography

Addis, J.P. (1957), *The Crawshay Dynasty*, Cardiff: University of Wales Press.

Alchian, A.A. and Demsetz, H. (1972), 'Production, Information Costs, and Economic Organization', *American Economic Review*, Vol. 62, No. 5: 777–795.

Allen, R.C. (1983), 'Collective Invention', *Journal of Economic Behaviour and Organization*, Vol. 4, No. 1: 1–24.

Armstrong, P. (1984), 'Competition between the Organizational Professions and the Evolution of Management Control Strategies', in Thompson, K. (ed.), *Work, Employment and Unemployment*, Philadelphia: Open University Press: 97–120.

——— (1986), 'Management Control Strategies and Inter-Personal Competition: The Cases of Accountancy and Personnel Management', in Knights, D. and Willmott, H. (eds.), *Managing the Labour Process*, Aldershot: Gower Publishing Co.: 19–43.

——— (1987), 'The Rise of Accounting Controls in British Capitalist Enterprises', *Accounting, Organizations and Society*, Vol. 12, No. 5: 415–436.

——— (1991), 'The Influence of Michel Foucault on Historical Research in Accounting: An Assessment', *Proceedings of the Accounting History Research Methodology Conference*, Oxford: University of Mississippi: 1–52.

——— (1994a), 'The Influence of Michel Foucault on Accounting Research', *Critical Perspectives on Accounting*, Vol. 5, No. 1: 25–55.

——— (1994b), 'Discussant's Commentary on "The Crux of Alternative Approaches to Accounting History: The Boulton and Watt Case"', *Proceedings of the Fourth Interdisciplinary Perspectives on Accounting Conference*, Manchester: University of Manchester: 1–3.

Aronowitz, S. and DiFazio, W. (1994), *The Jobless Future*, Minneapolis: University of Minnesota Press.

Arrington, C.E. and Francis, J.R. (1989), 'Letting the Chat out of the Bag: Deconstruction, Privilege and Accounting Research', *Accounting, Organizations and Society*, Vol. 14, No. 1/2: 1–28.

Arrington, C.E. and Puxty, A.G. (1991), 'Accounting, Interests, and Rationality: A Communicative Relation', *Critical Perspectives on Accounting*, Vol. 2, No. 1: 31–58.

Arthur, A. (1993), 'Accounting Theory and Practical Philosophy: Applying the Tools', *Critical Perspectives on Accounting*, Vol. 4, No. 3: 209–224.

Ashton, T.S. (1948), *The Industrial Revolution 1760–1830*, Oxford: Oxford University Press.

——— (1963), *Iron and Steel in the Industrial Revolution*, Manchester: Manchester University Press.

——— (1966), *An Economic History of England in the Eighteenth Century*, New York: Barnes & Noble.

Babbage, C. (1963), *On the Economy of Machinery and Manufactures*, New York: Augustus Kelley Publishers, reprint of 1835 edition.

Baber, C. and Atkinson, M. (1987), *The Growth and Decline of the South Wales Iron Industry 1760–1880*, Cardiff: University of Wales Press.

Baritz, L. (1965), *The Servants of Power*, New York: John Wiley & Sons.

Bernasconi, R. (1989), 'Seeing Double: Destruktion and Deconstruction', in Michelfelder, D.P. and Palmer, R.E. (eds.), *Dialogue and Deconstruction*, Albany: State University of New York Press: 223–250.

Bhimani, A. (1994), 'Accounting and the Emergence of "Economic Man"', *Accounting, Organizations and Society*, Vol. 19, No. 8: 637–674.

Birch, A. (1967), *The Economic History of the British Iron and Steel Industry 1784–1879*, London: Frank Cass & Co., Ltd.

Boreham, P., Clegg, S., and Dow, G. (1986), 'The Institutional Management of Class Politics: Beyond the Labour Process and Corporatist Debates', in Knights, D. and Willmott, H. (eds.), *Managing the Labour Process*, Aldershot: Gower Publishing Co.: 186–210.

Braverman, H. (1974), *Labor and Monopoly Capital*, New York: Monthly Review Press.

Brief, R.P. (1965), 'Nineteenth Century Accounting Error', *Journal of Accounting Research*, Vol. 3, No. 1: 12–31.

Briggs, A. (1959), *The Age of Improvement: 1783–1867*, London: Longmans Green.

Brown, R. (1905), *A History of Accounting and Accountants*, Edinburgh: C. & E.C. Jack.

Brown, R. (1991), *Society and Economy in Modern Britain, 1700–1850*, London: Routledge.

Buchanan, D.A. (1986), 'Management Objectives in Technical Change', in Knights, D. and Willmott, H. (eds.), *Managing the Labour Process*, Aldershot: Gower Publishing Co.: 67–84.

Burawoy, M. (1979), *Manufacturing Consent*, Chicago: University of Chicago Press.

——— (1985), *The Politics of Production*, London: Verso.

Bythell, D. (1969), *The Handloom Weavers*, Cambridge: Cambridge University Press.

Campbell, R.H. (1958), 'The Financing of Carron Company', *Business History*, Vol. 1, No. 1: 21–34.

——— (1961), *Carron Campany*, Edinburgh: Oliver & Boyd.

——— (1980), *The Rise and Fall of Scottish Industry 1707–1939*, Edinburgh: John Donald Publishers, Ltd.

Cantrell, J.A. (1984), *James Nasmyth and the Bridgewater Foundry*, Manchester: Manchester University Press.

Chandler, A.D. (1977), *The Visible Hand: The Managerial Revolution in American Business*, Cambridge: Harvard University Press.

——— (1980), 'The United States: Seedbed of Managerial Capitalism', in Chandler, A.D. and Daems, H. (eds.), *Managerial Hierarchies*, Cambridge: Harvard University Press: 9–40.

——— (1984), 'The Emergence of Managerial Capitalism', *Business History Review*, Vol. 58, No. 4: 474–503.

Chapman, S.D. (1967), *The Early Factory Masters*, Newton Abbot: David & Charles.

——— (1972), *The Cotton Industry in the Industrial Revolution*, London: Macmillan.

Chatfield, M. (1977), *A History of Accounting Thought*, Huntington, NY: Robert E. Krieger Publishing Co.

Chua, W.F. (1986), 'Radical Developments in Accounting Thought', *Accounting Review*, Vol. 61, No. 4: 601–632.

Chua, W.F. and Degeling, P. (1993), 'Interrogating an Accounting-Based Intervention on Three Axes: Instrumental, Moral and Aesthetic', *Accounting, Organizations and Society*, Vol. 18, No. 4: 291–318.

Clawson, D. (1980), *Bureaucracy and the Labor Process*, New York: Monthly Review Press.

Clegg, S.R. (1989), *Framework of Power*, London: Sage Publications.

Coase, R. (1937), 'The Nature of the Firm', *Economica*, Vol. 4, No. 16: 386–405.

Cooper, D.J. and Tinker, A.M. (1994), 'Accounting and Praxis: Marx after Foucault', *Critical Perspectives on Accounting*, Vol. 5, No. 1: 1–3.

Covaleski, M. and Aiken, M. (1986), 'Accounting and Theories of Organizations: Some Preliminary Considerations', *Accounting, Organizations and Society*, Vol. 11, No. 4/5: 297–319.

Crafts, N.R.F. (1985), *British Economic Growth during the Industrial Revolution*, Oxford: Oxford University Press.

Cronhelm, F.W. (1978), *Double Entry by Single: A New Method of Book-Keeping*, New York: Arno Press, reprint of 1818 edition.

Crossman, P. (1953), 'The Genesis of Cost Control', *Accounting Review*, Vol. 28, No. 3: 522–527.

Crouzet, F. (1985), *The First Industrialists*, Cambridge: Cambridge University Press.

Dallmayr, F.R. (1989), 'Hermeneutics and Deconstruction: Gadamer and Derrida in Dialogue', in Michelfelder, D.P. and Palmer, R.E. (eds.), *Dialogue and Deconstruction*, Albany: State University of New York Press: 75–92.

Dandecker, C. (1990), *Surveillance, Power and Modernity*, New York: St. Martin's Press.

Deane, P. and Cole, W.A. (1969), *British Economic Growth 1688–1959*, Cambridge: Cambridge University Press.

Derrida, J. (1989), 'Three Questions to Hans-Georg Gadamer', in Michelfelder, D.P. and Palmer, R.E. (eds.), *Dialogue and Deconstruction*, Albany: State University of New York Press: 52–54.

Dickinson, H.W. (1937), *Matthew Boulton*, Cambridge: Cambridge University Press.

——— (1967), *James Watt, Craftsman and Engineer*, Newton Abbot: David & Charles.

Dilworth, T. (1810), *The Young Book-Keepers Assistant*, London: Thomas Wilson & Son.

Dobb, M. (1973), *Theories of Value and Distribution since Adam Smith*, Cambridge: Cambridge University Press.

Dreyfus, H.L. and Rabinow, R. (1982), *Michel Foucault: Beyond Structuralism and Hermeneutics*, Chicago: University of Chicago Press.

Duboff, R.B. and Herman, E.S. (1980), 'Alfred Chandler's New Business History: A Review', *Politics & Society*, Vol. 10, No. 1: 87–110.

Edwards, J.R. (1989), 'Industrial Cost Accounting Developments in Britain to 1830: A Review Article', *Accounting and Business Research*, Vol. 19, No. 76: 305–317.

Edwards, J.R. and Baber C. (1979), 'Dowlais Iron Company: Accounting Policies and Procedures for Profit Measurement and Reporting Purposes', *Accounting and Business Research*, Vol. 9, No. 34: 139–151.

Edwards, J.R. and Boyns, T. (1992), 'Industrial Organization and Accounting Innovation: Charcoal Ironmaking in England 1690–1783', *Management Accounting Research*, Vol. 3, No. 2: 151–169.

Edwards, J.R. and Newell, E. (1991), 'The Development of Industrial Cost and Management Accounting Before 1850: A Survey of the Evidence', *Business History*, Vol. 33, No. 1: 35–57.

Edwards, R. (1979), *Contested Terrain*, London: Heinemann.

Edwards, R.S. (1937), 'Some Notes on the Early Literature and Development of Cost Accounting in Great Britain', *The Accountant*, Vol. 97: 193–195, 225–231, 253–255, 283–287.

Elbaum, B. and Lazonick, W. (1984), 'The Decline of the British Economy: An Institutional Perspective', *Journal of Economic History*, Vol. 44, No. 2: 567–583.

Elias, M. (1960), *Iron in the Making*, London: Butler & Tanner, Ltd.

Elson, D. (1988), 'Market Socialism or Socialization of the Market?', *New Left Review*, No. 172: 3–44.

England, J. (1959), 'The Dowlais Iron Works, 1759–1793', *Morgannwg: Transactions of the Glamorgan Local History Society*, Vol. 3: 41–60.

Englander, E.J. (1987), 'The Individual Contract System of Production and Organization', *Labor History*, Vol. 28, No. 4: 429–446.

Euphemia, K. (1973), *Letters of Josiah Wedgwood*, Didsbury: E.J. Morten, Ltd.

Ezzamel, M.A., Hoskin, K.W., and Macve, R.H. (1990), 'Managing It All by Numbers: A Review of Johnson and Kaplan's *Relevance Lost*', *Accounting and Business Research*, Vol. 20, No. 78: 153–166.

Fama, E. (1980), 'Agency Problems and the Theory of the Firm', *Journal of Political Economy*, Vol. 88, No. 2: 288–307.

Farnie, D.A. (1979), *The English Cotton Industry and the World Market*, Oxford: Clarendon Press.

Feyerabend, P. (1978), *Against Method*, London: Verso.

Fisher, G. (1799), *The Instructor or Young Man's Best Companion*, London: privately published.

Fitton, R.S. and Wadsworth, A.P. (1958), *The Strutts and the Arkwrights 1758–1830*, Manchester: Manchester University Press.

Fleischman, R.K. (1985), *Conditions of Life Among the Cotton Workers of Southeastern Lancashire, 1780–1850*, New York: Garland Publishing, Inc.

——— (1993), 'James Watt, Jr.: Accountant-Entrepreneur', *Accounting Biography Conference Proceedings*, Oxford: University of Mississippi: 1–5.

——— (1996), 'A History of Management Accounting Through the 1960s', in Lee, T.A., Bishop, A., and Parker, R.H. (eds.), *Accounting History from the Renaissance to the Present*, New York: Garland Publishing, Inc.: 119–142.

Fleischman, R.K., Hoskin, K.W., and Macve, R.H. (1995), 'The Boulton & Watt Case: The Crux of Alternative Approaches to Accounting History?', *Accounting and Business Research*, Vol. 25, No. 99: 162–176.

Fleischman, R.K., Kalbers, L.P., and Parker, L.D. (1996), 'Expanding the Dialogue: Industrial Revolution Costing Historiography', *Critical Perspectives on Accounting*, Vol. 7, No. 3: 315–337.

Fleischman, R.K. and Parker, L.D. (1990), 'Managerial Accounting Early in the British Industrial Revolution: The Carron Company, A Case Study', *Accounting and Business Research*, Vol. 20, No. 79: 211–221.

——— (1991), 'British Entrepreneurs and Pre-Industrial Revolution Evidence of Cost Management', *Accounting Review*, Vol. 66, No. 2: 361–375.

——— (1992), 'The Cost-Accounting Environment in the British Industrial Revolution Iron Industry', *Accounting, Business and Financial History*, Vol. 2, No. 2: 141–160.

Fleischman, R.K., Parker, L.D., and Vamplew W. (1991), 'New Cost Accounting Perspectives on Technological Change in the British Industrial Revolution', in O.F. Graves (ed.), *The Costing Heritage: Studies in Honor of S. Paul Garner*, Harrisonburg, VA: Academy of Accounting Historians: 11–24.

Fleischman, R.K. and Tyson, T.N. (1993), 'Cost Accounting during the Industrial Revolution: The Present State of Historical Knowledge', *Economic History Review*, Vol. 46, No. 3: 503–517.

——— (1996), 'Archival Researchers: An Endangered Species?', working paper.

Flinn, M.W. (ed.) (1957), *The Law Book of the Crowley Ironworks*, Durham: Andrews & Co.

Flinn, M.W. (1962), *Men of Iron: The Crowleys in the Early Iron Industry*, Edinburgh: Edinburgh University Press.

——— (1966), *Origins of the Industrial Revolution*, London: Longmans Green.

——— (1984), *The History of the British Coal Industry*, Vol. 2, Oxford: Clarendon Press.

Follett, M.P. (1918), *The New State: Group Organization—The Solution of Popular Government*, New York: Longmans Green.

——— (1951), *Creative Experience*, New York: Peter Smith.

Forget, P. (1989), 'Argument(s)', in Michelfelder, D.P. and Palmer, R.E. (eds.), *Dialogue and Deconstruction*, Albany: State University of New York Press: 129–149.

Foucault, M. (1979), *Discipline and Punish*, New York: Vintage Books.

——— (1980), *Language, Counter-Memory, Practice*, Ithaca: Cornell University Press.

——— (1984), *The Foucault Reader*, New York: Pantheon Books.

——— (1988), *Politics, Philosophy, Culture*, New York: Routledge.

Francis, J.R. (1994), 'Auditing, Hermeneutics, and Subjectivity', *Accounting, Organizations and Society*, Vol. 19, No. 3: 235–269.

Frank, M. (1989), 'Limits of the Human Control of Language: Dialogue as the Place of Difference between Neostructuralism and Hermeneutics', in Michelfelder, D.P. and Palmer, R.E. (eds.), *Dialogue and Deconstruction*, Albany: State University of New York Press: 150–161.

Friedman, A. (1977), *Industry and Labor*, London: Macmillan.

Gadamer, H.G. (1986), *Truth and Method*, New York: Crossroad.

——— (1989), 'Text and Interpretation', in Michelfelder, D.P. and Palmer, R.E. (eds.), *Dialogue and Deconstruction*, Albany: State University of New York Press: 21–51.

Gane, M. (ed.) (1986), *Towards a Critique of Foucault*, London: Routledge & Kegan Paul.

Garcke, E. and Fells, J.M. (1887), *Factory Accounts, Their Principle and Practice*, London: Crosby, Lockwood & Son.

Garner, S.P. (1954), *Evolution of Cost Accounting to 1925*, University, AL: University of Alabama Press.

Garnsey, E. (1984), 'The Rediscovery of the Division of Labor', in Thompson, K. (ed.), *Work, Employment and Unemployment*, Philadelphia: Open University Press.

Giddens, A. (1976), *New Rules of Sociological Method: A Positive Critique of Interpretative Sociologies*, New York: Basic Books.

Gordon, D.M., Edwards, R., and Reich, M. (1982), *Segmented Work, Divided Workers*, Cambridge: Cambridge University Press.

Greenbaum, J. (1994), 'The Forest and the Trees', *Monthly Review*, Vol. 46, No. 6: 60–70.

Grey, C. (1994), 'Debating Foucault: A Critical Reply to Neimark', *Critical Perspectives on Accounting*, Vol. 5, No. 1: 5–24.

Habakkuk, H.J. (1962), *American and British Technology in the Nineteenth Century: The Search for Labor-Saving Inventions*, Cambridge: Cambridge University Press.

Habermas, J. (1987), *The Philosophical Discourse of Modernity*, Cambridge: MIT Press.

——— (1990), *Moral Consciousness and Communicative Action*, Cambridge: MIT Press.

Hamilton, H. (1928), 'The Founding of Carron Ironworks', *Scottish Historical Review*, Vol. 25, No. 97: 185–193.

Hamilton, R. (1777), *An Introduction to Merchandise*, Edinburgh: privately printed.

Harley, C.K. (1982), 'British Industrialization Before 1841: Evidence of Slower Growth during the Industrial Revolution', *Journal of Economic History*, Vol. 42, No. 2: 267–289.

Harris, J. R. (1988), *The British Iron Industry, 1700–1850*, London: Macmillan.

Heaton, H. (1931–1932), 'Benjamin Gott and the Industrial Revolution in Yorkshire', *Economic History Review*, Vol. 3, No. 1: 45–66.

Hegel, G.F.W. (1975), *Logic*, Oxford: Clarendon Press.

Held, D. (1980), *Introduction to Critical Theory: Horkheimer to Habermas*, Berkeley: University of California Press.

Hill, C. (1986), *The Collected Essays of Christopher Hill*, Vol. 3, Amherst: University of Massachusetts Press.

Hobsbawm, E.J. (1957–1958), 'The British Standard of Living 1780–1850', *Economic History Review*, Vol. 10, No. 1: 46–68.

——— (1968), *Industry and Empire*, New York: Pantheon Books.

——— (1972), 'Karl Marx's Contribution to Historiography', in Blackburn, R. (ed.), *Ideology in Social Science*, New York: Pantheon Books: 265–283.

Hogarth, R.M. (1991), 'A Perspective on Cognitive Research in Auditing', *Accounting Review*, Vol. 66, No. 2: 258–270.

Hopper, T.M. and Armstrong, P. (1991), 'Cost Accounting, Controlling Labour and the Rise of Conglomerates', *Accounting, Organizations and Society*, Vol. 16, No. 5/6: 405–438.

Hopper, T., Cooper, D., Lowe, T., Capps, T., and Mouritsen, J. (1986), 'Management Control and Worker Resistance in the National Coal Board: Financial Controls in the Labour Process', in Knights, D. and Willmott, H. (eds.), *Managing the Labour Process*, Aldershot: Gower Publishing Co.: 109–141.

Hopper, T., Storey, J., and Willmott, H. (1987), 'Accounting for Accounting: Towards the Development of a Dialectical View', *Accounting, Organizations and Society*, Vol. 12, No. 5: 437–456.

Hopwood, A.G. (1987), 'The Archaeology of Accounting Systems', *Accounting, Organizations and Society*, Vol. 12, No. 3: 207–234.

Hopwood, A.G. and Johnson, H.T. (1986), 'Accounting History's Claim to Legitimacy', *International Journal of Accounting Education and Research*, Vol. 21, No. 2: 37–46.

Hoskin, K.W. (1994), 'Boxing Clever: For, Against and Beyond Foucault in the Battle for Accounting Theory', *Critical Perspectives on Accounting*, Vol. 5, No. 1: 57–85.

Hoskin, K.W. and Macve, R.H. (1986), 'Accounting and the Examination: A Genealogy of Disciplinary Power', *Accounting, Organizations and Society*, Vol. 11, No. 2: 105–136.

——— (1988), 'The Genesis of Accountability: The West Point Connections', *Accounting, Organizations and Society*, Vol. 13, No. 1: 37–73.

——— (1991), 'Boxing Clever: For, Against and Beyond Foucault in the Battle of Accounting Theory', *Proceedings of the Third*

Interdisciplinary Perspectives on Accounting Conference, Manchester: University of Manchester: 1–34.

——— (1994), 'Reappraising the Genesis of Managerialism: A Re-examination of the Role of Accounting at the Springfield Armory, 1815–1845', *Accounting, Auditing and Accountability Journal*, Vol. 7, No. 2: 4–29.

Hudson, P. (1977), 'Some Aspects of Nineteenth Century Accounting Development in the West Riding Textile Industry', *Accounting History*, Vol. 2, Part 2: 4–22.

——— (1986), *The Genesis of Industrial Capital*, Cambridge: Cambridge University Press.

Hudson, P. (ed.) (1989), *Regions and Industries, A Perspective on the Industrial Revolution in Britain*, Cambridge: Cambridge University Press.

Hutton, C. (1788), *A Complete Treatise on Practical Arithmetic and Book-Keeping*, London: Robinson & Baldwin.

Hyde, C.K. (1977), *Technological Change and the British Iron Industry, 1700–1870*, Princeton: Princeton University Press.

Inglis, W. (1800), *Book-Keeping by Single and Double Entry*, London: W. & R. Chambers.

Jensen, M.C. and Meckling, W.H. (1976), 'Theory of the Firm: Managerial Behavior, Agency Costs and Ownership Structure', *Journal of Financial Economics*, Vol. 3, No. 4: 305–360.

John, A.H. (1950), *The Industrial Development of South Wales 1750–1850*, Cardiff: University of Wales Press.

Johnson, H.T. (1972), 'Early Cost Accounting for Internal Management Control: Lyman Mills in the 1850s', *Business History Review*, Vol. 46, No. 4: 466–474.

——— (1981), 'Toward a New Understanding of Nineteenth-Century Cost Accounting', *Accounting Review*, Vol. 56, No. 3: 510–518.

——— (1986), *A New Approach to Management Accounting History*, New York: Garland Publishing, Inc.

——— (1991), 'Managing by Remote Control', in Temin, P. (ed.), *Inside the Business Enterprise: Historical Perspectives on the Use of Information*, Chicago: University of Chicago Press: 41–65.

Johnson, H.T. and Kaplan, R.S. (1987), *Relevance Lost: The Rise and Fall of Management Accounting*, Boston: Harvard Business School Press.

Jones, G.S. (1972), 'History: The Poverty of Empiricism', in Blackburn, R. (ed.), *Ideology in Social Science*, New York: Pantheon Books: 96–115.

Jones, H. (1985), *Accounting, Costing, and Cost Estimation: Welsh Industry 1700–1930*, Cardiff: University of Wales Press.

Jones, T.C. (1992), 'Understanding Management Accountants: The Rationality of Social Action', *Critical Perspectives on Accounting*, Vol. 3, No. 3: 225–257.

Keenan, M.G. (1996), 'A Defence of Traditional Historical Research Methodology for Accounting History Research', working paper.

Kelly, P. (1802), *The Elements of Book-Keeping*, London: J. Whiting.

Knights, D. (1990), 'Subjectivity, Power and the Labour Process', in Knights, D. and Willmott, H. (eds.), *Labour Process Theory*, London: Macmillan: 297–335.

Knights, D. and Collinson, D. (1987), 'Discipline on the Shopfloor: A Comparison of the Disciplinary Effects of Managerial Psychology and Financial Accounting', *Accounting, Organizations and Society*, Vol. 12, No. 4/5: 457–478.

Knights, D. and Willmott, H. (1986), 'Introduction', in Knights, D. and Willmott, H. (eds.), *Managing the Labour Process*, Aldershot: Gower Publishing Co.: 1–18.

——— (1990), 'Introduction', in Knights, D. and Willmott, H. (eds.), *Labour Process Theory*, London: Macmillan: 1–45.

Kuhn, T.S. (1970), *The Structure of Scientific Revolutions*, Chicago: University of Chicago Press.

Lee, C.H. (1972), *A Cotton Enterprise 1795–1840*, Manchester: University of Manchester Press.

——— (1986), *The British Economy since 1700: A Macro-economic Perspective*, Cambridge: Cambridge University Press.

Lister, R.J. (1983), 'Accounting as History', *International Journal of Accounting*, Vol. 18, No. 2: 49–68.

Littler, C.R. (1986), *The Development of the Labour Process in Capitalist Societies*, Aldershot: Gower Publishing Co.

——— (1990), 'The Labour Process Debate: A Theoretical Review 1974–88', in Knights, D. and Willmott, H. (eds.), *Labour Process Theory*, London: Macmillan: 46–94.

Littler, C.R. and Salaman, G. (1982), *Class at Work*, London: Batsford Academic.

Littleton, A.C. (1933), *Accounting Evolution to 1900*, New York: American Institute Publishing Co., Inc.

Loft, A. (1986), 'Towards a Critical Understanding of Accounting: The Case of Cost Accounting in the UK, 1914–1925', *Accounting, Organizations and Society*, Vol. 11, No. 2: 137–169.

——— (1990), *Coming into the Light*, London: Chartered Institute of Management Accountants.

Lukes, S. (1974), *Power: A Radical View*, London: Macmillan.

Machlup, F. (1967), 'Theories of the Firm: Marginalist, Behavorial, Managerial', *American Economic Review*, Vol. 57, No. 1: 3–33.

Mackie, J.D. (1964), *A History of Scotland*, Harmondsworth: Penguin Books, Ltd.

Madison, G.B. (1989), 'Gadamer/Derrida: The Hermeneutics of Irony and Power', in Michelfelder, D.P. and Palmer, R.E. (eds.), *Dialogue and Deconstruction*, Albany: State University of New York Press: 192–198.

Mair, J. (1749), *Book-Keeping Methodized*, Edinburgh: W. Sands, A. Murray, & J. Cochran.

Marshall, D. (1973), *Industrial England 1776–1851*, New York: Charles Scribner's Sons.

Marshall, G. (1980), *Presbyteries and Profits*, Oxford: Clarendon Press.

Marx, Karl (1977), *Capital: A Critique of Political Economy*, Vol. 1, New York: Vintage Books.

McCloskey, D.N. (1983), 'The Rhetoric of Economics', *Journal of Economic Literature*, Vol. 21, No. 2: 481–517.

McConnel & Co., Ltd. (1906), *A Century of Fine Cotton Spinning*, Manchester: George Falkner & Sons.

McGaw, J.A. (1985), 'Accounting for Innovation: Technological Change and Business Practice in the Berkshire County Paper Industry', *Technology and Culture*, Vol. 26, No. 4: 703–725.

McKendrick, N. (1970), 'Josiah Wedgwood and Cost Accounting in the Industrial Revolution', *Economic History Review*, Vol. 23, No. 1: 45–67.

McLean, T. (1997), 'Agent's Reputation, Accounting and Costing in Organizational Control Structures', forthcoming.

Meek, R.L. (1976), *Studies in the Labor Theory of Value*, New York: Monthly Review Press.

Megill, A. (1979), 'Foucault, Structuralism and the Ends of History', *Journal of Modern History*, Vol. 51, No. 3: 451–503.

Meiksins, P. (1994), 'Labor and Monopoly Capital for the 1990s: A Review and Critique of the Labor Process Debate', *Monthly Review*, Vol. 46, No. 6: 45–59.

Mepham, M.J. (1988), *Accounting in Eighteenth Century Scotland*, New York: Garland Publishing, Inc.

Merino, B.D. and Mayper, A.G. (1993), 'Accounting History and Empirical Research', *Accounting Historians Journal*, Vol. 20, No. 2: 237–267.

Michelfelder, D.P. and Palmer, R.E. (1989), 'Introduction', in Michelfelder, D.P. and Palmer, R.E. (eds.), *Dialogue and Deconstruction*, Albany: State University of New York Press: 1–18.

Miller, P. (1987), *Domination and Power*, New York: Routledge and Kegan Paul.

Miller, P., Hopper, T.M., and Laughlin, R.C. (1991), 'The New Accounting History: An Introduction', *Accounting, Organizations and Society*, Vol. 16, No. 5/6: 395–403.

Miller, P. and Napier C. (1993), 'Genealogies of Calculation', *Accounting, Organizations and Society*, Vol. 18, No. 7/8: 631–648.

Miller P. and O'Leary, T. (1987), 'Accounting and the Construction of the Governable Person', *Accounting, Organizations and Society*, Vol. 12, No. 3: 235–265.

Mills, P.A. (1993), 'Accounting History as a Social Science: A Cautionary Note', *Accounting, Organizations and Society*, Vol. 18, No. 7/8: 801–803.

Mokyr, J. (1985), *The Economics of the Industrial Revolution*, London: Allen & Unwin.

——— (1987), 'Has the Industrial Revolution Been Crowded Out? Some Reflections on Crafts and Williamson', *Explorations in Economic History*, Vol. 24, No. 3: 293–319.

Montgomery, J. (1840), *The Cotton Manufacture of the United States Contrasted and Compared with that of Great Britain*, Glasgow: J. Niven.

Morrison, C. (1834), *A Complete System of Practical Book-Keeping*, Edinburgh: Stirling & Kenney.

Musson, A.E. (ed.) (1972), *Science, Technology and Economic Growth in the Eighteenth Century*, London: Methuen.

Napier, C.J. (1989), 'Research Directions in Accounting History', *British Accounting Review*, Vol. 21, No. 3: 237–254.

Neimark, M.K. (1990), 'The King is Dead. Long Live the King!', *Critical Perspectives on Accounting*, Vol. 1, No. 1: 103–114.

——— (1994), 'Regicide Revisited: Marx, Foucault, and Accounting', *Critical Perspectives on Accounting*, Vol. 5, No. 1: 87–108.

Neimark, M.K. and Tinker, A.M. (1987), 'Identity and Non-Identity Thinking: A Dialectical Critique of the Transaction Cost Theory of a Modern Corporation', *Journal of Management*, Vol. 13, No. 4: 661–673.

Norris, C. (1991), *Deconstruction Theory and Practice*, London: Routledge.

Oldroyd, D. (1996), 'The Costing Records of George Bowes and the Grand Allies in the North-east Coal Trade in the Eighteenth Century: Their Type and Significance', *Accounting, Business and Financial History*, Vol. 6, No. 1: 1–22.

O'Neill, J. (1986), 'The Disciplinary Society: From Weber to Foucault', *British Journal of Sociology*, Vol. 37, No. 1: 42–60.

Owen, J.A. (1972), *A Short History of the Dowlais Iron Works*, Merthyr Tydfil: Merthyr Tydfil Borough Council.

Parker, M.S. and Reid, D.J. (1972), *The British Revolution 1750–1970: A Social and Economic History*, London: Blandford Press.

Parker, R.H. (1969), *Management Accounting: An Historical Perspective*, New York: Augustus Kelley Publishers.

——— (1986), *The Development of the Accountancy Profession in Britain to the Early Twentieth Century*, London: Academy of Accounting Historians.

——— (1987), 'The Study of Accounting History', in Bromwich, M. and Hopwood, A. (eds.), *Essays in British Accounting Research*, Bath: Pitman: 279–293.

Pawson, E. (1979), *The Early Industrial Revolution: Britain in the Eighteenth Century*, London: Batsford Academic.

Perren, A. (1944), 'The Development of Cost Accounting in Europe', *N.A.C.A. Bulletin*, Vol. 25, No. 19: 1059–1076.

Pollard, S. (1965), *The Genesis of Modern Management*, Cambridge: Harvard University Press.

——— (1990), 'Industrial Management and the Beginnings of Industrialization in Europe', *L'Impresa Industria Commercio Banco*, Secc. 13–18: 95–118.

Porter, D.M. (1980), 'The Waltham System and Early American Textile Cost Accounting 1813–1848', *Accounting Historians Journal*, Vol. 7, No. 1: 1–15.

Previts, G.J., Parker, L.D., and Coffman, E.N. (1990a), 'Accounting History: Definition and Relevance', *Abacus*, Vol. 26, No. 1: 1–16.

——— (1990b), 'An Accounting Historiography: Subject Matter and Methodology', *Abacus*, Vol. 26, No. 2: 136–158.

Puxty, A.G., Sikka, P., and Willmott, H.C. (1994), 'Systems of Surveillance and the Silencing of UK Academic Accounting Labour', *British Accounting Review*, Vol. 26, No. 2: 137–171.

Raistrick, A. (1970), *Dynasty of Iron Founders*, Newton Abbot: David & Charles.

Randall, J. (1879), *The Wilkinsons*, Madeley, Shropshire: J. Randall.

Ricoeur, P. (1965), *History and Truth*, Evanston: Northwestern University Press.

Rimmer, W.G. (1960), *Marshalls of Leeds Flax-Spinners 1788–1886*, Cambridge: Cambridge University Press.

Risser, J. (1989), 'The Two Faces of Socrates: Gadamer/Derrida', in Michelfelder, D.P. and Palmer, R.E. (eds.), *Dialogue and*

Deconstruction, Albany: State University of New York Press: 176–185.

Roll, E. (1968), *An Early Experiment in Industrial Organization*, New York: Augustus Kelley Publishers, reprint of 1930 edition.

Rose, M.B. (1977), 'The Role of the Family in Providing Capital and Managerial Talent in Samuel Greg & Company 1784–1840', *Business History*, Vol. 19, No. 1: 37–54.

Rosenberg, N. (1985), *Perspectives on Technology*, Armand, NY: Sharpe.

Rostow, W.W. (1960), *The Stages of Economic Growth: A Non-Communist Manifesto*, Cambridge: Cambridge University Press.

Saul, S.B. (1970), *Technological Change: The United States and Britain in the Nineteenth Century*, London: Methuen.

Scorgie, M.E. (1996), 'Genealogies of Calculation: A Comment', working paper.

Scrivenor, H. (1967), *History of the Iron Trade*, London: Frank Cass & Co., Ltd., reprint of 1854 edition.

Shepardson, C. (1989), 'Imagine Understanding', in Michelfelder, D.P. and Palmer, R.E. (eds.), *Dialogue and Deconstruction*, Albany: State University of New York Press: 186–191.

Sheridan, A. (1980), *Michel Foucault: The Will to Truth*, New York: Tavistock.

Shusterman, R. (1989), 'The Gadamer-Derrida Encounter: A Pragmatist Perspective', in Michelfelder, D.P. and Palmer, R.E. (eds.), *Dialogue and Deconstruction*, Albany: State University of New York Press: 215–221.

Slaven, A. (1975), *The Development of the West of Scotland: 1750–1960*, London: Routledge & Kegan Paul.

Smart, B. (1983), *Foucault, Marxism, and Critique*, London: Routledge & Kegan Paul.

Smith, C., Whipp, R., and Willmott, H. (1988), 'Case Study Research in Accounting: Methodological Breakthrough or Ideological Weapon', *Advances in Public Interest Accounting*, Vol. 2: 95–120.

Smith, V. (1994), 'Braverman's Legacy', *Work and Occupations*, Vol. 21, No. 4: 403–421.

Solomons, D. (1952), *Studies in Costing*, London: Sweet & Maxwell, Ltd.

——— (1968), 'The Historical Development of Costing', in Solomons, D. (ed.), *Studies in Cost Analysis*, London: Sweet & Maxwell, Ltd.

——— (1991), 'Accounting and Social Change: A Neutralist View', *Accounting, Organizations and Society*, Vol. 6, No. 3: 287–295.

Stacey, N.A.H. (1954), *English Accountancy 1800–1954*, London: Gee & Co., Ltd.

Stewart, R.E. (1992), 'Pluralizing Our Past: Foucault in Accounting History', *Accounting, Auditing and Accountability Journal*, Vol. 5, No. 2: 57–73.

Stinchcombe, A.L. (1968), *Constructing Social Theories*, Chicago: University of Chicago Press.

Stone, W.E. (1973), 'An Early English Cotton Mill Cost Accounting System: Charlton (sic) Mills, 1810–1889', *Accounting and Business Research*, Vol. 4, No. 17: 71–78.

Tann, J. (ed.) (1981), *The Selected Papers of Boulton and Watt*, London: Diploma Press.

Thiele, P. (1986), 'Foucault's Triple Murder and the Modern Development of Power', *Canadian Journal of Political Science*, Vol. 19, No. 2: 243–260.

Thompson, E.P. (1964), *The Making of the English Working Class*, New York: Pantheon Books.

——— (1967), 'Time, Work-Discipline, and Industrial Capitalism', *Past and Present*, No. 38: 56–97.

Thompson, K. (ed.) (1984), *Work, Employment and Unemployment*, Philadelphia: Open University Press.

Thompson, P. (1984), 'The Labour Process and Deskilling', in Thompson, K. (ed.), *Work, Employment and Unemployment*, Philadelphia: Open University Press: 67–86.

——— (1989), *The Nature of Work*, London: Macmillan.

Thompson, W. (1777), *The Accountant's Oracle*, York: N. Nickson.

Tinker, A.M. (ed.) (1984), *Social Accounting for Corporations*, Manchester: Manchester University Press.

Tinker, A.M. (1985), *Paper Prophets*, London: Holt, Rinehart & Winston.

——— (1988), 'Panglossian Accounting Theories: The Science of Apologizing in Style', *Accounting, Organizations and Society*, Vol. 13, No. 2: 165–190.

——— (1991), 'The Accountant as Partisan', *Accounting, Organizations and Society*, Vol. 16, No. 3: 297–310.

——— (1992), personal correspondence.

Tinker, A.M., Lehman, C., and Neimark, M.K. (1991), 'Falling Down the Hole in the Middle of the Road: Political Quietism in Corporate Social Reporting', *Accounting, Auditing and Accountability Journal*, Vol. 4, No. 2: 28–54.

Tinker, A.M., Merino, B.D., and Neimark, M.K. (1982), 'The Normative Origins of Positive Theories: Ideology and Accounting Thought', *Accounting, Organizations and Society*, Vol. 7, No. 2: 167–200.

Tinker, A.M. and Neimark, M.K. (1988), 'The Struggle Over Meaning in Accounting and Corporate Research: A Comparative Evaluation of Conservative and Critical Historiography', *Accounting, Auditing and Accountability Journal*, Vol. 1, No. 1: 55–74.

Toynbee, A. (1884), *Lectures on the Industrial Revolution of the Eighteenth Century in England*, London: Longmans Green.

Trinder, B. (1973), *The Industrial Revolution in Shropshire*, London: Phillimore.

——— (1974), *The Darbys of Coalbrookdale*, Chichester: Phillimore.

von Tunzelmann, G.N. (1978), *Steam Power and British Industrialization to 1860*, Oxford: Clarendon Press.

——— (1981), 'Technical Progress during the Industrial Revolution', in Floud, R.C. and McCloskey, D.N., *The Economic History of Britain Since 1700*, Vol. 1, Cambridge: Cambridge University Press: 143–163.

Tyson, T.N. (1990), 'Accounting for Labor in the Early Nineteenth Century: The US Arms Making Experience', *Accounting Historians Journal*, Vol. 17, No. 1: 47–59.

——— (1992), 'The Nature and Environment of Cost Management among Early Nineteenth Century US Textile Manufacturers', *Accounting Historians Journal*, Vol. 19, No. 1: 1–24.

——— (1993), 'Keeping the Record Straight: Foucauldian Revisionism and Nineteenth Century US Cost Accounting History', *Accounting, Auditing and Accountability Journal*, Vol. 6, No. 2: 4–16.

Unwin, G. (1924), *Samuel Oldknow and the Arkwrights*, Manchester: Manchester University Press.

Urwick, L. and Brech, E.F.L. (1964), *The Making of Scientific Management*, London: Sir Isaac Pitman & Sons, Ltd.

Vamplew, W. (1983), 'Industrial Revolution or Economic Evolution? Was There Really a Take-off in the British Economy in the Late Eighteenth Century?', *Tradition*, Vol. 24: 4–7.

Walsh, E.J. and Stewart, R.E. (1993), 'Accounting and the Construction of Institutions: The Case of a Factory', *Accounting, Organizations and Society*, Vol. 18, No. 7/8: 783–800.

Watts, R.L. and Zimmerman, J.L. (1979), 'The Demand for and Supply of Accounting Theories: The Market for Excuses', *Accounting Review*, Vol. 54, No. 2: 273–305.

Webster, W. (1781), *An Essay on Book-Keeping According to the True Italian Method*, London: Bettesworth, Hitch, & King.

Wells, M.C. (1977), 'Some Influences on the Development of Cost Accounting', *Accounting Historians Journal*, Vol. 4, No. 2: 47–61.

——— (1978), *Accounting for Common Costs*, Urbana, IL: Center for International Education and Research in Accounting.

——— (1987), 'A Market Simulation Theory of Accounting', *Waseda Business & Economic Studies*, No. 23: 65–79.

Whitley, R.D. (1986), 'The Transformation of Business Finance into Financial Economics: The Roles of Academic Expansion and Changes in US Capital Markets', *Accounting, Organizations and Society*, Vol. 11, No. 2: 171–192.

——— (1988), 'The Possibility and Utility of Positive Accounting Theory', *Accounting, Organizations and Society*, Vol. 13, No. 6: 631–645.

Williamson, O.E. (1971), 'The Vertical Integration of Production: Market Failure Considerations', *American Economic Review*, Vol. 61, No. 2: 112–123.

——— (1973), 'Markets and Hierarchies: Some Elementary Considerations', *American Economic Review*, Vol. 63, No. 2: 316–325.

——— (1975), *Markets and Hierarchies: Analysis and Antitrust Implications*, New York: Free Press.

——— (1985), *The Economic Institutions of Capitalism*, New York: Free Press.

Willmott, H.C. (1996), 'Managing the Academics: Commodification and Control in the Development of University Education in the UK', working paper.

Yamey, B.S. (1949), 'Scientific Bookkeeping and the Rise of Capitalism', *Economic History Review*, Vol. 1, No. 2/3: 99–117.

——— (1960), 'The Development of Company Accounting Conventions', *Three Banks Review*, Vol. 47: 22–37.

——— (1981), 'Some Reflections on the Writing of a General History of Accounting', *Accounting and Business Research*, Vol. 2, No. 42: 127–135.

Young, W.A. (1923–1924), 'Works Organization in the 17th Century: Some Accounts of Ambrose and John Crowley', *Transactions of the Newcomen Society*, Vol. 4: 73–101.

Author Index

Firm Index

Subject Index